The SAS Fighting Techniques Handbook

NEW AND REVISED

The SAS Fighting Techniques Handbook

NEW AND REVISED

TERRY WHITE

The Lyons Press
Guilford, Connecticut
An imprint of The Globe Pequot Press

To buy books in quantity for corporate use
or incentives, call **(800) 962–0973,**
or e-mail **premiums@GlobePequot.com.**

10 9 8 7 6 5 4 3 2 1

Printed in the United States of America

ISBN 978-1-59921-081-0

Library of Congress Cataloging-in-Publication Data is available on file.

Contents

Acknowledgments

I WOULD LIKE TO EXPRESS MY GRATITUDE to Jim Shortt who provided me with a wealth of interesting insights into close personal protection and counterterrorism. A former member of the British Parachute Regiment and Special Air Service, Jim has trained presidential bodyguard teams in the Baltic republics. My thanks also to Mark Lloyd who drew upon his long career in the British Army to provide material on intelligence SOF and agent support networks. Finally, I would like to express my appreciation to Tony Randell who drew the illustrations for this work.

Introduction

IT WAS STILL DARK WHEN THE RECRUITS set off from the Talybont
Reservoir. Melting ice and snow combined with grass tussocks to topple the
unwary. A bitterly cold wind cut through the soldiers' thin windproof
smocks, and in the valleys it carried a freezing rain which soaked the men
in minutes, adding to the weight of their 40-lb. Bergens. On the tops of the
mountains, where the selectors had placed their checkpoints, the rain
turned to driving snow. Later an officer would describe events on that day
to a coroner's court in undramatic language, simply reporting the weather
conditions as being of "minimal visibility"—after all a military guerrilla
unit is expected to live in the field under all conditions.

The two groups of men moving across the hills were recruits just
embarking on "Long Drag," Britain's 22nd SAS Regiment's final selection
march. Their 40-mile route would take them across some of the highest
peaks in the Brecon Beacons. The march was demanding enough under the
mixed weather conditions experienced on the hills in September but this
was the first recruit cadre of the year, the infamous "Winter Selection."

One soldier was unusual. He walked alone, moving quickly toward his
first RV. Mike Kealy was an experienced 33-year-old SAS major, decorated
during the Oman campaign, returning to a sabre squadron after a long

period on staff duties. He was not part of the selection course but wanted to test himself, to see if he could complete the endurance march in the permitted twenty hours, before returning to the operational duties. With his smock and trousers soaked by the rain, Kealy was last seen on an exposed ridge by a section of the course who were forced to turn back to seek shelter in the valley below. He was later discovered staggering in the snow, already suffering from hypothermia. Refusing aid from a party of recruits, Kealy slumped in the snow, allowing a jacket placed over his shoulders to blow away. Two recruits attempted to lead him off the hills but, stumbling behind, he became lost in the darkness. He was discovered again by an SAS officer and corporal seven hours after the march had started. They placed the unconscious Mike Kealy in a hurriedly constructed snow-hole and the officer set off to raise the alarm. When the officer arrived at SAS rescue headquarters, the exercise had been abandoned and several other groups of soldiers were missing. Flying was nearly impossible, and when a helicopter was finally able to reach the snow-hole early the next morning, Kealy was dead.

In the Taiwan Straits, just after Red China's two abortive attempts to invade the Nationalists' stronghold on the offshore islands, another more hair-raising selection course played itself out. The islands of Taiwan, Quemoy, and Matsu were held by Chiang Kai-Shek's huge army. On both sides of the straits, the Chinese were on a war-footing and batteries on Quemoy and Matsu engaged in artillery duels with Communist guns on the mainland. Both sides used combat swimmers to probe the others' defenses but the Red Chinese gave these operations a neat twist.

Communist commandos were taken close to the coast of Taiwan by boat or submarine when completing their training. Slipping into the water, the swimmers penetrated the coastal and beach defenses before changing into civilian clothes and leaving their equipment in a cache on the beach. The Taiwanese were experiencing newfound prosperity, and across the island cinemas had sprung up to provide nightly entertainment for the workers. A young man bought two movie tickets, left the line, and waited a short while before walking away. Just another factory worker stood up by his date? On a commando's return to China, the Communist instructors demanded proof that he had penetrated the Nationalists' defenses, and a movie ticket was a favored souvenir.

This book is about the practical aspects of the SAS and other special forces' warfare; the nuts and bolts of slipping undetected through the enemy's defenses and going to war in his backyard. Each technique or skill has been taken from the manual of a unit which specializes and therefore excels in that task. The problems of landing on hostile beaches are seen through the eyes of covert undersea warfare units, while the descriptions of secret parachute descents and resupply missions were written for units which use the parachute as their primary means of going into battle. What is the safest way to negotiate a river when the enemy may be waiting in ambush behind the next bend? What are the rules for operating a clandestine radio, meeting an agent, or directing attack aircraft to a concealed target? How do you set up a safe house or pass information to an agent you will never meet? What are the ingredients of a successful hostage rescue mission and what precautions can a bodyguard take to protect his client from attack by criminals and terrorists? These and many more topics are described for the reader as they are taught to the men who volunteer to risk their lives carrying out special operations.

Today, Special Operational Forces (SOF) are more important than ever before. In battle they take the war into the enemy's camp. In peacetime, they find themselves at the sharp end of foreign policy, stepping into the breach to fight secret undeclared wars when diplomacy fails. Volunteers for these dangerous duties are selected for a variety of attributes, all of which must be honed to perfection. They must be able to reach the same level of fitness as professional athletes. Their missions require almost superhuman stamina in hostile environments such as the tundra, jungle, and desert. They must be intelligent and learn new tasks easily. Their new trade involves mastering an endless series of weapons, equipment, and techniques as well as special skills required for particular operations. They must be determined and able to keep going when the going gets very rough. Even when exhausted, they must remain observant and careful—they have a job to do and their first mistake could be their last.

Currently, many countries maintain self-contained organizations capable of carrying out special operations, which, for the most part, are under direct political control. Britain deploys the UK Special Forces Group, America the United States Special Operations Command, and Australia the Special Action Forces, to mention just three. While the high-profile commando units are well known, a much wider range of military and civilian personnel support their operations or are engaged in specialized duties of their own. Indeed, one American defense analyst defines SOF as:

> Small, carefully selected military, paramilitary, and civilian units with unusual (occasionally unique) skills, which are superlatively trained for specific rather than general purposes, and are designed to undertake unorthodox tasks that ordinary units could accomplish only with far greater difficulty and far less effectiveness, if at all.[1]

So who are these military, civilian, and paramilitary personnel who are selected and trained for secret missions?

▰ Army SOF

Army SOF include elite light infantry units such as rangers, commandos, and paratroops used for shock action: strikes, raids, ambushes, and the temporary seizure of bridges, road junctions, and strong points behind the battlefield or invasion beaches. Once behind enemy lines, these troops may fight as conventional infantry but are lightly armed and have few defenses against enemy armor and mechanized infantry. Consequently, their operations tend to be short-term. They are relieved by conventional forces or quickly extracted by sea or air.

In contrast, units such as the American Special Forces ("Green Berets") or the British, Australian, and New Zealand SAS are trained to spend long periods deep behind enemy lines. Dedicated to special operations, these units are seen as lacking "sufficient fire-power for shock action, staying power for sustained combat, and mobility for use as maneuver units." Consequently, they conduct raids and

---

[1] *Green Berets, Seals and Spetsnaz: US and Soviet Special Military Operations* by J. M. Collins. Written as a handbook for Congress and the American Special Operations Panel.

ambushes against enemy headquarters, supply units, or lines of communication such as roads and railways, before melting away to strike elsewhere. Such actions weaken the enemy's reinforcements and supply lines and force him to deploy units away from the front line in an attempt to protect his rear areas.

Another important task is intelligence gathering behind the front line (reconnaissance and surveillance) and providing detailed information about specific targets, enemy reserve units, or enemy road and rail traffic. Such intelligence-gathering teams may be assigned to acquire particular targets for friendly air strikes. During the Gulf War, British and American Special Forces teams located the mobile launchers firing Scud missiles at Israel from sites in western Iraq. This was deemed a high-priority mission as Israel's entry into the war might have resulted in the Arab countries withdrawing from the alliance.

A no less important mission is the rescue of pilots, VIPs, prisoners of war, and hostages from behind enemy lines. During the invasion of France in 1944, the British SAS rescued more than sixteen badly needed aircrew, shot down behind the battlefield. During the Vietnam War, the American commandos provided the cutting edge to an intelligence program designed to rescue American POWs. More recently, four American pilots were rescued by SOF personnel in the Gulf.

Some units are more specialized. The American Special Forces are proficient at raids, ambushes, and sabotage, but their primary role is to train, organize, equip, and direct foreign troops in guerrilla or counterguerrilla warfare. Rather than applying direct force, the raising of indigenous units had a powerful "force multiplication" effect when they operate in conjunction with conventional forces. The British SAS and "Jedburgh Teams" trained and armed thousands of Maquisards living in the French forests and mountains after the D-Day invasion. The SAS later trained and organized tribesmen in Borneo and Oman as guides, intelligence gatherers, or counterguerrillas. In Vietnam, the American Special Forces organized Montagnard tribesmen into irregular militia to fight both the Vietcong and the regular North Vietnamese army invading the South. In South and Central America, the Americans trained elite army and police units in counterrevolutionary warfare to help stem the tide of the numerous insurgencies in "America's backyard."

Navy and Marine SOF

American Sea-Air-Land (SEAL) Teams and Britain's Special Boat Service (Royal Marines) are trained for the same type of mission as their Army Special Forces and SAS counterparts but excel at maritime and riverine operations. Deployed in support of naval operations, their targets include shore installations, beach defenses, merchant and warships in port, or, indeed, any target that can be approached from the shore or an accessible waterway. The American Navy's Special Boat Squadrons are equipped with a range of surface craft to support SEAL operations, while the SEAL Delivery Vehicle Teams deploy ten six-man mini-submarines which can be carried to their target by parent Polaris or attack submarines converted for special operations use.

A Pentagon study undertaken in the early 1980s revealed that of the 113 cities considered to be important to US interests, 80 were within 100 km of the sea. As a consequence, the US Marine Corps made two of their Marine Expeditionary Units special operations capable (MEU-SOC) and have prepared them for a range of missions such as amphibious raids and show of force operations, the rescue of civilian hostages, and civic action and disaster relief tasks. The Marines also deploy the "Recons" for more specialized tasks. Force Recon Company deploys four-man teams to support Marine operations by intelligence gathering, raiding, acquiring targets for artillery and naval gunfire, and forward air-controlling strike aircraft. These men are trained for high-risk missions, and all are trained in combat swimming (military diving and surface swimming techniques), parachuting, and small-boat handling. Their counterparts, the Battalion Recon Companies, are less specialized and less intensively trained, being used to gather intelligence on the beaches and coastline within the area of a Marine amphibious assault.

Britain's Royal Marines field similar special units. The Special Boat Service, mentioned above, serves Royal Marine operations and is part of the UK Special Forces Group. The Mountain & Arctic Warfare Cadre provides instruction in climbing techniques and Arctic warfare. In wartime it would conduct long-range reconnaissance patrols (LRRPs) and deep raiding tasks for HQ Commando Forces. Comacchio Group is tasked with internal security and defending naval bases, oil rigs, and Britain's nuclear arsenal. A fourth specialized subunit, 539 Assault Squadron, provides small boats and landing craft for amphibious operations. In addition, the British Navy's Naval Gun Fire Observers are a small unit of commando-trained parachutists skilled in directing naval gunfire onto coastal targets.

▄▄ Air Force SOF

The Air Force's SOF play a vital role in supporting army and naval operations. Teams may need to be parachuted or air-landed close to their target and then resupplied constantly by covert parachute drops. The Air Force SOF may also be called upon to provide fire support. Finally, aircraft extraction may be the only means of snatching the team to safety at the end of the mission. In order to penetrate air defenses bristling with radar and surface-to-air missile (SAM) sites, the aircrew must be capable of flying for long distances at treetop level at night and under poor flying conditions and then finding a small drop zone or landing strip.

While the majority are drawn from the cream of the Air Force's helicopter and fixed-wing aircrew, some American Air Force SOF personnel are trained to work on the ground. These are the Special Operations Combat Control Teams (SOCCT) which provide two- or three-man elements to direct air strikes onto difficult or concealed targets (forward air control). The pilots of the attacking aircraft may be given verbal instructions over a radio link or the SOCCT may place navigation aids and target designators close to the objective. These operators are also trained as air traffic controllers and may be asked to establish communications and control the flow of friendly aircraft landing at an airfield seized by commando elements such as the Rangers. Like their commando counterparts, these teams are trained as divers and high-altitude parachutists, allowing them to penetrate deep into hostile territory. Working with local guerrillas or underground movements, they are also trained to select, survey, construct, and operate clandestine reception sites such as dropping zones, airstrips, or recovery zones, thus facilitating the insertion and recovery (extraction) of special mission teams.

Intelligence SOF

Intelligence organizations, such as the American CIA, Russia's KGB, Britain's MI6, the French DGSE, and Israel's Mossad, have small numbers of covert operations personnel at their disposal. Although numbers are classified, their presence is revealed by spectacular operations. Many are ex-soldiers with elite unit experience who have been given extensive training in intelligence work.

French divers and intelligence-support personnel destroyed the Greenpeace organization's *Rainbow Warrior* in Auckland Harbor (1985). An Israeli sabotage team destroyed a nuclear reactor being built in France for Iraq as part of Saddam Hussein's bid for nuclear weapons (1979), and the Mossad has launched numerous assassinations and raids against terrorists and their sponsors. Accounts of kidnappings and assassinations by the former Soviet Bloc intelligence services are legion. The Bulgarian defector, Georgi Markov, was poisoned after being stabbed with an umbrella in a London street (1978). Other attempts to kill Bulgarian and Romanian defectors living in France either failed or were scotched by the French security service. North Korea used both military SOF and intelligence agents in at least three attempts on the lives of South Korean presidents. In 1987, a North Korean intelligence team used a bomb concealed in unattended baggage to destroy Korean Airlines flight KAL 858.

Other covert operations have involved working with local forces. During America's war in Southeast Asia, the Geneva Accords prevented an overt American military presence in Laos, but Communist infiltration was resisted by local forces, funded, armed, organized, and led by field officers from the CIA's Covert Action Branch. When Borneo was under attack from Indonesian insurgents, Britain came to its assistance. While the military were limited to tracking and eliminating Indonesian patrols and launching preemptive strikes just across the border, MI6 officers trained tribesmen for raids deep inside Indonesia. During the same period, small numbers of the same tribesmen, under British intelligence officers, later fought briefly alongside their American counterparts, organizing and training Montagnard troops in Vietnam's Central Highlands.

The major role of intelligence is, of course, the collection and analysis of information. However "illegal" agents, operating under deep cover, may provide support for military commandos by supplying them with safe houses, drop zones, weapons and equipment dumps, documents, and funds (see chapter 9).

▧ Civilian SOF

Other civilians who might find themselves fighting alongside military or intelligence SOF personnel are resistance or guerrilla movements. Britain, America, and the Soviet Union used commandos or intelligence staff to organize, arm, and direct the many guerrilla and resistance movements which sprang up in the countries occupied by the Germans and Japanese during World War II. In the nuclear stand-off which followed the war, the Soviet Union and its allies supported more than thirty insurgencies in Africa, South America, and the Middle East. America, likewise, supported rebellions or began programs in Third World countries to raise indigenous troops to counter internal subversion or external threats.

The use of terrorist groups, mercenaries, and even criminal organizations on special operations distances the authors of the operation from any political repercussions. During the Vietnam War, Chinese and North Vietnamese mercenaries were used on American special operations inside Laos, Cambodia, and North Vietnam. When the government of North Yemen was toppled by an Egyptian-backed coup in September 1962, Britain used a mercenary force composed of French, Belgian, and British ex-SAS soldiers to organize and direct the royalist forces faced with fighting a guerrilla war. The CIA and MI6 are reputed to maintain links with offshore companies which recruit ex-SAS personnel for freelance operations.

Eastern Bloc countries and Libya have provided training bases, arms, and information to terrorist groups. The North Koreans supplied training facilities for Japanese Red Army operations to disrupt the 1988 Olympics. The attempted assassination of Pope John Paul by a right-wing Turkish terrorist is reputed to have had a Bulgarian-KGB connection. In 1973, the South Korean CIA are reputed to have employed a Japanese-based Korean *yakuza* family to kidnap a political opponent of President Park.

A range of other civilians may be asked to assist in special operations. Some will occupy key positions in organizations formed to institute political, economic, and social reforms designed to redress the inequalities which fuel insurgencies. In Vietnam, the CIA, United States Information Agency, and the US Agency for International Development all contributed to improving life in South Vietnamese hamlets and villages. Other specialists may be drawn into the fighting. At least four anthropologists, with an intimate knowledge of the local people, organized resistance to the Japanese during World War II. Two ran intelligence networks in Malaysia and Thailand, a British woman academic led tribes against the Japanese army in northern Burma, and Professor W.E.H. Stanner raised a force of locals in northern Australia to operate behind the Japanese lines in the event of invasion. Other civilians with highly specialized operational knowledge may be asked to volunteer for these dangerous missions. When British paratroops hijacked a German radar installation on the northern French coast (1942), an RAF radar technician went with them to identify key components. Similarly, radar technicians accompanied Israeli paratroops when they hijacked a Soviet radar device in a fortified site on the Egyptian coast (1969). The Israeli team which sabotaged the French-built nuclear reactor took with them a nuclear physicist who showed the saboteurs where to lay their charges for the greatest effect. When Israeli aircraft finally attacked the Osirak nuclear plant outside Baghdad on June 7, 1981, a French technician was recruited to take a target designator into the critical area of the plant to complement the navigation beacons laid by an Israeli pathfinder team.

The problem with using civilians on special ops is that most are untrained in the various techniques required to get teams in and out of hostile territory. SOF planners have been forced to come up with solutions such as the tandem HALO rig. In this instance, the specialist can accompany a free-fall team, slung underneath an experienced parachutist in much the same way as a piece of additional baggage. Once the operation is completed, the specialists, now a liability to the team, can be quickly extracted by means of the Surface to Air Recovery (STAR) system. A specially adapted recovery aircraft approaches a pre-arranged extraction point, which is little more than a small field or clearing. The civilian is strapped into a harness connected to a helium balloon by a long suspension rope and left sitting with his back to the aircraft's approach route. When the aircraft snags the suspension rope, the civilian is pulled into the air and winched aboard.

■ Peacetime Covert Operations

The SAS and, indeed, special forces of any description are expensive to equip and train, and their operations consume valuable funds and resources, often at the expense of conventional units and operations. The US Special Operations Command's budget for fiscal years 1992 and 1993 was $3.1 billion and $2.95 billion respectively. Although these forces represent an irreplaceable pool of talent and experience, and can no longer be created from scratch in the same way as the World War II commando units, many would not have survived to the present day if their only purpose were to support full-scale military operations in wartime.

Off the battlefield, these covert forces can be used to bridge the gap between diplomacy and war. In 1931, Secretary of War Patrick J. Hurley described the very special role of the US Marines in American foreign policy: "The Marines can land on foreign territory without it being considered an act of war, but when the army moves on foreign territory, that is an act of war and that is one of the reasons for the

Corps." Under the nuclear umbrella, the strategic balance became more delicate and use of the Marines was no longer a practical option. In the wake of its defeat in Vietnam, America found itself locked into a dilemma in responding to international crises. Short of nuclear confrontation, it could send in the Marines or it could do nothing. Senior intelligence officers with experience in covert action insisted that the United States ". . . should also consider the third option, the use of insurgency and counterinsurgency techniques and covert action to achieve policy goals. In our view, paramilitary skills would give the United States an additional arrow in its national defense quiver."

A few years ago, two US senators introduced bills that recommended sweeping changes in US Intelligence. One, Sen. David Boren, saw the CIA's covert operations directorate becoming "the Marines of the intelligence community." Other observers argued that the CIA's directorate should be disbanded, that ". . . it is a standing invitation to mischief. Special operations units within the regular military branches are adequate for any likely threat." In other countries, it is probable that covert intelligence teams will continue to handle missions too sensitive for an armed group of commandos. Mercenaries or local forces may act as proxies, or national teams may enter and leave the target country under civilian cover on normal civilian transport. Alternatively, both military and intelligence teams may continue to work together within the areas in which each excels. This was the case when the French government decided that they would meet Greenpeace's anti-nuclear protests in the Pacific with a surgical strike to sink the organization's flagship *Rainbow Warrior*.

The intelligence-support and command personnel for this operation entered New Zealand aboard normal commercial flights. Two operatives, Major Alain Mafart and Captain Dominique Prieur, arrived in the country in late June 1985, travelling on forged Swiss passports, and posing as a honeymoon couple. Renting a camper, presumably they reconnoitered a beach landing site (BLS) and may have conducted close target reconnaissance of the *Rainbow Warrior*. At the same time, three military divers from the Navy Frogman Training Center (CNIC) at Aspretto, Corsica, arrived in New Zealand aboard the chartered yacht *Ouvea*, posing as the crew of a wealthy playboy. Apparently leaving the harbor at Whangarei for Norfolk Island, some 625 miles to the north, the *Ouvea* turned south and kept its rendezvous with Mafart and Prieur at a BLS somewhere north of Auckland on the night of July 10. A single diver, his equipment, limpet mines, and an inflatable dinghy were loaded in the camper and driven to the northern shore of Auckland Harbor where witnesses later saw the dinghy being launched. Presumably the diver approached to within striking distance of his target before beginning his underwater swim. At around 9:30 p.m., witnesses saw a man abandoning an inflatable dinghy near the Outboard Boating Club in Hobson's Bay, before being driven away in a camper. Later that evening, the two limpet mines on the hull of *Rainbow Warrior* exploded during a party, and the boat settled on the bottom, taking with it a young Portuguese photographer.

At this point the differences in the job descriptions and relative risks involved in the military and intelligence-type roles become apparent. The diver disappeared, possibly leaving New Zealand by a regular flight but more likely being returned to the BLS where he rejoined the *Ouvea*. Once the yacht was in international waters, the military element was away and free. By the time the New Zealand police interviewed the crew in Norfolk Island on July 15, they had rehearsed their apparently watertight alibi. When the New Zealand investigators asked to look for forensic evidence, the yacht disappeared. Ostensibly leaving for the French island of New Caledonia on July 16, the *Ouvea* made a preplanned rendezvous with the French nuclear submarine *Rubis*. When the divers were safely aboard, the yacht was scuttled.

The intelligence personnel, well trained in espionage tradecraft, were left behind to cover their tracks. The camper was to be returned and all bills paid before the honeymooners left New Zealand. It was this careful attention to detail, much a part of intelligence training, that led, ironically, to their capture. Mafart and Prieur, now linked by witnesses to the camper, returned the vehicle to the rental agency and requested a refund on their rental agreement. Already alerted, the rental firm contacted the police. The French press soon ferreted out details of the operation, including the identities of other agents involved. The French government, caught with its hand in the till, claimed that the attack was a rogue intelligence operation and the Defense Minister, Charles Hernu, resigned. DGSE Chief Admiral Lacoste was sacked. The French would have been forced to create some very imaginative explanations if the entire team had been drawn from the military. Equally, a military unit, completely detached from the armed services and dedicated to covert operations, would simply be an intelligence organization under a different title.

CHAPTER 1

Mission Preparation

THE FAILURE OF THE OPERATION to rescue the hostages held in the American Embassy in Tehran (Operation Eagle Claw) underscored the value of the old military maxim KISS—Keep It Simple Stupid. The plan involved inserting the rescue force and support teams into Iran by rotary- and fixed-wing aircraft. After refueling at the first staging post (Desert One) in southern Iran, Operational Detachment Delta and elements of the 10th Special Forces Group were to continue their airborne insertion to a covert landing zone, Desert Two, within 50 miles of the Iranian capital. The American commandos planned to enter Tehran in six Mercedes trucks provided by a ground support team. After the assault, the soldiers and hostages were to be evacuated by helicopter to a disused airfield at Manzariyh, where a security force of Rangers and a fleet of C-141 Starlifter transports would be waiting to fly the soldiers and released prisoners out of the country. In the early hours of April 25, 1980, the large, complex, and expensive operation, already flawed by a lack of command and control, was finally foiled by equipment failure, adverse weather (seasonal dust storms), and a disastrous collision between a helicopter and a C-130 tanker, which turned Desert One into an inferno.

Operation Eagle Claw was attempted by the world's most powerful military power, with one of the largest multiservice cadres of SOF, equipped with state-of-the-art technology. Its operational target was a Third World country. Its failure illustrates the complexity and dangers of special operations. In preparing for such contingencies, SOF planners must take into account a web of interconnecting factors: training, command and control, insertion technology, weather, climate, terrain, logistics, and equipment. A failure at any point can result in a political and military disaster and the loss of the special mission team.

■ Training

The training program for special operations is broken down into a series of progressively testing phases:

Endurance selection phase All teams operating inside enemy territory must develop a well-honed fitness, physical conditioning, and mental toughness. Teams may be required to cover long distances between their insertion point and target and may be forced to undertake arduous escape journeys, carrying loads in excess of 150 lbs., in an effort to break control with enemy forces. In addition they are expected to maintain a high state of alertness while exhausted and must continue to function for long periods despite illness and inadequate nutrition.

Military (*Spetsnaz*), police (*Spetsnazovtsy*), and intelligence/internal security (*Osnaz*) units of the Confederation of Independent States (CIS), the former Soviet Union, are expected to reach the same sort of standards as their SAS and American Special Forces counterparts. Among other tests, the aspiring candidate will be faced with a 3-km run which must be completed in 13–15 minutes, a 5-km ski course (26–29 minutes), a 5-meter hand-over-hand rope climb, and a 14-obstacle assault course which has to be completed within 4–5 minutes. These are only the basic physical requirements. On operations, the Soviet commando will be expected to travel long distances under arctic conditions, walking or skiing more than 30 miles per day and swimming across icy rivers and frozen swamps carrying his 60–100 lb. load of personal kit, plus any additional team equipment.

"Hacking" into enemy territory

Penetrating a well-defended foreign country may be compared to hacking into a high-security computer. Like any SAS or other Special Forces operator, the hacker is self-selected and highly trained, often having extensive experience of computer programming and networking. He has to gain access to a military network of which his target computer forms one of many nodes. This can often be achieved by penetrating a computer within a university department or factory linked into military computer nets for the purposes of communicating by electronic mail.

The target computer itself will require a valid identity and password. However, if there is reason to believe that the security assumes that only valid users have access to the military network, the hacker may be afforded the opportunity to log in through a backdoor in the system, using "GUEST" or "VISITOR" with no password requirement. Alternatively, he may write a dictionary program which systematically runs through thousands of words until the correct password is entered; or he may attempt to log himself into the computer, using electronic mail. These are the hacker's "insertion vehicles" and the "enemy's" border defenses.

Once inside the system, the hacker finds himself in a very user-unfriendly environment. He requires passwords to gain access to his ultimate target—the user files—and the computer log will have recorded the intrusion. By placing a "Trojan Horse" program within the system's command files, the hacker can acquire "super user" status, normally only afforded to database managers and service engineers. Now, with access to the command files, he inserts a second program, which faithfully records the names and passwords of everyone logging into the apparently well-protected information files, and deletes the record of his intrusion in the computer log. This is the reconnaissance and infiltration phase of his operation.

The hacker will return time and time again to milk the information files, but, aware of the principles of countersurveillance, he is continually alert for the presence of other knowledgeable persons using the system. Once discovered, he will be ambushed. Further access will be denied by carefully concealed ploys, while a wiretap is arranged to trace the hacker and his modem-linked computer through miles of telephone cable.

Consequently, the experienced hacker needs an escape and evasion plan. In order to buy time and conceal his identity, he will enter the military net by way of commercial networks spanning several foreign countries. If discovered, the wiretap will lead initially to the university department or defense installation where staff will be subjected to a long and fruitless security screening. Even if the security team sees through this ruse, the continuing hunt through the commercial networks will come to an abrupt end at the national border. The cooperation required for international wiretap operations can take months to arrange.

Finally, like the Special Forces operator, the hacker will attempt to hid his tracks by clearing the computer logs along his path. He may then destroy the target computer system by inserting a logic bomb or virus. During the late 1980s, German-based Soviet spies were able to penetrate many American defense computers by means of these techniques. Computer hacking provides an analogy for the problems facing special operations. If the target country is well defended, the problems begin again before the enemy's border or coast is even sighted.

Basic training This covers the "common-core" skills vital for long unsupported missions in hostile territory. The training covers map-reading and navigation, radio communications, emergency first aid, small-patrol procedures and survival, evasion, resistance to interrogation and escape (SERE).

Specialist training Having completed basic training, each patrol and team member is faced with specializing in a vital skill such as combat medicine, demolitions, radio communications, or weapons.

This training phase is intensive and places great demands on the man's intellectual abilities. A weapons specialist on a US Special Forces "A" Team, for example, is required to have an intimate knowledge of more than sixty of the world's small arms. Similarly, the medical specialist undergoes a sixteen-week medical course, so tough that a Training Company Commander, Major Rocky Farr, boasted: "Put the average medical student on our schedule, and he probably couldn't make it." The combat engineer is taught the quickest way to build a sturdy bridge or the most economical way of destroying it. If the team runs out of military explosive, he can manufacture comparable charges from agricultural and industrial chemicals. The team signaler must not only acquire a proficiency in high-speed morse and aerial theory but must become familiar with a wide range of radio sets and their repair and servicing under field conditions. Candidates who learn these skills are usually faced with training within the "A" Team to absorb combat losses.

Insertion and advanced training Most soldiers are taught the basic techniques for penetrating enemy territory. These include static-line parachuting, helicopter and boat landings, or surface swimming. Some, with the aptitude for high-altitude parachuting or military diving, will specialize in the relatively few methods of penetrating the formidable array of defenses mounted by developed countries (see below). All of the techniques require constant training and practice; consequently, these highly trained cadres are placed in dedicated subunits and would operate together in wartime.

Other advanced training covers vehicle-mounted, small-boat, and arctic and mountain warfare operations. These involve additional clusters of skills. Vehicle operations in the desert require, among other things, a thorough knowledge of navigational astronomy and satellite navigation, while cold-weather warfare requires skiing, climbing, and abseiling aptitudes. Other advanced training includes small-patrol skills, where the soldiers learn the arcs of fire and responsibilities of each person within the patrol. They must also know the contact drills in the event of an ambush or when being pursued by an enemy force. Above all, they must learn to remain invisible and spot the enemy first. Target interdiction, or sniper courses, emphasize concealment, stalking and surveillance, and the precise long-distance shooting techniques needed to eliminate personnel and equipment. Operations and intelligence courses teach how to plan and administer operations, what types of field intelligence to collect, and how to assess its importance.

Unit role training Candidates who have survived the training so far now need to assimilate the skills necessary for their unit's wartime role(s). For example, a reconnaissance team may need to build up a picture of the enemy from road and rail traffic or from tracks and abandoned encampments. The raw intelligence indicators need to be distilled into size, activity, location, unit, time, and equipment (SALUTE), which requires an expert knowledge of the enemy's formations and equipment; and this in turn means many hours spent memorizing uniforms, badges, weapons, and the silhouettes of hardware such as tanks and vehicles. Supply dumps and bases must be approached, avoiding sentries and electronic surveillance equipment, in order for detailed maps and drawings to be made. This information has to be radioed back to headquarters without alerting the enemy's electronic warfare units. The team may be required to direct the resulting air strike. Finally, the team will use their preplanned exfiltration or escape and evasion corridors to link up with friendly forces.

Area of operations training All operational tasks need to be carried out in one or more operational areas which may involve survival under jungle, desert, temperate, or arctic conditions. Each American Special Forces Group is assigned to a specific global area, allowing them to learn the languages, customs, culture, and politics of a restricted number of countries. In contrast, the less specialized US Rangers rotate through an arduous and continuous training cycle in a variety of climates. Foreign weapons courses familiarize the soldiers with a wide range of small arms, support weapons, and ammunition likely to be encountered within their area of operations. Once behind the lines, the team may need to rely on captured weapons and ammunition, particularly when training and organizing local forces.

Specific mission training Certain missions may require special training. For example, the 10th Special Forces contingent, which took part in the abortive Iranian rescue, were faced with the rescue of three American diplomats held on an upper floor of the Iranian Foreign Ministry. Rather than fight their way through the building, floor by floor, they decided to scale the outside walls, using suction cups. Other operations may require special weapons, communications or insertion equipment, or the specialized knowledge necessary to attach unusual military or industrial targets.

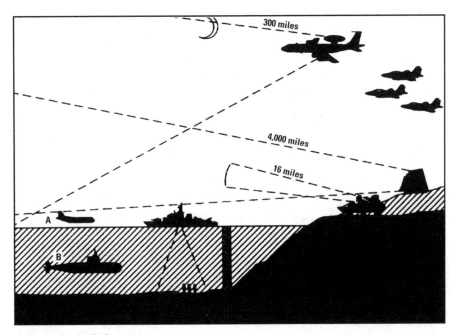

Sea and air defenses

The low-flying C130 (A) faces a formidable gauntlet of obstacles attempting to insert an SAS or any other special forces team inside a developed country. Phase-array radar watches for intruders well beyond the national borders. Inside enemy airspace Airborn Warning and Control System aircraft, such as the E3A Sentry, target hostile aircraft for attacks by fighters and surface-to-air missile sites.

The submarine (B) circumvents the air defenses while it remains submerged but must survive patrols by submarine-hunting ships and aircraft, palisades of sonar buoys and underwater beach defenses.

■ Planning Matrix

What are the main factors to be considered when planning an operation? First and foremost, the mission must be feasible and a way found to get the team in and out of hostile territory. The overall defenses of a country are part of the "enemy situation" and serve to determine which type of insertion offers the best chance of success. This may require the specialized services of air force or navy SOF who will carry the team in and then try to retrieve them again. Today, this is no easy matter, as most advanced countries are protected by concentric rings of sophisticated defenses. A few examples of air and coastal defenses suffice to illustrate this point:

Air defense Over-the-Horizon (OTH) skywave radar compensates for the Earth's curvature by reflecting signals off the ionosphere to provide early warning of low-level intruders such as conventional and stealth aircraft and cruise missiles. Two OTH systems guard America's eastern and western seaboards. The Continental United States Over-the-Horizon-Backscatter (CONUS OTH-B) operated by the US Air Force permits electronic surveillance of aircraft at ranges of 500–1,875 miles. The Australian Jindalee OTH-B sites (Alice Springs, Central Queensland, and Western Australia), which are under construction, will provide coverage of the northern seaboard to a range of 2,500 miles. This system will provide early warning of aircraft and ships carrying illegal immigrants, drug smugglers, terrorists, or military teams which may seek to exploit Australia's sparsely populated northern coastline.

Even an intruder from outer space would find it difficult to arrive unannounced. Phased-array radar is replacing the traditional revolving dish. Arranged into chains of multiple elements, the system can transmit signals between many targets, determining their size, shape and speed; target positions can be updated in millionths of a second. The old adversaries in the Confederation of Independent States and the NATO countries continue to spy on each other. The radar code-named COBRA DANE sits on the edge of the Bering Sea, peering into the former Soviet Union. Designed to watch ballistic missile launches, it performs the workload of a battery of traditional rotating-dish radars. Its 15,360 elements, each 30 meters in diameter, can track hundreds of targets simultaneously.

Two AN/FPS-115 phased-array radars, codenamed PAVE PAWS, defend the seaboard and atmosphere above the eastern United States. Designed to provide early warning against a submarine-launched ballistic missile attack, the two sites, one on the coastline of Florida and the other on the coast of Massachusetts, search 5,500 km into space. Each site has two massive 31-meter diameter faces, each containing 1,792 aerial elements. Together, these cover a 240-degree field of view, to track and log suspicious objects against a background of thousands of satellites and bits of space junk. Two more PAVE PAWS sites have been built in Texas and Georgia, to cover the southern United States. Other phased-array radars defend the NATO countries; these sites at Thule, Greenland, and at Fylingdales, England, are part of the American-operated Perimeter Acquisition Radar Characterization System (PARCS).

Inside enemy airspace, the traditional microwave acquisition-radar searches the sky for likely targets, which are then handed to fire-control radar servicing surface-to-air missile (SAM) and anti-aircraft batteries. The rapid clicks of the three systems guarding the approaches to Moscow have earned these pulse-Doppler radar sites the title of "Russian Woodpecker." Radar pulses travelling at the speed of light are reflected by the target, the strength of the echo indicating size, the time of the return giving the distance to the target, and the direction of the echo providing the bearing of the target. Pulse radar works best against targets of large cross section. Radar employing the Doppler effect detects changes in frequency of the returning echo, caused by the change in displacement of the target with respect to the radar site—in short, it provides a very sensitive means of detecting moving objects such as aircraft.

In addition, the airspace above the frontier or battlefield may be under surveillance by Airborne Warning and Control System (AWACS) aircraft such as the Russian Tu-125 Moss and the American

E3A Sentry, The latter carries sophisticated radar and computer systems which are used to detect suspicious low-flying aircraft and clarify their friend or foe status. The system ensures the interception of hostile aircraft, while providing command and control facilities for friendly aircraft within range of the flying command post. Another airborne phased-array radar system, Joint Surveillance and Target Attack Radar System (JSTARS), acquires ground targets such as fighting vehicles. During the Gulf War, JSTARS was even able to pinpoint coils of barbed wire in the Iraqi defenses!

Misreading these defenses can mean the death of a lingering captivity. At the end of World War II, the American National Security Agency, which eavesdrops on signals and electronics transmissions, attempted to test and analyze the then "steam-driven" radar defending the Soviet border. By 1947, at least thirty of these "Ferret" flights had been shot down, with some survivors parachuting onto Soviet territory. The worst incident involved an Air Force C-130 packed with NSA intercept gear, which crossed into Soviet Armenia in 1958. The plane was intercepted by Mig fighters within minutes, and radio operators at an NSA SigInt (Signals Intelligence) post in Turkey were forced to listen in horror as Russian pilots described the aircraft breaking up under cannon fire. Although some parachutes were reported leaving the aircraft, all seventeen crew members were lost. Another eight American aircraft were shot down by the USSR in the 1950s. The twelve or more aircrew who were known to have survived these latter flights simply disappeared into the gulag prison system. Unlike the high-altitude reconnaissance pilot, Gary Powers, intelligence, SAS, and other special forces personnel are rarely repatriated.

Maritime defenses Coastal seas, shipping routes, and major harbors are watched by a similar array of devices. Land and ship-based groundwave OTH radar can detect ships beyond 190 miles but smaller, more covert craft may be lost in the returning echoes produced by the waves ("Bragg Spectrum"). The American Inshore Undersea Warfare Groups (Naval Special Warfare Group) are charged with defending beaches and anchorages against enemy combat swimmers. This task is undertaken by means of the Mobile Inshore Detection and Surveillance System (MIDASS)—a network of high-frequency radar and sonar buoys—and the Battle Area Surveillance System (BASS), which provides a network of land and underwater electronic sensors. Surface and underwater sonar networks also watch Western and Russian ballistic missile submarines as they pass through natural choke points such as the Greenland—Iceland—Faroes Gap, the Barents Sea, and the narrow straits separating the Japanese island group. Shore and shipborne surveillance radar maintain a similar watch on surface vessels.

Close to the coast, intruders may have to contend with thermal imagery and electronic sensors, designed to detect bubbles and chemical emissions, and high-frequency sonar pulses designed to kill or disable divers. On the beach, the traditional defenses of minefields, barbed wire, and guard dogs are reinforced by microwave fences and flammable, sticky petroleum-based Astrolite fields triggered by sensor devices.

An early type of Astrolite field may have incinerated a party of German commandos who attempted a landing on Britain's Norfolk coast during World War II. This area had a number of high-security installations, and an enduring legend has it that a number of Germans were buried secretly in Norfolk churchyards. The story suggests that the party was detected as they approached the beach, but by then it was too late. Trapped in a sea of flames, the commandos were burnt beyond recognition and many of those who were asked to dispose of the remains were sickened and horrified by the carnage. The story also claims that the government of the day classified all documents relating to the incident as "Top Secret" and that more recently the records were destroyed to prevent their release.

Special operations personnel even run the risk of being killed by underwater defenses in home harbors. On April 18, 1956, Communist Party Secretary Nikita Khrushchev and Soviet Prime Minister Marshal Nikolai Bulganin arrived in Portsmouth Harbor for a goodwill visit to Britain. They travelled on the cruiser *Ordzhonikidze* accompanied by a destroyer. Britain's intelligence community were very anxious to learn more about the *Ordzhonikidze's* propeller design as the boat could travel much faster than British naval experts had calculated. This had originally been attempted in Russian waters but the mini-submarine and combat swimmers were unable to penetrate the harbor defenses. Now offered a second chance, Britain's MI6 asked Commander Lionel "Buster" Crabb, a pioneer and expert in underwater warfare, to conduct an underwater inspection of the Soviet vessel. Early on the morning of April 19, Crabb slipped into the uninviting dark green waters of Portsmouth Harbor, briefly returning for extra weights to overcome a buoyancy problem, before setting off for the cruiser. He was never seen again. Although there have been some wild stories that Crabb was taken to the USSR to help train Soviet frogmen, it is likely that he was killed or disabled by the cruiser's underwater defenses, before being recovered by Soviet divers and taken aboard the *Ordzhonikidze* through an underwater chamber. On June 9, 1957, a fisherman pulled a body from the water outside Chichester Harbor. The body, which was dressed in a black rubber diving suit, had no head and the hands were missing. The mystery deepened when a close friend claimed, quite definitely, that the corpse was not that of Crabb. Whatever the final truth of the "Crabb affair," the diver's body was laid to rest in Portsmouth cemetery.

The "enemy situation," of course, also covers the size and level of training of the target country's armed forces, the sophistication of its security apparatus, and the resulting level of surveillance and control exerted on the civilian population. For their part, the operational planners will seek to exploit weaknesses or, if necessary, create their own gaps in the defenses. We shall examine these techniques in later chapters. This, then, is one component of the planning matrix that is used to assess the feasibility of the operation and consequently the risk of discovery and subsequent political repercussions.

Another component of the planning matrix is the level of training of the units at the planners' disposal. The securest forms of insertion, such as high-altitude parachuting and underwater penetration, require special training to attain and maintain proficiency. As a consequence, only relatively small cadres are trained in these techniques. It may be necessary to examine the feasibility of less specialized techniques such as surface swimming, static-line parachuting, or an unassisted entry through a neighboring neutral or friendly country.

If used, a specialized insertion vehicle must meet the operational requirements. A submarine may offer the most secure means of insertion and exfiltration, but its use requires extensive rehearsal and interservice cooperation. Such cooperation is usually available for air operations but, although aircraft are capable of inserting ground or swimmer teams together with a considerable weight of equipment, security depends upon the aircraft remaining undetected. Assault craft and other surface vessels also require interservice cooperation and, while they can deliver the team and their equipment close to the coast, they provide the least clandestine means of insertion.

Terrain and climate of the operational area Once behind the border defenses, bleak, rugged, and uninhabited areas of wilderness such as moors, mountains, swamps, deserts, jungle, tundra, and heavy bush can offer a "geographical backdoor" to an otherwise well-defended country. The Alaskan/Canadian tundra and the arid northern Australian coastline are two examples of such regions: consequently these countries maintain their own special warfare surveillance units to meet this potential threat. The team must be equipped and trained to survive for long periods in an inhospitable environment. While the military aspects of operations in sparsely inhabited areas are simplified, the terrain poses its own challenge, requiring specialized equipment or vehicles.

Usually, the terrain dictates the campaign. The unsuccessful insertion of an SAS team onto the Fortuna Glacier during operations to retake South Georgia on April 21, 1982 necessitated the use of sledges, skis, tents, and arctic clothing. The problems associated with the glacier had been obvious during the planning phase and had led some observers to suggest that the mission was untenable. Nevertheless, it did offer a means of landing unseen on South Georgia. The 200-lb. equipment-laden sledges, 80-lb. Bergens (rucksacks), frequent blizzards, and the every-present danger of falling into a crevasse resulted in the team covering only half a mile after an exhausting five-hour trek.

MISSION PLANNING MATRIX	
Mission	The mission may require rapid deployment into the operational area, thereby indicating the most expeditious method of infiltration. In other cases, however, mission success may depend on maintaining secrecy with speed of secondary importance.
Enemy Situation	Enemy capabilities, disposition, and security measures affect the means selected for infiltration: a heavily guarded border may preclude land infiltration; a strongly defended and patrolled coastline may eliminate infiltration by water; the enemy's air detection and defense systems may reduce air delivery potential.
Terrain	Land formations must be considered in selecting the method of infiltration/exfiltration. Terrain affects the selection of altitudes, approach and exit routes, and landing areas of mission aircraft. Mountains could force aircraft to fly at higher altitudes, resulting in greater exposure to enemy air detection and defense systems.
Weather	Seasonal weather conditions affect infiltrations/exfiltrations. Factors to be considered include temperature, precipitation, visibility, clouds, and wind. High surface winds and their effect upon surf conditions or periods of reduced visibility may prohibit the use of parachutes, inflatable boats, or surface/subsurface swimming as entry/recovery techniques. These same conditions generally favor land infiltration/exfiltration. The adverse weather aerial delivery system (AWADS) reduces the impact of weather as a limiting factor on air infiltrations.
Hydrography	In maritime operations, hydrography is the science of describing the sea and marginal land areas and their effects on such operations. The selection of water as a means of infiltration/exfiltration is influenced by the hydrographic conditions

Hydrography (Cont.)	on the foreshore and the nearshore sea approach, such as the offshore water depth; beach gradients; the nature of tide, surf, currents, and sea bottom; and the location of reefs, sandbars, seaweed, or natural/manmade obstacles.
Astronomical Conditions	Periods of twilight, sunrise and sunset, moon phase, and moonrise and moonset must be considered for infiltrations/exfiltrations.
Distance	The distance to the objective area must be considered in selection of infiltration means.
Training	The training given to the SAS and other special forces is usually sufficient to prepare them for any means of infiltration/exfiltration. However, it is not anticipated that all members of a selected operational element will be equally proficient in a given skill or technique at any given time. Should areas be discovered in which weaknesses exist, added emphasis is placed on such areas. A properly balanced training program will produce a reasonably proficient team member. Special training programs are required to attain and maintain proficiency for: • Surface and open-water swimming • SCUBA • Military free-fall (MFF) parachuting • Submarine operations • Inflatable boat handling • Insertion/extraction techniques • Survival, evasion, resistance, and escape
Accompanying Equipment / Supplies	The quantity and types of accompanying equipment/supplies carried on initial infiltration are influenced by: • The situation in the UWOA • The size of the resistance force • The enemy threat • The capabilities/limitations of the mission air/naval craft

Assessing the risk of launching a special operation

The risk incurred by the proposed operation must be set against the potential threat. The greatest level of threat is posed by the high-intensity conflict, or total war, where there is the real risk that nuclear, biological, and chemical (NBC) weapons will be employed at the strategic, tactical, and theater levels. The prospective high-intensity battlefield is perceived as a chaotic and immensely destructive clash between massed armored and mobile infantry forces, with the employment of modern, highly lethal NBC systems.

A lower threat is posed by the mid-intensity conflict, involving a clash between major armed forces, carrying the prospect of the limited use of weapons of mass destruction but with little real threat to national survival (e.g., World War II; the Korean War, 1950–53; and the Gulf War, 1991).

By contrast, the low-intensity conflict involves a fraction of a country's armed forces in a range of operations such as counterinsurgencies, counterterrorism, border and territorial disputes, and the rescue of civilians or hostages (e.g., the Falklands War, 1982; Grenada, 1983). Lastly, peacetime operations are unusual in combining the lowest threat to national survival with a high risk of political repercussions if the mission is discovered or fails (e.g., the abortive rescue of the Tehran hostages, 1980; and the *Rainbow Warrior* affair, 1985).

Most wilderness areas are bedeviled by adverse seasonal weather conditions. While the Iraqi and Coalition armies faced each other across the Saudi-Kuwait border during the 1991 Gulf War, the longer border between Iraq and Saudi Arabia offered every possibility for covert insertion. Iraqi patrols were confined to the few existing roads (a single route, the Tapline road, ran along the Saudi side of the border), the terrain hindered cross-country mobility, and there were large navigable gaps between the dispersed Iraqi units. However, the border ran across the top of the notorious An-Nafud desert. During the summer, the ground is burnt barren, there is no standing water and gale-force winds bury livestock, people, and even whole encampments. Towering sandstorms and dust devils reduce visibility, interfere with radio communications, and disable vehicles. In winter, high arctic fronts from Russia interface with the southeast sleet and snow, turning the desert into a frozen quagmire.

The missile launchers firing Soviet-built Scuds at Israel from the H3/H2 area of western Iraq were important targets for Allied Special Forces teams. The tyranny of distance, the need for precise navigation and secure communications, and the necessity of carrying rations and ample water were solved by employing a range of vehicles that served as self-contained life-support systems. The Americans used the Chenowth Fast Attack Vehicle, a low-slung, armed, hi-tech dune-buggy. The British firm Longline had provided the SAS with a similar design, but while the British Special Forces were impressed by the speed and mobility of the Light Strike Vehicle, they found that its cargo and fuel capacity restricted missions, forcing them to return to their tried and tested Land Rovers. Two types of SAS mission were launched into the "Scud boxes" of western Iraq. The first put road-watch surveillance teams close to Iraqi roads to report the presence of Scud convoys and, when possible, acquire them for American attack aircraft. These eight-man teams, consisting of two four-man patrols, were initially dropped by helicopter 140–180 miles behind enemy lines and, once in their static Ops (Observation Post), were left to their own devices. Dependent upon helicopters for resupply and ex-traction, if these teams found themselves in trouble, they were faced with a dangerous and arduous journey back to the forward base of the Saudi border or Syria, the only immediate friendly country (Jordan handed one evader, and American pilot, back to the Iraqi Army).

The second type of mission employed twelve or more armed Land Rovers and trucks, organized into half-squadron (thirty-man) fighting columns. Four such columns, each carrying 1.5 tons of supplies and ammunition and accompanied by motorcycle scouts acting as lead and flank scouts, established themselves behind enemy lines. Armed with .50 calibre heavy machine guns, general purpose machine guns, 40mm grenade launchers, Milan wire-guided antitank missiles, and Stinger anti-aircraft missiles, these fighting columns attacked mobile Scud launchers, Iraqi bases, and communications equipment.

How Saddam Hussein lost his SCUD missiles

The hostile environment of western Iraq and the resupply navigation and communication problems it presented forced the majority of British and American teams to operate with their own transport. While static roadwatch teams could only pinpoint Scud convoys as they passed in front of their hides, Delta Force Teams in Fast Attack Vehicles (A) and SAS fighting columns in Land Rovers (B) were able to shadow the convoys, constantly updating their positions for American attack aircraft or attacking the launchers in running ambushes.

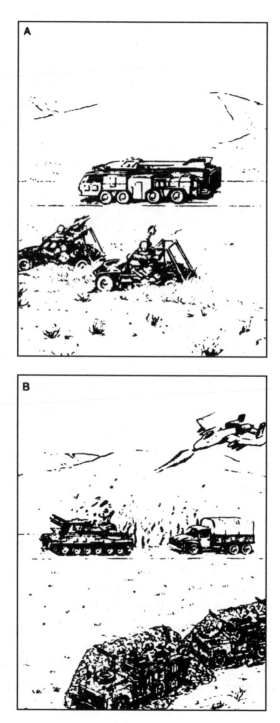

Local weather and astronomical conditions can also have a dramatic effect on the insertion. Reduced visibility may offer air operations some degree of concealment; but although modern equipment can be used to navigate to the precise area, moonlight and minimum meteorological conditions may be necessary if the pilot is to recognize the drop zone (DZ) and determine the necessary approach path to drop his parachutists safely. Air-landing and high-altitude parachuting are particularly dependent upon local conditions. At least two major World War II operations to land parachutists or gliders in Norway (Gunnerside and Rype) were defeated by the severe winter conditions. Operational necessity required both to be launched into the teeth of winter storms with the consequential loss of aircrew and special mission teams.

Hydrographical conditions such as tides, currents, surf, beach topography, and underwater obstacles can affect maritime operations. It may take swimmer reconnaissance teams and experienced naval personnel to identify the hidden dangers of a particular area. For example, tides are minimal in protected seas such as the Mediterranean, while the Bristol Channel can experience 50-ft. tides. More unusually, the Channel Islands enjoy four tides each day rather than the usual two. Currents and tides are influenced by the gravitational pull of the moon, and an otherwise weak current can pose a serious threat to combat swimmers during the full-moon period. Two attempts to land Sea-Air-Land (SEAL) teams on an island off the North Vietnamese coast, close to the Red River estuary, to rescue escapees from a prison camp were scotched by the powerful river currents at low tide, resulting, indirectly, in the deaths of two swimmers. Attempts to land American SEALs and Air Force SOCCT commandos close to Salines airfield during the invasion of Grenada on the night of October 23, 1983 also failed when a number of men were killed parachuting into the sea at night. The survivors pressed on but the rough seas swamped the boats. Similar efforts to land British reconnaissance teams onto the beaches of South Georgia were defeated by equipment failure, strong winds, and glacial ice which punctured the inflatables.

Russian air defenses

▲   Air Force HQS
●   Missile complexes
   Concentrations of air defense forces

Logistics A special mission team needs a mass of equipment to support their independent operations. The mission itself may require special equipment, and a distant target country may be reached by a succession of different transport (e.g., aircraft, submarine, and finally small boat) employing a range of additional specialized kit such as parachutes, diving equipment, and inflatables with outboard motors. Different terrains and climates demand further concessions. Machetes, hammocks, insect repellent, foot powder, and a range of antimicrobial drugs are required for jungle operations, while waterproof and thermal clothing, skis, snowshoes, ice picks, crampons, and abseiling equipment may be required for arctic and mountain operations.

Top on the inventory is the soldier's personal kit. An operator's main protection from the elements is his camouflage fatigues. These must also be role-compatible. They must allow freedom of movement when worn under a parachute harness and serve as a rugged, weatherproof outer shell, which accommodates carrying heavy loads over long distances. Some of the first fatigues to meet these criteria were the British World War II "windproofs." Designed as a loose-fitting smock and trousers, the tin material provided a wind-resistant outer shell which, although not waterproof, dried quickly with the soldier's body heat. The Royal Marine's Special Boat Service retained the full suit for a period after the war, while the SAS tended to use the smock only—in fact it became their unofficial badge. The new Disruptive Pattern Material (DPM) smock in NATO camouflage is available commercially and is employed more widely.

Other countries have turned to the more expensive "breathable" fabrics. Pores in the material allow perspiration to escape, thus preventing the inner garments from becoming soaked in sweat, while the outside remains wind- and waterproof. Some French parachute reconnaissance units use an outer Gore-Tex camouflaged uniform with an inner layer of Thinsulate, which has the same properties as goose down and gives protection against extreme cold in mountain operations. Underneath this shell, the parachutists wear a "guerrilla" uniform of jacket and trousers. Specially designed for recon teams, the jacket has deep pockets and a large collar that keeps the neck and back of the head warm. The trousers are worn with suspenders to prevent them sagging when the pockets are full. Chasseur-type gaiters protect the calves and keep the insides of the soldier's boots dry in snow or wet conditions.

Some camouflaged shells are designed specifically for the operational terrain. American Special Forces units in Vietnam found that tiger-striped fatigues blended well with the mountainous jungle, while plain cotton-poplin fatigues, sprayed with black paint, enabled them to pass as VC guerrillas or peasants. In the Gulf, US Special Forces teams who were inserted into the patchwork of fields and canals in the Euphrates Valley were provided with green-and-brown camouflage rather than the "chocolate chip" desert fatigues worn by other Coalition forces. However, while superfluous items such as unit badges, parachute wings, and flashes are scrupulously removed to deny the enemy intelligence, unusual uniforms still identify the wearer as "special."

Minor foot and ankle injuries can slow or even disable a team member. Consequently, the choice of boots becomes very important. A snug fit will avoid friction injuries and blisters, while parachutists require firm support around the ankle to prevent sprains and fractures on landing. "High" boots, however, can restrict the calf muscles, resulting in injury to the Achilles tendon when crossing steep ground. The boots must be light and comfortable but hard-wearing over a range of terrains. The soles should provide traction on wet ground without the tread becoming caked with mud and stones. Many European units favor "Adidas" hiking boots or "Danner" combat boots, but, again, special boots leave distinctive prints for enemy tracking teams. To counter this problem, American teams in the Gulf taped cardboard over the soles of their boots.

Another major problem is to keep the feet dry and warm. The wet conditions encountered on the Falklands led to many cases of trench-foot—a disabling injury that results from continual immersion in cold water. Some SAS teams avoided this problem by using NBC (nuclear, biological, chemical) overboots. Another method is to place a plastic bag over the foot, followed by heavy woolen socks and a second plastic bag. Spare socks and laces are also important. Pairs of socks can be rotated, with the wet pair placed under clothes to dry with the soldier's body heat.

A soldier's equipment has to be carried in some sort of rucksack. It must have sufficient capacity to carry 80–150 lbs. of equipment and also serve as an equipment container on parachute descents. The British SAS and other special forces formerly used the GS Bergen, originally designed for ski troops. This served as an admirable equipment container but it rode low on the soldier's back and had a relatively low capacity. The new large-capacity "high" Bergen owes much to advances in commercial climbing packs, with a high center of gravity and additional external pockets and attachment points for further kit. This pack, which has a sturdy but heavy steel frame to withstand the shock of parachute landings, is used by para and SAS/SBS troops.

A place must be found within the pack for the soldier's individual personal and military equipment and the kit assigned to him on the basis of his role within the team (e.g., a radio set or ammunition for a support weapon). Surveillance and reconnaissance teams may share bulky items, such as "kit mats" and sleeping bags, as a section of the team will always be left on guard or observing the target. Stoves and eating utensils can be shared for the same reason. Extra canteens of water may form a large part of a team's load where water sources are few or under enemy surveillance. On four-day reconnaissance missions inside Iraq, each member of a Special Forces "A" Team carried five gallons of water, sufficient for the mission, and an additional two days' supply in case their extraction was delayed. Although personal hygiene is particularly important under hot, moist field conditions, soap and other toiletries leave distinctive traces. On short operations, medicated wipes provide a useful alternative. Plastic bags are essential, too, for waterproofing valuable equipment and for containing and, if necessary, storing bodily wastes.

Other necessities are divided between individual and team equipment. Each man will have his own watch, map, and compass. Accurate multifunction watches, recording both local and Greenwich Mean Time, provide a means of calculating longitude. Watches or a time signal are also vital for obtaining a position, using the techniques of navigational astronomy. A more recent and convenient system of checking position can be provided by the team's Global Positioning System (GPS) manpack. GPS or satellite navigation equipment compares the time taken by a series of satellites to transmit signals to Earth with the time they are actually received. This allows the team's position to be triangulated to an accuracy of 50 ft. (the simultaneous signals from three satellites are needed for an exact two-dimensional fix).

A team also needs good radio communications with base, with the pilots of combat aircraft called upon for assistance, and with the boat or helicopter crews detailed to extract them. These different military communication nets often require different radios. In the Gulf, American teams carried three radio sets covering the FM, UHF, and SATCOM bands. The LST-5 was linked to a heavy satellite dish, which passed coded signals to and from military communications satellites.

The highly directional line of sight transmissions were almost impossible for the Iraqis to intercept. However, the redundancy of carrying three or more transmitters into battle (more than 175 lbs. of equipment) has since persuaded USSOCOM (United States Special Operation Command) to invest a new multichannel radio called Joint Advanced Special Operations Radio System (JASORS).

The team must also be able to cope with battlefield injuries and minor illnesses, as the medical evacuation of a single soldier can endanger the whole team or even scotch the entire operation. Each man will have a field dressing as an immediate treatment to cover wounds and reduce blood loss. Other necessities may be carried by the medic or divided among the team. Such a kit includes morphine syrettes and other painkillers, inflatable splints, plasma expanders (to stabilize casualties with severe blood loss), and a range of anti-inflammatory and antibiotic creams and capsules to treat minor infections and skin lesions. Rapid treatment of minor skin disorders is particularly important in hot, humid environments, where cuts and bites quickly turn septic. Instrument packs also enable the medic to perform necessary surgery and dental repair.

What happened to the Spetsnaz when the Soviet Union was dissolved?

Most former Soviet special forces units have been retained by the Confederation of Independent States. Russian forces are being withdrawn to bases within Russia's borders, while many of the former republics have created their own special units for internal defense.

Russian Spetsnaz are now realigned toward the defense of its borders and countering terrorism and disorder inside the former republics. Another peacetime task is the organization and support of partisan forces to counter a potential invasion. The principal wartime missions remain the conduct of sabotage, diversion, and reconnaissance under the direction of planning staff at the front and army levels. Such missions include identifying nuclear weapons, command and control centers, and reserve formations for nuclear and conventional missile strikes.

In wartime, Spetsnaz units would be tasked by the Ministry of Defense through the Military Intelligence Directorate (GRU) of its General Staff. Peacetime missions will be conducted under KGB control. This dual control is apparent in the structure of the 5th Spetsnaz Brigade based at Maryina Gorka near the city of Minsk. The 5th Brigade has three operational parachute battalions, a reserve battalion which acts as a training unit, and a special mine company which deploys nuclear mines and antitank weapons. An operations section (around ten majors and captains) plans and executes operations under the command of the army chief of staff. The secret service section consists of two or three GRU officers who liaise between the brigade and agents in their area of operations. A KGB section, drawn from Departments Three and Eight, handles new official missions, nuclear mine safety, secret communications, and counterintelligence. Other command and control groups include administrative and financial sections and an officers company.

The Spetsnaz brigade is the basic SOF unit, comprising around 400–1,300 men, into 200-man *otryady*. Each *otriad* is divided into three fighting companies and a signals company. During operations, a company would be further divided into three sections, each of three patrols containing four to five men. Five such brigades, highly trained in specialist assassination and diversionary roles, are reputed to be under the wartime command of the GRU Second Directorate, while another twenty brigades are under Group of Forces or District control.

In addition, each of the four fleets deploy a naval Spetsnaz brigade subordinate to the Intelligence Directorate at Naval Headquarters. These consist of a parachute battalion, combat-swimmer battalion, mini-submarine battalion, and a special missions company. The naval Spetsnaz role is to seize beachheads, guide in the naval infantry, and eliminate any enemy forces which attempt to oppose the landing. Naval infantry then fight their way out of the beachhead, followed by successive waves of conventional army units. Two further Spetsnaz units are tasked below district level. Long Range Reconnaissance Regiments, divided into six or seven companies, are attached to

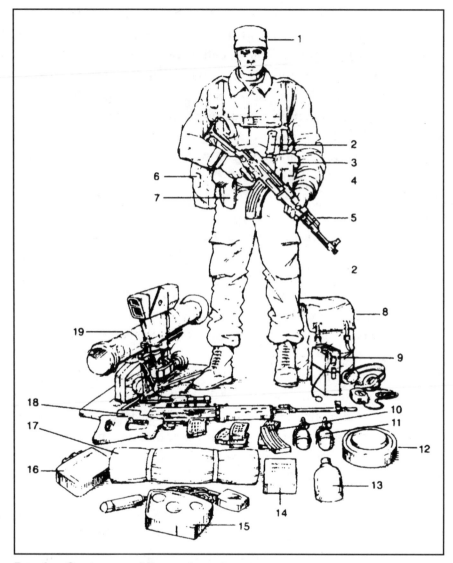

Russian Spetsnaz soldier and equipment

1. Cap—the majority of his body heat is lost from the head and neck.

2. Fighting/survival knife. Spetsnaz use three types of fighting knife, including one with a spring-propelled blade.

3. Map case—carried by officers and NCOs.

4. Pouch for NBC respirator worn on belt at back.

5. 5.45mm AKS-74 or AK-74 assault rifle.

6. Pouch for magazines.

7. Pouch for Bi-8 infrared binoculars.

8. RD-54 paratrooper's rucksack with detachable pouches containing binoculars and hand grenades.

9. R-392 VHF radio transmitter for group-level voice communications. The Spetsnaz group will also use R-357 HF radio with burst transmission for communicating with base and the secure R-255PP "receive only" radio for retrieving air drops and the issue of orders inside the group.

10. Spare ammunition magazines.

11. RGD-5 and F-1 hand grenades.

12. PMN-2 antipersonnel mine.

13. Water.

14. Rations—although Spetsnaz will often "live off the land."

15. RRS-1 passive receiver for detecting enemy radar sites, a prime Spetsnaz target. The group may also carry the "Trapetsiya" 299 receiver which detects the enemy's underground communication lines.

16. The Mon-50 Claymore-type mine. Triggered by trip wire, its fragmentation zone exceeds 150 ft.

17. "Dozhd" paratrooper poncho/air mattress.

18. 7.62mm Dragunov sniper rifle.

19. AT-4 "Spigot" antitank missile. The group also carries RPG-18 and RPG-7D rocket-propelled grenades. These are not necessarily for use against armored vehicles. The North Vietnamese Army (NVA) used antitank rockets directly against strong points or fired the missiles into the tree canopy above trench-lines to produce a fragmentation effect. In some Vietnam War battles, every second NVA soldier carried a rocket-propelled grenade launcher, and every man carried RPG ammunition. British Marines and Paras and Russian special forces excelled in using antitank missiles against strong-points during the Falklands and Afghanistan conflicts respectively.

Other group equipment (not shown) includes PSN (parachute, Spetsnaz) steerable parachute, GK-30 container parachutes, one- and two-man hang gliders, 200 g and 400 g blocks of plastic explosive, the PMN-1 antipersonnel mine, and the MS-1, MS-2 and MS-3 booby-trap mines.

each tactical theater and one Independent Company (headquarters and three parachute platoons) is attached to each Army.

Rations are always a problem and may be instrumental in determining mission duration. As rucksacks get heavier, a vicious circle develops where the increase in weight demands more work and thus more energy-producing food. In Vietnam, a partial solution to this unfavorable equipment/weight ratio was suggested in the patrol reports from teams maintaining surveillance on the North Vietnamese supply routes known as the Ho Chi Minh Trail. Intelligence analysts calculated that on average, 100 Communist porters moved 30 tonnes of supplies over 30 miles on an individual consumption of 2.7 lbs. of food per day. In an attempt to emulate this, the Americans produced Long Range Reconnaissance Patrol (LRRP) Rations, containing 1,200 kilocalories of freeze-dried food in a package that weighed only 11 ounces. However, the new rations generated two additional problems. Firstly, they were "energy depleted," containing 1,200 kilocalories less than the normal C-Rations. This shortfall had to be made up from sugar and protein-rich foods scavenged from C-Ration packs. Secondly, the freeze-dried rations required an additional weight- and space-consuming canteen of water per ration pack. Large quantities of water were naturally required in the hot, humid jungles of Southeast Asia. Well aware of this, Vietcong guerrillas ambushed or booby-trapped the local water sources. In a running firefight, the water often ran out before the ammunition.

Vietnam veteran and Ranger, Jim England, summarized these problems in a manual written for special operations teams:

> When looking at mission duration and comparing it to ration requirements, missions very much in excess of 7–14 days can be hard to justify. A team could become virtually immobile due to the weight of needed supplies. . . . Mobility and stealth are decreased when loads become too heavy, and the soldier is too often physically worn down by midday. Fatigue affects alertness, making him more vulnerable to detection and error.

Longer missions are dependent upon resupply. The traditional resupply operation damages team security and is dangerous to the air or naval support crews who are asked to undertake the long and difficult journey. Alternative logistical support may be provided by pre-positioned supply dumps or caches. A team may enter an area with additional supplies, which are left in a line of concealed caches for use on the return journey. Alternatively, previous operations may have created a network of supply caches within the operational area. Unfortunately, caches may involve using the same route twice and thus passing through enemy forces already alerted to the team's presence. Additionally, a cache may already have been discovered and ambushed, or may be difficult to find again in rough terrain (desert and jungle). During the Vietnam War, 30–60 day patrols into Communist-held areas of Laos were supported by caches disguised as unexploded napalm canisters. These were dropped by combat aircraft along the patrol's route, while a real air strike nearby completed the deception. An excellent idea in theory, it ignored the Communists' habit of carefully locating and cannibalizing unexploded bombs for their own booby traps and munitions.

If the mission turns sour, team members may have to fend for themselves until they can be rescued or reach the safety of friendly forces or a neutral country. Escape and evasion (E&E) and survival equipment is usually carried in pockets or pouches on an escape belt. The reason for this is simple: with the enemy closing in, rucksacks are dumped, rigged with explosives to deny the enemy an intelligence harvest of specialized kit and documents. However, the soldiers will still retain aircraft panels and heliographs with which to attract rescue aircraft, and a cloth map and compass for navigation. Filters and sedimentation bags can be used to purify water, while fishing lines, nets, and snares can be used to catch game. Survival shelters can be constructed with survival knives, wire saws, and a little know-how. Where security permits, a small fire provides the evader with cooked food, sterilized water, and warmth. Waterproofed matches or cigarette lighters give a fast, reliable means of starting a fire.

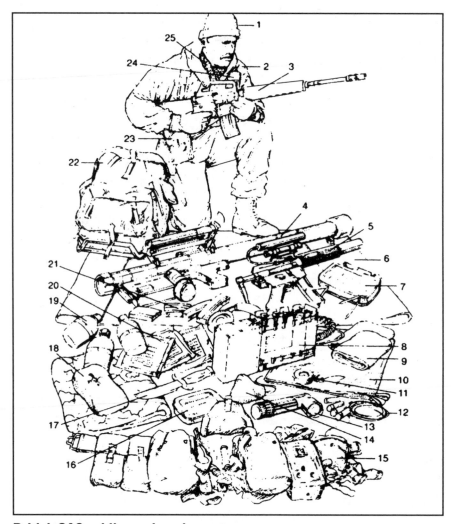

British SAS soldier and equipment

1. Woollen hat.

2. Windproof smock.

3. 5.56mm M16A2 assault rifle. Also use M16s fitted with the M203 40mm grenade launcher.

4. FIM-92A Stinger anti-aircraft missile. SAS Land Rovers and foot patrols may also carry the Milan antitank missile and the 40mm M79 grenade launcher.

5. Silenced 9mm Meckler & Koch MP5-SD6. The submachine gun of choice for the British SAS and American Special Forces during the Gulf War.

6. Rubber kit mat. Arctic and desert sleeping bags may be carried by every second man.

7. Claymore mine (detonated by command wire, time fuse, or trip wire).

8. PRC-319 HF/VHF radio transmitter with data, voice, and continuous wave and burst Morse facility. The SAS also use the Clansman HF transmitter for voice and inter-Troop communications, the MIL/UST-1 satellite ground terminal (SATCOM), the vehicle-mounted PRC-320 radio, and several experimental American radio transmitters.

9. Plastic bags. Large plastic bags can serve as emergency sleeping bags and are used as waterproof linings for Bergens. Small plastic bags are used to store rubbish and human waste.

10. Map.

11. Prismatic compass. SAS also use satellite navigation equipment.

12. Wire for trip wires, fishing lines, and assorted uses.

13. Torch with red filter and spare batteries.

14. String or twine. Variety of uses including "basher" (one-man shelter) construction, tying down equipment, and communications cord used to connect soldiers in surveillance or overnight rest stops.

15. Escape belt. Contains food, escape and evasion equipment, spare ammunition, a water bottle, weapon cleaning kit, and other essentials. Becomes a life-saver if the soldier is forced to abandon his Bergen.

16. Survival kit inside old cigarette tin (wire snares, fishing line, matches, button-compass, and water purification tablets). Held in escape belt together with water sedimentation bag, heliograph, Search and Rescue radio beacon, escape map, foreign currency, survival chocolate, and cooker.

17. Survival knife.

18. Medical kit.

19. Water. One entire Bergen may be used to carry additional water.

20. Dehydrated rations.

21. Additional ammunition.

22. Bergen with steel frame (serves as an equipment container during parachute descents).

23. Binoculars and night-vision scopes inside respective waterproof pouches.

24. Field dressing taped to webbing.

25. Camouflaged face veil worn as a scarf. Used in personal camouflage.

Surveillance missions also require hides and, depending upon the area to be covered, may also employ a range of electronic remote surveillance equipment such as microphones, magnetometers, and seismic probes. During the ground war in the Gulf, American eight-man teams from the 5th Special Forces set up road watches on Highway Eight, the main route from Baghdad to Basra, to provide early warning of Iraqi reinforcements rushing to the front. Close to the road, the teams used NVG/PVS-7 night-vision goggles to help them identify traffic at night. Their four-man hides consisted of 9-foot-square holes dug in the sand and covered with camouflaged canvas tarpaulins. These were covered in turn with a foot or so of sand and some vegetation for concealment. The amount of soil on top proved critical. During pre-mission training in Saudi Arabia, some teams discovered, to their horror, that a little too much sand collapsed the roof, burying the men inside the hide.

With each man carrying up to 150 lbs. of equipment, personal weapons must be light, dependable, and yet capable, in concert, of putting down a concentrated barrage of fire to get the team out of trouble. The aforementioned 5th Special Forces teams carried four standard M16A2 carbines, two M203 grenade launchers (a 40mm grenade launcher mounted beneath an M16A2), and two Heckler & Koch suppressed MP5SD submachine guns. In addition, each man carried a 9mm Beretta pistol for close-quarter battle.

Russian Spetsnaz teams tasked with wide-ranging raids and sabotage require a greater range of weapons and munitions. The Russian commander and his deputy in a seven-man team may be armed with an AKS-74 5.45mm assault rifle or 7.62mm AKMS with silencer; Makarov 9mm automatic pistol with silencer, hand grenades (RGD-5 and F-1), grenade launchers (RPG-18 or RPG-22), an R-392 VHF radio set (Spetsnaz field net), passive night-vision binoculars (BN-1), and Bi-8 infrared binoculars. The radio operator is equipped with an AKS-74, Makarov pistol, hand grenades and grenade launcher, and a burst-transmission R-357 HF radio set for communications with headquarters. Reconnaissance personnel carry the AKS-74 and grenades and grenade launcher. Antitank men carry the RPG-7D antitank rocket launcher and five rockets, hand grenades, and a Makarov pistol or the shortened version of the AKS-74; the 5.45mm AKS-U.

Spetsnaz favors fighting knives, and each group member may carry the AKS-74 bayonet, the MR-1 throwing knife, and the NR-2 "silent-fire" knife which hurls a blade at the opponent and has an effective range of around 50 ft. Group equipment includes the R-255PP receive-only radio, for intergroup and aircraft communications, the 7.62mm SVD sniper rifle, NSPU night-vision equipment, AT-4 Spigot antitank missiles, and specialized EW equipment for pinpointing enemy radio and radar emissions. Mines can have a devastating effect on enemy lines of communications (see chapter 6). Spetsnaz groups may carry the OZM-72 antipersonnel jumping mine, MON-50 antipersonnel directional mine, PMN-1 and PMN-2 antipersonnel mines, and the MS-1, MS-2 and MS3 booby-trap mines. For demolition tasks, Spetsnaz uses standard 200–400g nitrotoluene (TNT) briquettes, "Plastit 4" plastic explosive, and a range of cumulative, concentrated, or shaped charges.

■ Exfiltration

At the end of the mission, the team must be extracted from enemy territory or find their own way out. Extraction not only requires a commitment to put an aircraft or boat inside enemy territory but to perform a precision link-up with the team at the right time and place. This, in turn, requires covert radio communications, the double-edged nature of which may threaten security (see chapter 5).

Occasionally, circumstances dictate that the soldiers are left to their own devices. During the Falklands conflict, the British SAS planned to strike at airfields inside Argentina. Their targets were the Super Etendard aircraft and their Exocet missiles which were attacking the British fleet. The crew of one Sea King helicopter, having inserted a reconnaissance team close to Rio Gallegos airfield, had orders to ditch at sea and escape into neutral Chile. However, weather conditions forced the helicopter to crash-land on the Chilean coast, threatening the security of a politically sensitive operation that might have brought Venezuela and Peru into the war. The operation was aborted, forcing the eight-man SAS team to make their own way across the Chilean border.

In the event of a disaster overtaking the operation, or individuals becoming separated from the team, the soldiers must have an escape and evasion (E&E) plan. Ingredients include local money—or a universal currency such as gold—an acquaintance with the local language, survival training, and a feasible destination. E&E plans are usually divided into three phases. The first set of contingency plans covers the need to abort the insertion, the aircraft crash-landing, or discovery at the insertion site. This may entail avoiding the enemy until an emergency extraction can be arranged. The second plan covers discovery close to the target and may ensure that the mission can still be completed successfully. The third phase provides against discovery after the mission has been accomplished and may involve heading for a neutral country or hiding for several days prior to making for an alternative extraction RV. Had the operation to rescue the hostages in Tehran failed at a later stage, the operators had orders to head for the Turkish border. SAS teams operating inside western Iraq during the Gulf War were told to make their way to Syria.

The first special operational techniques

In the mid-eighteenth century, seven Independent Companies of Rangers were formed by British colonists to fight the French army and their Indian mercenaries for control of northeast America. The Rangers were an invaluable asset because conventional units of the day were poorly suited to the guerrilla-style tactics used by the enemy. Conventional forces were also ill-equipped to fight in the trackless forests, mountain ranges, and Great Lakes which formed many of the battlefields during the French and Indian Wars (1754–63). Probably the first military special force, the Rangers were used primarily as intelligence gatherers and pathfinders but often carried out raids and ambushes against French columns and Indian camps. In 1759, their commander, Major Robert Rogers, drafted a set of Standing Orders to be used on all operations. Two hundred years later, General

Westmorland had Rogers' Orders printed onto cards which he personally issued to troops beginning their tour in Vietnam:

1. Don't forget nothing.

2. Have your musket clean as a whistle, hatchet scoured, sixty rounds powder and ball, and be ready to march at a minute's warning.

3. When you're on the march, act the way you would if you was sneaking up on deer. See the enemy first.

4. Tell the truth about what you see and what you do. There is an army depending on us for correct information. You can lie all you please when you tell other folks about the Rangers, but don't never lie to a Ranger or officer.

5. Don't never take a chance you don't have to.

6. When we're on the march we march single file, far enough apart so one shot can't go through two men.

7. If we strike swamps, or soft ground, we spread out abreast, so it's hard to track us.

8. When we march, we keep moving till dark, so as to give the enemy the least possible chance at us.

9. When we camp, half the party stays awake while the other half sleeps.

10. If we take prisoners, we keep 'em separate till we have had time to examine them, so they can't cook up a story between 'em.

11. Don't ever march home the same way. Take a different route so you won't be ambushed.

12. No matter whether we travel in big parties or little ones, each party has to keep a scout 20 yards ahead, 20 yards on each flank and 20 yards in the rear, so the main body can't be surprised and wiped out.

13. Every night you'll be told where to meet if surrounded by a superior force.

14. Don't ever sit down to eat without posting sentries.

15. Don't sleep beyond dawn. Dawn's when the French and Indians attack.

16. Don't cross a river by a regular ford.

17. If somebody's trailing you, make a circle, come back on your own tracks, and ambush the folks that aim to ambush you.

18. Don't stand up when the enemy's coming against you. Kneel down. Hide behind a tree.

19. Let the enemy come till he's almost close enough to touch. Then let him have it and jump out and finish him up with your hatchet.

CHAPTER 2

Insertion Across Borders and War Zones

AIR AND MARITIME DEFENSES ARE DANGEROUS and require sophisticated support to overcome them. A relatively simple and secure alternative may involve the team breaching the enemy defenses by making an unassisted infiltration across a national frontier or war zone. At a time when some of the most formidable border defenses are being dismantled, a daunting barrier still divides the Korean Peninsula. This maze of walls, fences, minefields, and antipersonnel devices, running across plains and heavily wooded mountains, has been crossed by several North Korean special mission teams, whose tasks have included the attempted assassination of South Korean President Park Chung Hee (the 1968 "Blue House Raid"). Operational details of their missions have been gleaned from the captured survivors of these operations.

After undergoing extensive training for their mission, the North Korean teams were driven to a border post on one of the wilder stretches of the frontier, where they were briefed on the American and Republic of Korea (ROK) units facing them and the terrain on the Republic's side. Where there was no clear infiltration route, the mission team established an observation post (OP) on high ground overlooking the border. From their vantage point the observers could compare the terrain to aerial reconnaissance maps. Of particular interest to the team commander would have been:

1. The frequency of aerial and ground patrols.
2. The limits of areas covered by ground patrols.
3. The positions and frequency of static guard posts and the intervals of guard rotation.
4. The location of mines, flares, obstacles, and antipersonnel devices.

Armed with this information, and crossing under the cover of darkness, a team would seek to avoid identifiable danger areas such as guard posts, tethered dogs, obstacles, patrols, potential night-ambush sites, minefields, roads, and villages. The men may have carried wooden or bamboo wands which are used to probe for antipersonnel devices and trip wires—not metal probes such as bayonets which can complete the circuit on electrically activated mines and mantraps.

Crossing borders and war zones is a race against time. Obstacles on a national frontier are not constructed to prevent penetration but rather to slow the intruders and increase the likelihood of their discovery by mobile patrols. NATO forces employ three security categories: a Category "A" obstacle is rated at one hour, Category "B" at two to six hours, with Category "C" as a low-security designation. As yet, no obstacle has been devised that cannot be penetrated with good training and a thorough understanding of security technology. Even untrained Eastern European civilians were able to flee across heavily defended borders to the West. One Russian, who attempted to escape across the Finnish border and was captured twice, ascribed the success of his third attempt to simple good luck.

Military operations, however, are not based upon luck. An SAS or any other special forces team will rely on training and speed to overcome concentric layers of defenses, but the two principal assets that will swing the balance of probability in the team's favor— detailed intelligence and pathfinding skills—are provided by other

Guides provide the necessary intelligence to overcome obstacles on a hostile border.

specialists. American Special Forces' doctrine states that to cross borders or front lines:

> Generally, guides are required. If guides are not available, the detachment must have detailed intelligence of the route. Routes are selected to take maximum advantage of cover and concealment and to avoid enemy outposts, patrols, and installations. . . . The location and means of contacting selected individuals (local agents or partisans) who will furnish assistance are provided to the detachment. These individuals may be used as local guides and sources of information, food and shelter (safe houses).

The North Koreans, of course, had their own border guides who provided a wealth of information about the United Nations Command (UNC) lines which they constantly observed. The guides also probed for weaknesses and created safe corridors by deactivating mines and antipersonnel devices.

■ Borders

National boundaries may be marked by a line of posts. Several meters inside a hostile frontier, there is likely to be a 10–15-ft. high security fence. The strip of land between the posts and fence may be occasionally patrolled and may also contain covert observation posts used to see the other side of the border. Electrified fences represent an additional hazard but can be identified by the presence of dead animals and by insulators or sparks produced by short circuits or local thunderstorms. A damp twig or grass stem, held close to the wire, is said to transmit a mild warning shock. Fine-mesh fences, designed to prevent an intruder gaining a purchase with his fingers and toes, can be countered with the aid of specially designed "climbing claws" and strong arms.

Climbing the fence, however, silhouettes intruders and forces them to negotiate deliberately designed overhangs and razor- or barbed wire defenses laid along the top. It also activates motion-detector alarms, rigged to detect the slightest movement in the wire. In addition, the team needs to ferry their equipment over the fence. Antipersonnel devices and seismic ground probes, laid close to the other side of the fence, are activated by vibrations as men or kits land heavily on the ground.

Cutting a hole in the fence announces the presence of intruders. Faced with moving carefully to negotiate further obstacles, a team might find themselves trapped between the alerted border patrols and the inner defenses. If a wire fence is patrolled every hour and is found to be breached, it can be assumed that the intrusion has occurred sometime in the last sixty minutes. An estimate of the speed at which the intruders can overcome further obstacle belts in their path can be used to define an area of probability within which the intruders are likely to be found. This area is immediately searched by foot patrols and tracker dogs.

Climbing or cutting fences, therefore, are methods of last resort. One American manual, written to personnel moving through enemy territory, recommends that its students find ways of passing beneath

Soldier uses a wooden wand to probe for trip wires.

This wire, running across the soldier's front, is connected to a fence mine.

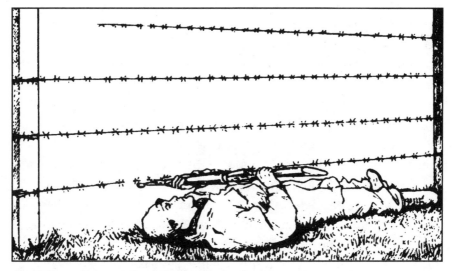

A soldier edges under a barbed wire fence.

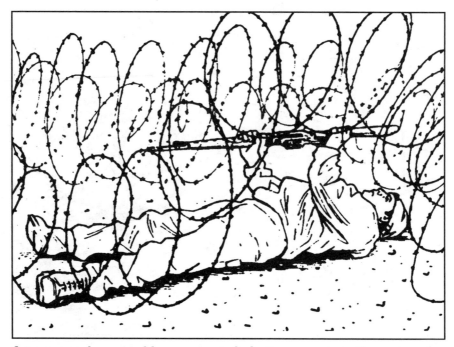

A team member uses his weapon to help cross a concertina wire obstacle.

obstacles such as fences. After first checking for the presence of antipersonnel devices, either concealed within the fence or on the other side of the wire, the evader is advised to use a wand or staff to raise the bottom of the wire so that he can slip under on his back. If the fence is dug into the ground, he is advised to burrow underneath. Care must be taken to push the soil to the other side, so that the hole can be refilled and the turf replaced to conceal the entry. The same technique can be used to crawl underneath concertina wire barriers that are not secured to the ground. If the wire is secured, the manual advises crawling through the obstacle, one coil at a time. Gaps can be created by using shoelaces or string to tie the coils apart. These are later removed to erase evidence of entry. When forced to climb walls and log fences, the evader is told to maintain a low silhouette by keeping his body pressed tightly against, and parallel to, the top of the wall.

Crossing hi-tech defenses

Increasingly, the ears and eyes of sentries and guard dogs are being replaced by a range of electronic devices. Seismic probes and microphones respond to vibrations or sounds produced by intruders walking close to the device, but their usefulness may decline in bad weather, when nearby telegraph poles or tree root systems move in the wind and set up their own vibrations and background noise. Systems such as the Canadian Sentrax convert a conventional security fence into a hi-tech barrier, using two wires that create a capacitance field between them. An intruder alerting the electrostatic properties of the fence triggers a silent alarm. Each control station can monitor thirty-two lengths of alarm wire, each of 500 ft., or a total perimeter of three miles. Variants of this system use buried cables (close-proximity wiring or perimeter intruder cables) to create an invisible fence. Hand-held devices can detect the electrostatic or radio field around obstacles, but the use of electronic countermeasures (ECM) to jam or interrupt the signal only alerts the guards to the presence of intruders.

Nevertheless, the two Achilles heels of these modern systems are the cost of securing an entire border and their exquisite sensitivity. At maximum sensitivity, electronic surveillance equipment can be triggered by natural phenomena such as the passage of snowflakes, leaves blown by the wind, and small foraging animals. Guards, constantly turned out of bed in response to a series of apparently false alarms, may reduce the system's sensitivity or fail to respond to a real incursion. "Trojan Horse" activities may be used to increase the system's false alarm rate (FAR) to an intolerable level, destroying the guard force's confidence in the barrier and engendering dangerous complacency. The SAS and all the other special forces are familiar with all these systems, since they also use them to defend installations or covert ops in the field or for collecting remote intelligence (see chapters 6 and 8). However, successful penetration still requires prior reconnaissance which uses valuable time. When the United Nations Command Lines were strengthened in response to repeated incursions, the North Koreans turned to tunnelling under the Demilitarized Zone (DMZ) or landing on the Republic's coast.

The Israeli border

Israel is virtually surrounded by an electrified, hi-tech security fence. The 8 ft.-high steel posts support a closely woven mass of barbed wire interspersed with alarm wires that signal breaks and disturbances. Defenses behind the fence include excavated tank ditches and machine guns. Some of the latter are set on fixed lines and triggered by infrared sensors. At some places the soil has been used to create a large earth wall. Behind the obstacles is a dirt road that is patrolled regularly by guard vehicles. These trucks tow a mass of tangled barbed wire which leaves a characteristic lined pattern in the dirt, designed to record faithfully the tracks of infiltrators. Beyond the road there are guard posts that act as monitoring stations for the electronic surveillance equipment on the obstacle belt. The Israelis also employ a series of tethered balloons, or "aerostats," which carry sophisticated surveillance equipment, including radar to monitor air traffic and pinpoint hostile artillery batteries. (In the early hours of August 2, 1990, similar surveillance balloons along the northern Kuwaiti border provided sufficient warning of the Iraqi invasion to enable the escape of the Emir and his family.)

Overall, the fortifications are designed to identify intrusions and delay entry until a military response can be mounted, whether the infiltrators are a modern army or a group of Arab terrorists. The border defenses are reported to have curtailed, but not eliminated, infiltrations by guerrillas.

The area behind the fence may be ploughed (to record tracks and footprints), mined, and crisscrossed with trip wires. A corridor must be cleared by probing carefully for mines and wires Trip wires may be attached to illumination flares, alarm devices, or booby traps and set from a couple of inches to several feet off the ground. Cutting the wire can be disastrous as it may be attached to a device with a pressure-release arming mechanism or an electrical mechanism that becomes activated when it no longer detects the presence of a small current flowing through the wire. When found, the wires can be tagged with small strips of light paper or cloth removed by the last man, to eradicate evidence of entry. Team members might consider

The Russian-Finnish border

On some frontiers man-made barriers are complemented by the terrain and climate. The Russian-Finnish border runs across 800 miles of hills and forests from the Gulf of Finland to within 100 miles of the Barents Sea. On the Russian side, the obstacle belt is often 12 miles deep and includes a series of three security fences—at least one of which is electrified—interspersed with ploughed areas covered in trip wires connected to alarm devices. The fences and the forest close to the border are patrolled by KGB border guards with dogs. The tall walls of fir and pine trees are dwarfed by a line of closely spaced 100 ft.-high observation towers. The forest is also interspersed with a series of cleared trails running parallel to the border. In the summer, dog teams conduct 25-mile patrols along the forest paths.

The long, bitterly cold winter nights are a fickle ally, providing some cover for the intruder but often producing conditions so hostile that survival is possible only below ground in a snow hole. As the winter storms relent, ski and snowmobile patrols search the forest trails carefully for the presence of footprints in the snow. One weakness on their border is the long distances that the guards and their dogs patrol, inducing fatigue in both men and animals. Additionally, the 150–200-yard distance at which a dog can reliably scent an intruder is affected by the direction and speed of the wind, the cold, and the thick forest and undergrowth.

Prior to the collapse of the Soviet Union, the heavily guarded frontier, established by the 1948 treaty, might be seen merely as a barrier to the exodus of Soviet citizens to the West. Indeed, until recently, Soviet escapees who were picked up by the Finnish security police were repatriated to face reeducation in a psychiatric institution followed by a term of forced labor. However, the so-called "secret" of this frontier reflected Soviet concerns about intrusions from the West. This secret was a 2½-mile-wide restricted zone on the *Finnish* side of the border. Lighting a match, shining a torch, using binoculars, taking photographs, or even shouting was punishable by a fine or two years' imprisonment. Doctors, taxi drivers, and domestic oil carriers all required a permit to enter the zone. Farmers living within this area were not even permitted to have their relatives stay with them. While the situation on this border has now been defused, it is still patrolled, the KGB's current preoccupation being the myriad smugglers' routes carrying Russian icons and other artifacts to buyers in the West.

An idealized representation of the former East-West German border

Typical of many hostile borders, in this section the national frontier follows the line of a river (A). The East German bank was occasionally patrolled by troops or watched by covert OPs. The two border fences contained an area which was either ploughed and mined or was guarded by war dogs on running leads (B). A road behind the inner fence was regularly patrolled by two-man motorcycle groups (C). Their rosters were kept secret and frequently changed; each patrol included a married man to deter defections to the West. The road was also overlooked by 4-meter (D) and 2-meter (E) guard posts and was floodlit (G). Behind the guard posts lay areas of mines (F) and antitank ditches and obstacles (H). The inner "forbidden zone" (5–15 miles in depth) was restricted to permit holders who had to observe a 10 p.m. curfew. Even farm laborers were accompanied by border guards and the local villages were hidden from the West by hessian-type screens (I).

A soldier carefully cuts a lid of turf before burrowing under a chain-mesh fence.

crawling across the cleared corridor on their backs, balancing their kit on their chests, to avoid leaving footprints, but not tracks, in the ploughed earth.

Illumination flares may be as bright as 20,000 candlepower and light an area with a radius of 1,000 ft. Most army manuals advise men to crouch low and remain motionless as soon as the "pop" of the activated flare is heard. If the intruders cover their eyes, their night vision will be spared, but the guards, whose attention will be drawn by natural curiosity toward the incident, may become temporarily night-blind after the flare is extinguished. If the flare results in an immediate response, the team, contained by unknown obstacles in front of them, can only hope to escape back across the border.

Crude defenses of this nature tend nowadays to be replaced increasingly by "hi-tech" obstacles. Infrared cameras watch the security fence while remote-activated strobe lights, replacing illumination flares, blind the intruders and offer little chance of escape. Closely interwoven microwave and infrared fences pass invisible beams between alternating emitters and receivers. An intruder passing through the area interrupts the beam, triggering a silent alarm. The weak points in these defenses are the posts themselves, where the beams are thinnest and where the post can be scaled to avoid the beam. However, the well-constructed obstacle consists of two lines of staggered posts, with the beams interweaving between the two fence lines. This type of construction ensures that each post is itself guarded by one of the beams.

The ploughed zone is usually contained by a second security fence, behind which a concrete path or road provides the guards with access to the border. This will be patrolled regularly by motorized units. In flat country the team might choose to cross the road on a straight stretch to avoid being surprised by the patrols, In wooded or mountainous country, the insides of bends offer the best concealment. Scouts may be placed on either of the crossing point to give warning of approaching patrols. The team's reconnaissance will have identified the timing and regularity of road patrols and the presence of "tail-end Charlies," positioned to catch intruders who cross immediately after the patrol has passed. Further security is offered by trees and bushes whose shadows are cast across the road in strong moonlight. Culverts and drains running under roads also offer a concealed crossing, but the openings are likely to be booby-trapped.

On the other side of the obstacles there is likely to be a series of guard posts. On the Communist side of the former East–West German border, for example, there were two types of observation tower, each 30 ft. high and positioned 300–800 ft. apart. Large 12 ft.-square permanently manned posts were equipped with telephones and linked into electronic surveillance devices. These were interspersed with smaller 6 ft.-square positions manned only during periods of heightened alert. Areas in front of the observation towers were floodlit, and the guards kept a careful watch on the areas between the posts.

Elimination of the guards, Rambo-style, might be tempting but would probably avert catastrophe only until the next routine telephone check or the arrival of the guards' relief. The team's best hope of crossing this type of obstacle covertly would be to keep close to the ground, using available shadows and ground cover as shields against night-vision equipment such as image intensifiers and thermal imagers. Areas of ground heated by the afternoon's sun and thick wooded areas with dense ground vegetation emit their own thermal image, offering some concealment. Alternatively, the intruders might choose a crossing point between or under the posts where the guards are less alert—many observation towers are deliberately kept unheated to sharpen concentration.

A soldier uses a culvert to cross a road.

These are likely to be booby-trapped in high-security areas.

Most borders under the shadow of hostilities have a rear defensive zone consisting of tank traps and anti-vehicle ditches. The ditches, 10–20 ft. deep, may contain further mines, barbed wire obstacles, and trip wires, and will need to be probed carefully before being negotiated by the team. Some hostile frontiers also have an inner 6–18-mile restricted zone. All personnel within this area must have a permit or be accompanied by a border guard. Patrols, an eight- to ten-hour curfew, regulations prohibiting gatherings or strangers, and the probability that civilians will report chance sightings make this area potentially hostile. A group of woodcutters alerted the ROK security forces to the presence of the "Blue House" mission team. With three exceptions, the North Koreans were either killed or took their own lives when capture became inevitable.

■ War Zones

The front line between hostile armies forms a different sort of frontier. The difficulty in crossing the lines depends upon whether the opposing forces are advancing, retreating, dispersed, or in heavily defended static positions. Numerous engagements have been fought in jungle and desert environments against a dispersed enemy. In World War II, large Chindit forces were able to cross the Japanese lines in Burma. During the Soviet involvement in Afghanistan, Spetsnaz units were inserted by helicopter close to guerrilla positions. Dressed in local garb, the commandos commandeered the nearest flock of animals which they drove across the insurgents' lines. Similar tactics were used by German military intelligence officers crossing Allied lines in Italy: although hundreds of German agents who were mingling with refugees were caught and executed, the "shepherds" managed the crossing with the loss of only a few sheep. The mountains and moorland of East Falkland, scene of much British SAS activity, witnessed the greatest concentration of Argentine forces around Stanley. Some isolated settlements on the islands never saw a single Argentine soldier throughout the entire conflict.

Remaining invisible

A soldier keeps his body parallel to the top of a log fence (or wall) to maintain minimum visibility, while his companion uses the shadow of a tree to cross a road.

Retreating forces may also offer welcome gaps to a team infiltrating through the lines. One commando-trained soldier, with a British armored regiment in Holland during the German retreat in 1944, inadvertently crossed the lines while investigating a suspected minefield. This was the first of many forays. Wearing an old German parachute smock over his battledress and avoiding isolated pockets of enemy troops, the soldier was able to move through the German rear

Remaining invisible

A special mission team uses the night and bad weather to cross a heavily defended frontier. A demoralized guard peers into the darkness as the patrol scout digs a hole under the chain-link fence, and the second soldier uses shadow to crawl under the guard tower. On the Finnish-Russian border an escapee ascribed his successful getaway to his technique of passing lines of guard posts by crawling underneath one of the towers.

areas. Brought up in the country, he was able to sustain himself on the two- to three-day journeys by living off the land. His technique, however, proved less successful in urban areas, and he had to abandon his dangerous pastime after narrowly escaping capture by German field police checking documents in a small town.

Office of Strategic Services (OSS) chief and later director of the CIA, William Casey, initially infiltrated agents into Germany across the same lines. But as the Germans began to concentrate troops in

> ## Using the weather
>
> Most special operational personnel agree that border/war zone crossings should be made under the cover of adverse weather conditions. Rain, snowstorms, mist, and fog obscure moon and stars, reducing the effectiveness of normal vision and passive infrared scopes. Clouds deepen shadows, wind causes foliage to rustle, obscuring other noises, and fog or mist deadens sound and hides movement. Rain can offer all of these advantages, additionally washing away tracks and footprints. It may also reduce the alertness of the guards. The "Blue House Raid" team crossed under the cover of a Korean winter. Yet weather conditions can be manipulated to advantage. In Vietnam, the Americans observed that fewer Buddhist monks turned out to demonstrate when it was raining. Subsequently, silver iodide crystals were used to produce showers during the Buddhist unrest of 1963. Potassium and chloride aerosols were also dispersed by aircraft to "seed" the clouds above North Vietnam. This is said to have produced excellent overcast conditions for American commandos infiltrating into the North.

heavily fortified defensive positions, Casey estimated that the probability doubled of an agent being killed or captured. The OSS then turned to parachute insertion because experience showed that their agents had an excellent chance of survival once inside Germany.

James England's manual *Long-Range Patrol Operations* offers advice for patrols faced with crossing a heavily defended front line. During the initial phase, the patrol moves to the forward line of friendly troops to observe the infiltration route and to be briefed by guides or reconnaissance patrols which have penetrated or probed the enemy's defenses. The briefing also provides information on gaps in the defense line and safe routes, emergency signals, and passwords to be used if the mission is aborted and the team is forced to return to its own lines. The soldiers may use deception by dressing in enemy uniform with insignia that match those forces directly to their front. The team is then placed on hold to await ideal conditions—a wet, stormy night with no moon.

Phase two ends when the team comes within visual distance of the first enemy defense line. The decision to continue or abort the mission depends primarily on whether the team can move fast enough to penetrate the primary defensive line in the remaining hours of darkness. Colonel David Hackworth, said to be the most outstanding American battalion commander in Vietnam, and the reputed model for Colonel Kurtz, the guerrilla commander in *Apocalypse Now*, formed a group of commandos in Korea to conduct ambushes and raids behind the Chinese lines. Hackworth notes that even though friendly artillery fire targeted the infiltration route to provide cover for his "Rangers," the Chinese defenses were often so concentrated that it might take five hours to crawl 100 yards.

Identifying a gap in the enemy positions requires patience and lots of nerve. Recce patrols may have determined the enemy's eating and sleeping habits. A soldier, woken from sleep, may take half an hour or so to become fully alert and gain his night vision, and may spend the last half-hour of his guard duty thinking about his sleeping bag. The soldier who has just eaten may be less attentive and slower to react. Inexperienced or low-grade troops may be careless—the flare of a cigarette lighter can be seen for many hundreds of yard and a sentry who takes up his guard position only to discover that his weapon is on "safe," or uncocked, can betray his position when he releases the safety lever or pulls back the cocking handle. Other night sounds, such as metal on metal, conversation, or men mumbling in their sleep, may provide an indication of both position and numbers. Contacts along the front line or wild firing at night terrors can betray the enemy's position. The number of seconds between the flash and the bang, multiplied by 400, provides an indication of distance in meters. The characteristic signature and rate of fire can identify the type of weapon being used. One British manual instructs its SAS students:

> If you watch for up to two hours some enemy soldier will give away his position by noise, movement or normal sentry relief. Once a position is located pass as near to it as you safely can. If challenged, learn at least one phrase in his language like 'Don't shoot you bloody fool,' but you must be able to say it fluently.

Once the team has passed the initial defenses, guides are allowed to return to friendly lines. While their capture recrossing the lines may jeopardize the mission, an untrained man compromises the team.

Phase three ends when the first defensive line is crossed successfully. If the entire enemy defenses cannot be crossed in a single night, the next day is spent in a pre-prepared hide. When the team is 1,000 yards beyond the last major defensive position, the men assume their own uniforms and equipment carried in their rucksacks. This type of unsupported infiltration limits the duration and type of mission. The team will have to wait to link-up with advancing friendly forces or risk a second dangerous crossing. Reconnaissance of the acquisition targets for friendly air-and-artillery strikes is compatible with this type of insertion. By contrast, raids and other "boom and bang" operations will place the local enemy forces on a state of heightened alert.

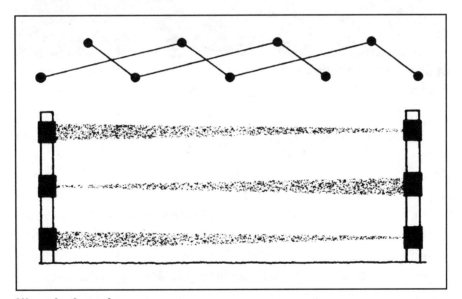

Hi-tech obstacles

Each post emits and receives three beams, and when one or more beams are interrupted, a silent alarm is activated. However, it might still be possible to cross this hi-tech fence by scaling the posts themselves. With this in mind, most security fences of this nature interweave the beams between two lines of staggered fence posts. This ensures that each post is, in turn, protected by a beam.

A Special Operations Team crosses a front line behind a creeping artillery barrage.

An advancing enemy offers the safest and most secure form of insertion—stay-behind. During World War II, the British left stay-behind parties in Malaysia, and American OSS reconnaissance teams were placed in front of the German Ardennes offensive. The team and their equipment are concealed in underground bunkers or hides while they wait for the enemy forces to pass by them. The stay-behind forces may be troops who lack training in infiltration techniques, or they may be used by an army involved in a high-intensity war where the necessary superiority to execute air and sea operations is lacking. However, this technique creates problems for exfiltration and medical evacuation, which require the establishment of protected routes across the front line.

Some American light-infantry units have trained in the stay-behind role, moving into action as soon as the main thrust of armor and infantry has passed, to acquire targets for friendly artillery and air strikes. As interdiction strikes slow the momentum of the enemy's attack, American forces launch their counteroffensive. At this point the stay-behind forces start to raid and ambush targets of opportunity, finally linking up with friendly "heavy" mechanized units to plunge deep into the enemy's rear areas, isolating his battle groups in the front line.

Other stay-behind parties such as the American Long Range Patrol (LRP) and Long Range Surveillance (LRS) units, are intelligence gatherers. Although stay-behind simplifies insertion, the soldiers soon find themselves in one of the most hostile areas on the battlefield. NATO planners, facing the specter of an East-West high-intensity clash in Europe, calculated that stay-behind parties would experience 50 percent casualties in the first twenty-four hours of operations. The Soviets expected similar losses. An original force allocation of sixty Spetsnaz teams within an area behind NATO lines was expected to lose twelve teams per day.

CHAPTER 3

Air Operations

US ARMY MANUAL FM 7-93 WARNS its students: "The infiltration phase is the most complicated and dangerous aspect of any operation. During this phase the danger of discovery is greater than during any other phase." Inserting teams on foot or by vehicle has obvious disadvantages in terms of operational range and the amount of equipment that can be carried. These factors are crucial to mission duration. During World War II, teams were deposited on distant landing sites by small boat or static-line parachute. In the postwar era, electronic surveillance and increasing counterintelligence efforts have limited the effectiveness of such operations. One American official summed up, for writer and journalist Tom Mangold, the Central Intelligence Agency's (CIA's) attempts to insert paramilitary teams or partisans into the Eastern Bloc at the start of the Cold War:

> We had agents parachuting in, walking in, boating in. Virtually all of these operations were complete failures. After the war, we also had a whole stay-behind network of agents in Eastern Europe. They were all rolled up.

Modern military operations to place soldiers behind the lines have relied on technology to bypass enemy defenses, and on high-level

training combined with tried and tested standard operating procedures (SOPs) to safeguard the team on the ground.

Sneaking through the Air Defenses

Even crude air defense weapons can have a devastating effect on air
operations, as evidenced by the effect of Viet Minh artillery at Dien
Bien Phu and the appearance of the shoulder-fired SA-7 anti-aircraft

Ways of penetrating enemy airspace: stealth and brute force

The Russian AN-2 biplane's minimum speed of 56 mph is too slow to be detected
by Doppler radar and its fabric-covered hull provides near invisibility to pulse
radar. Flying at treetop level and rising to the minimum drop height to deliver its
fourteen Spetsnaz commandos, this old World War II aircraft is a flying ghost (A).
The helicopter also flies low to avoid detection, using hills and valleys to mask
the aircraft (B). Another technique is to punch holes in the enemy's air defenses
by suppressing or jamming critical radar sites (C).

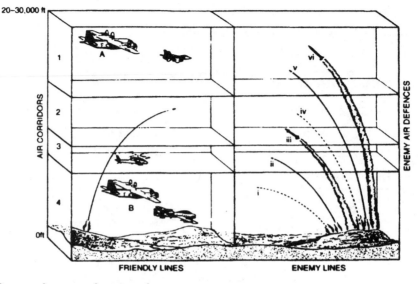

Constraints on air operations

Friendly airspace will be divided into air corridors to accommodate:

1. High performance aircraft.
2. Field artillery.
3. Helicopter operations.
4. Field artillery and low-level aircraft.

An air corridor through enemy airspace is determined by the type and strength of their air defense weapons. Weapons seeking to dominate the lower air corridors include:

i)   Heavy machine guns (ceiling 5,000 ft.).
ii) ZU-23 Anti-aircraft guns (ceiling 8,200 ft.).
iii) Shoulder-fired SA-7 surface-to-air missiles (ceiling in excess of 11,500 ft.).

Higher level air defenses include:

iv) 20mm anti-aircraft cannon (ceiling 13,000 ft.).
v)   ZSU-57-2 self-propelled anti-aircraft gun (ceiling 20,000 ft.).
vi) SA-11 surface-to-air missile (ceiling 45,000 ft.).

Strong low-level air defenses might result in the air force attempting high altitude operations, inserting the team by HALO of HAHO parachuting (A).

Strong high-level air defenses may force a low-level insertion (B) or abandoning air operations for some other means of insertion.

missile on the Cambodian battlefields. However, several modern operations have demonstrated that sophisticated air defense systems can be neutralized by paralyzing or circumventing the enemy's radar. This can be achieved by using concealment, by jamming the signal, or by destroying the radar installation.

"Stealth" or radar transparency technology attempts to lower the radar cross section of aircraft and achieve an overall configuration which ensures that much of the electromagnetic energy is deflected

---

Finding gaps in the radar defenses

Electronic warfare (EW) aircraft, such as the "Ferret" flights mentioned in chapter 1, probe foreign airspace deliberately, inducing the potential enemy to activate his defenses, thereby allowing the EW specialists to characterize individual radar installations. Two pieces of information gathered by these operations are of prime importance: the beam width—how much sky can be scanned at one time—and the pulse repetition rate. A radar pulse travels at the speed of light and has to reach its target and return to the receiver before the next pulse can be emitted. This knowledge, combined with the pulse repetition rate, allows the radar's maximum operational range to be calculated.

One often-quoted example concerns the German Freya tracking radar, which threatened British bomber streams during World War II. These installations were determined to have a pulse repetition rate of 500 pulses per second. The speed of the radar pulses equalled 186,281 miles per second (speed of light), and consequently a single pulse could travel 373 miles (186,282 ÷ 500) before another pulse was emitted. However, as the pulse had to reach a target and return to the radar antennae before the next pulse was released, the target could not be more than 186 miles from the radar site.

The characterization of all the radar sites within a particular area may allow a route to be plotted to circumvent these sites. If, in addition, the pilot flies sufficiently low to maximize the masking effects of hills and undulating country, his aircraft has a good chance of remaining invisible to the enemy.

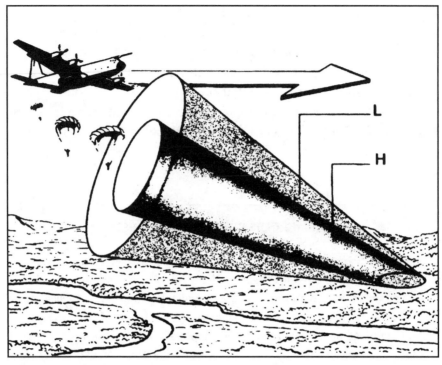

HAHO parachuting

Stand-off parachuting is a great idea; the aircraft remains in friendly airspace and the parachutists float unseen into enemy territory. In fact, the problems start when the canopies open. In conditions of low wind speeds (L) the parachutists have considerable leeway in maneuvering to avoid under- or overshooting the DZ. In high wind speeds (H) the restricted wind-cone calls for great skill on the part of the parachutists.

away from the radar receiver. Other design features act to reduce the strength of the radar echo. The aircraft are covered in radar-absorbent material, and sensors embedded in the "skin" act to distort the reflected by flying close to the ground where the aircraft are "lost" in the spurious echoes from hills, trees, and buildings—the so-called "ground return." The frequency-shift clutter of moving objects such as waves, sea spray, and trees blown by the wind confuses Doppler systems as they attempt to track the low-flying aircraft.

Although, at present, there are no transport aircraft with "Stealth" characteristics, several slow, small, ground-hugging aircraft are available to the SAS and other special forces. The Soviets were reported to have experimented with Very Light Aircraft (VLA) such as powered hang-gliders, microlites, and ultralites. Powered hang-gliders have been used by Arab terrorists for several unsuccessful attacks on targets inside Israel. An older Russian aircraft, the An-2 Colt, worried Western defense experts during the Cold War. The 1947 biplane, which was designed to carry fourteen paratroops on wartime missions, was fabric-covered and could fly as slowly as 56 mph, making it difficult to detect by use either of pulse or Doppler radar.

Airborne Insertion

The air assault phase may include the establishment of an infiltration flight corridor across the border or front line. Precise passage points, times, and recognition signals avoid engagement by friendly forces. Entry into enemy airspace is coordinated with jamming or suppression of enemy air defenses concentrated along, and immediately behind, the border or front line. Deception operations may provide further cover for the insertion. Multiple feints or false insertions, using RPVs (Remote Piloted Vehicles) or aircraft, and cover operations, such as air strikes, ground operations, the leakage of false information, and fake radio transmissions, combine to deceive the enemy.

The aircrew may have rehearsed the operation, using computer flight simulation technology. The USAF is using the Evans and Sutherland Image Generation (ESIG-4000) flight simulator to train its crews for low-level special operations. The terrain over which the aircraft will fly is reconstructed from ground and satellite photographs and stereo-imagery, while towns and geographical features that will serve as navigation points and approach corridors are added later from a data library.

The mode of insertion depends upon the amount of equipment to be carried, the level of secrecy, and the degree of special training required. As a rule of thumb, the more difficult the insertion, the smaller the number of soldiers trained in the necessary infiltration techniques.

■ High-Altitude High-Opening (HAHO) Parachuting

HAHO, or "stand-off parachuting," allows the insertion aircraft to remain in friendly airspace. The parachutists may be released at altitudes of up to 25,000 ft. with a long flight to the DZ. After several seconds in free-fall, the rip cords are pulled, deploying the canopies. A standard parachute with a low glide ratio, opened at the same height, would simply drift on the prevailing wind. In the colder, thinner air at high altitude, the standard parachute would fall initially at an ankle-breaking speed of approximately 22 mph, finally slowing to around 16 mph closer to the ground. At an average wind speed of 10 knots, the parachutist would spend approximately 20 minutes in the air, landing only some three or four miles from the release point.

HAHO parachuting employs wing and foil canopies that enjoy the same aerodynamic properties as an aircraft wing. The low rate of descent and a high forward speed allow the parachutist to fly quickly to a DZ 20–35 miles inside hostile territory. A Ram Air canopy with a glide ratio of 4:1 can accomplish this at speeds of up to 30 mph, the parachutist spending 40–80 minutes in the air, depending upon the distance to be covered. Although fine in theory, however, this technique spawns a cluster of problems that must be solved if the team is not to find themselves captured or landing back behind their own lines:

Assembly and navigation For reasons of security, HAHO drops are usually attempted at night. Once the canopies are deployed, the team must assemble together with the aim of landing in a tight military formation. Some parachutes have panels coated with a chemiluminescent material, the dull glow of which allows the parachutists to remain in visual contact while avoiding midair collisions.

The flight to the DZ requires pinpoint accuracy. It is distant, shrouded in darkness, and may be masked by low clouds. Chest-pack navigation sets, based on the Global Positioning System (GPS), obtain their exact position with reference to navigation satellites such as NAVSTAR. This equipment provides up to 100 waypoints between the release point and the DZ, allowing the parachutists to check their position, heading, and altitude with respect to the flight path.

Getting the teams in by air

Two modified Blackhawk helicopters inserted American Special Forces team Operational Detachment Alpha 525 into Iraq at last light on February 23, 1991. Other "dummy" Blackhawk flights made simultaneous false insertions to confuse the enemy as to the actual LZ. While much of the Iraqi air defense systems had been knocked out by Coalition air attacks, nothing was left to chance. The helicopters were going in well under the emissions of any surviving radar sites. Flying at 140 knots and a mere 10 ft. above the desert, the pilots used night-vision goggles to see the undulating sand dunes. Suddenly, there was a loud bang and one of the helicopters lurched toward the sky. "What happened?" asked the worried team commander. "I just tore a wheel off on a sand dune, but don't worry about it," replied the pilot. In fact, only the instantaneous reactions of the pilot in lifting the aircraft's nose and increasing power prevented the mission from ending in a fireball.

America is the world leader in insertion technology. The "Air Commandos" of the 1st Air Force Special Operations Wing deploy forty Sikorsky MH-53J Pave Low III Enhanced aircraft, reputed to be the "most sophisticated helicopter in the free world." The chopper has a 600-mile range which can be extended by midair refueling. It has an array of electronic systems that enable it to penetrate hostile airspace. Forward-mounted infrared receivers, ground following/avoidance/ mapping radar, Doppler and inertial navigation equipment, and an on-board mission computer enable it to fly nap-of-the-earth, at night, and in poor weather conditions.

An additional array of electronic and infrared countermeasure devices are designed to confuse or block enemy weapons systems. It even has passive electronic equipment which will detect and locate new or previously unmapped radar sites. The instruments feed their information into warning devices and an on-board computer which replots the aircraft's route to avoid the new radar. A more recent addition is the Sikorsky MH-60G Pave Hawk, which, like its big brother, is equipped for low-level missions behind enemy lines but can be easily transported inside the Lockheed C141 Starlifter or C-5 Galaxy aircraft. Two modified Hercules, the MC-130E Combat Talon I and MC-130H Combat Talon II, can undertake longer missions, flying at altitudes as low as 50 ft. Both are equipped with sophisticated navigation systems, electronic warfare equipment, secure communications, and aerial refuelling systems. The MC-130H is also rigged for night operations and is fitted with the adverse weather aerial delivery system (AWADS). The MC-130C is rigged with the Fulton Surface-to-Air Recovery (STAR) system which allows the team to board the aircraft while in flight. Other versions include the MC-130EY, which is similar to the MC-130C but lacks the STAR system, and the MC-130S, which is equipped for electronic warfare and jamming missions. Massive fire support for teams on the ground is provided by the AC-130H Spectre gunships with their 105mm howitzer, 40mm Bofors cannon, and two M61 20mm Vulcan cannons.

Fine adjustments to position can be made by increasing speed, braking, flying into the wind ("holding-off"), or by maneuvering within the wind cone. The latter is an imaginary cone or triangle that places limits on the zigzag flight used by parachutists who find themselves up- or downwind of their expected position. Failure to observe these limits means under- or overshooting the DZ. The base of the cone is at the release point and the apex on the DZ. Consequently, the closer the parachutist is to the DZ, the less room he has to maneuver on either side of the flight path. The cone also becomes narrower and more restrictive at higher wind speeds.

Physiological problems. At high altitudes the air is cold, and there is insufficient oxygen to support respiration. As a rough approximation, the surface temperature drops 3.5°F for every 1,000 ft. of altitude. At 25,000 ft. the temperature could be as low as -50°F, requiring layers of warm clothing underneath the camouflaged outer shell. Gloves and a balaclava worn underneath the helmet and mask protect the extremities against frostbite. At this altitude, lack of oxygen would limit consciousness to around 3–5 minutes. Between 10,000 and 20,000 ft., hypoxia presents as drowsiness, sluggish muscle control, blurred vision, and slow, unreliable thought processes. Prior to jumping, the team hooks up to the crew's oxygen supply, but during the actual descent they must carry a bale-out bottle with sufficient oxygen to take them below 10,000 ft.

■ High-Altitude Low-Opening (HALO) Parachuting

HALO, or military free-fall, provides a fast, covert means of delivering a team onto the DZ. Soldiers leaving the aircraft at 30,000 ft. and maintaining a stable position would spend just over two minutes in free-fall and a further two to three minutes in flight, once the canopy is deployed at 2,000 ft. The problems associated with HAHO parachuting are magnified for the free-faller.

On leaving the aircraft, the parachutists adopt a stable or "frog" position. This has to be maintained with a heavy rucksack or Bergen, slung low on the back below the main parachute, and the personal weapon, held by the parachute harness along the side of the body. At these altitudes terminal velocity increases from 120 mph to 180 mph. Should the parachute need to be deployed in an emergency, the resulting 14G opening shock would do considerable damage to both the parachutist and his canopy.

Jamming or suppressing air defenses

Radar can be jammed by ground stations, electronic warfare aircraft, attack aircraft, or possibly ground teams with small disposable battery-powered jammers. In November 1970, the Americans launched a rescue operation to recover prisoners of war held at Son Tay. North Vietnam was well defended by 85mm and 100mm radar-guided anti-aircraft artillery and Soviet-supplied "Fansong" radar, which acquired targets for SA-2 or SA-3 SAMs. Consequently, 116 aircraft, flying from bases in Thailand, and three carriers in the Gulf of Tonkin supported the operation by locking out the SAM sites around Son Tay, saturating the Chinese/North Vietnamese radar defenses, carrying out decoy attacks, and trawling for the night fighters that presented a major danger to the helicopters carrying the special ops team. The operation is reported to have irreparably damaged North Vietnamese confidence in their air defense system.

Radar installations are particularly vulnerable to aircraft carrying anti-radiation missiles which home in on the radar beam. In June 1982, the Israelis supported their invasion of Lebanon by eliminating forty to fifty Syrian SA-6 and SA-8 SAM sites guarding the Bekaa Valley. When the Syrians switched on their radar, in response to a series of deception attacks employing small robotic planes or Remote Piloted Vehicles (RPVs), electronic warfare equipment characterized the radar frequencies. This information was used to calibrate the sensors on the anti-radiation missiles carried by the Israeli attack aircraft.

More recently, the assorted Allied aircraft, which started the 1991 Gulf air war by attacking Baghdad on the night of January 17, 1991, flew along a "radar-black" air corridor in the Iraqi defenses. Two key sites along the corridor had been destroyed by missile-equipped Apache helicopters, guided by SOF Pave Low helicopters. Air strikes inside Iraq were also covered by Wild Weasel F-4G Phantoms from the 81st Tactical Fighter Squadron. In the time it took Iraqi radar to "paint" a Coalition combat aircraft and unleash a SA-6 or SA-8 SAM, the Weasels could detect the radar, using their APR-47 Radar Homing and Warning System, and fire a High-Speed Anti-Radiation Missile (HARM) at the aggressor. Usually, the radar sites were hit while still guiding their SAM toward an allied aircraft, causing the missile to lose its "radar lock" and fall harmlessly to earth. When the Iraqi radar operators became familiar with the "Magnum" call sign used to warn friendly pilots of a HARM launch, they stayed off the air. This was picked up quickly by F-16 and Tornado pilots who yelled "Magnum, Magnum" on the radio, as they rolled in to attack their targets.

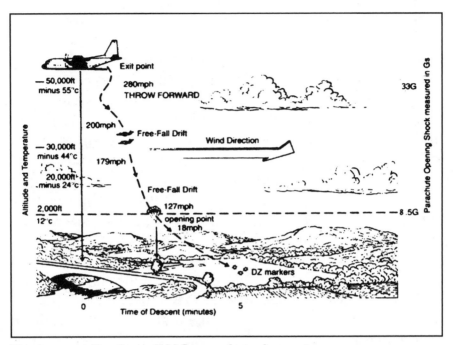

The factors affecting a HALO parachute descent

The team must exit close together because complicated aerial maneuvers such as turns are impossible in the thin air above 20,000 ft. Luminescent markers on the equipment serve as reference points in the darkness. While still in free-fall, the team will experience wind drift—approximately 10 ft. for every 100 ft. of fall and every knot of wind. Below 20,000 ft. the team can group into formation and track to compensate for drift away from the descent path. Tracking involves arching the body into a crude aerofoil so that the airflow is directed along the underside of the body. Swept-back arms lower the head and increase the rate of descent and horizontal movement. A good tracking position propels the parachutist across the sky at 35° from vertical and at speeds of around 18 mph. In order to open his canopy, the parachutist must first lose speed by maneuvering back into a stable position.

Hypoxia is a serious problem for the free-faller, but he need only carry two to three minutes' supply of oxygen. Loss of consciousness with streaming arms and legs might result in the parachutist inadvertently assuming a stable back-to-earth position. Alternatively, he may tumble through the sky until the barometric trigger deploys the canopy at 2,000 ft. While the parachutist will usually deploy his own canopy, barometric triggers, such as the British Irvin Hitefinder D/1 Mk4, act as a safety device. Fitted to the main or reserve parachute, the device activates the parachute-release mechanism when a critical altitude is reached. At 2,000 ft. the parachutist still has time (12–14 seconds) to deploy his reserve canopy if the main parachute malfunctions. However, if the parachutist is still tumbling when the parachute opens, the rigging lines and canopy may enclose him, quite literally, in a shroud.

Other dangers include stress-induced hyperventilation, which can lead to a severe lowering of blood carbon dioxide and unconsciousness, and barometric trauma, as a result of air in the intestine, ears, and sinuses expanding in response to the lower air pressure at high altitudes.

The free-faller will also experience lower temperatures than the HAHO parachutist. The ambient temperature, already cold, is further reduced as the soldier plummets through the air at 120–179 mph— the "windchill" factor. This may cause ice to form on the equipment. The parachutist's vital oxygen mask is particularly at risk from icing because, "windchill" aside, the mask experiences cooling as the compressed gas is released into the mouthpiece. In some systems this very dangerous situation is circumvented by warming the oxygen supply.

High altitude military parachuting is dangerous and requires constant training, employing not only practice jumps but acclimatization periods in high-altitude chambers. The superb physical conditioning and training of these troops prepare them for the medical problems associated with high altitudes. However, frequent medical examinations are necessary to identify problems that are incompatible with this work—in particular, any reduction in the amount of oxygen reaching the tissues as a result of anemia, drugs, alcohol, or poor circulation. Smoking is contraindicated as it reduces the oxygen transport capacity of the blood and adversely affects night vision (three cigarettes, smoked in quick succession, saturate 5 percent of the blood's oxygen-carrying capacity with carbon monoxide, producing the same oxygen stress as an altitude of 8,000 ft. above sea level).

Static-Line Parachuting

Static-line parachuting requires far less training but is often incompatible with the operational security required for covert missions. Its major roles nowadays are the movement of a large force across a battlefield to block an enemy advance, the insertion of forces to raid or hold objectives immediately behind the lines, and low-threat rapid deployment operations in the Third World. The survival of a large air armada depends on total air superiority, with friendly aircraft both protecting the transports and suppressing or jamming enemy air defenses.

A single aircraft carrying a special operations team might avoid the radar by flying at 50–100 ft., climbing only briefly to 400–500 ft. to dispatch the team. Although, ideally, the pilot will aim to dispatch his cargo in a single pass, wind drift and obstacles in the flight path influence the release point. This form of insertion allows the parachutist to carry between 50–150 lbs. of personal equipment packed into an equipment container. Once in the air, the container and personal weapon are released to hang below the parachutist on a suspension rope. This frees the soldier to adopt a landing position and execute a parachute roll which absorbs the shock of meeting the ground at 16 mph. Although simple in theory, this technique has its own problems.

Dispersion and lost parachutists Military static-line parachuting tends to employ poorly maneuverable parachutes. Less time is available for directed flight—approximately 30 seconds from 800 ft.—and high-performance canopies would increase the collision rate as the soldiers are thrown together in the darkness and turbulent slipstream. The parachutists are dispersed along the length of the DZ, but wind drift can cause further separation. Drifting away from the DZ, the darkened landscape can become a confusing patchwork of fields, trees, and hedgerows. Significant numbers of D-Day parachutists became lost in this fashion. Although German panic was increased by the myriad small battles that erupted behind their lines as the men landed, the paratroopers' main objectives had to be taken with greatly depleted forces.

Dispersion has remained a perennial problem. During the American invasion of Panama ("Just Cause") in December 1989, sticks of the 82nd Airborne Division were lost for several vital hours in the high elephant grass bordering the drop zones. Dispersion and the time spent hanging uselessly from the rigging lines have been reduced by designing Low-Altitude Low-Opening (LALO) parachutes which can be deployed at heights as low as 250 ft.

Obstacles and other dangers The success of static-line insertions is strongly dependent upon recent intelligence on the operational terrain and the aircrew's navigation. In Panama, a significant proportion of the 82nd Airborne's heavy-drop platforms—some containing much-needed tanks—were parachuted into a bog. It took two days to rescue all the equipment. Flooded areas on the flanks of the D-Day beaches claimed the lives of wartime parachutists, and the British 15th Parachute Battalion (TA) experienced a similar tragedy in the 1970s when aircrew mistook the lights of a German canal for DZ markers.

The relatively large areas required for static-line drops can also be identified by the enemy, with unfortunate consequences for parachutists dropping "blind." A pilot ferrying a small special ops team into Burma during World War II miscalculated the release point so that the team landed in the jungle—a dangerous descent likely to leave parachutists swinging in the tree canopy some 100–200 ft. off the ground. However, when the team finally disentangled themselves, they discovered that a far greater danger had awaited them on the DZ. The Japanese, aware that clandestine forces were operating in the area, had identified all the large jungle clearings and covered them with punji stakes designed to impale the unwitting intruders.

The British SAS attempted to do without DZs during its counter-insurgency operations in postwar Malaysia. In the jungle, suitable clearings were scarce and attempts to use them often resulted in soldiers landing in the surrounding forest. This persuaded the Regiment to jump into virgin jungle. "Tree-jumping" depended upon the parachute being snagged on a tree, allowing the parachutist to lower himself to the jungle floor down a 100-ft. rope. However, for covert insertion, the technique became self-defeating as the inevitable casualties required helicopter evacuation.

■ Air Landing

Landing troops by aircraft requires little specialized training and provides a rapid method of deploying infantry and heavy equipment. With an adequate approach path, a light aircraft can land on a 300-ft. airstrip, but medium transports require a runway three to four times this length. Conventional operations may seek to use an established airfield, behind enemy lines, which is seized, held, and cleared of obstacles by an initial parachute assault. Such a technique was employed during the American invasion of Grenada, but that operation serves to highlight the shortcomings of air landings. The US Rangers were allotted the task of taking Salines airfield and holding it for successive waves of transports carrying the 82nd Airborne. A small, lightly armed force of Grenadan militia and Cuban advisors nevertheless resisted the assault from the eastern end of the runway. When the first wave of C-130s appeared overhead, the balance of the Ranger battalion was forced to parachute. After the airfield was finally secured by the Rangers, it was found that the airstrip was unable to accommodate the continuous wave of transports, compelling the C-130s and C-141 Starlifters to spend more time circling the island than had been spent flying from the United States.

More covert operations can be serviced by light aircraft, but this usually requires help from indigenous forces in building and maintaining the landing zone (LZ). British Special Duties Lysanders serviced partisan forces in Europe and the Far East. In France the strip was often little more than a long fallow field, but in Burma some all-weather runways were constructed from gravel and bamboo to defy the monsoon rains. The Americans' Balkan Air Terminal Service (BATS) built heavy-duty airstrips inside partisan-held areas in Yugoslavia. Transports such as Dakotas used the airfields to repatriate American aircrew shot down over the Balkans. During America's subsequent war in Indochina, a series of airfields of "Lima Sites" were built across the Plain of Jars to support the CIA's private army in Laos, and Special Forces' bases in Vietnam were serviced by aircraft.

As the operational range and payload capability of helicopters increased, they offered an alternative to insertion by fixed-wing aircraft. Rotary-wing aircraft have the advantage of being able to fly low and take maximum advantage of the concealment offered by the terrain. This nap-of-the-earth flying may be used to confuse the enemy about landing areas. Helicopters can land in small areas at relatively steep angles or hover to load or disembark troops and supplies. Additionally, they can remain within the immediate vicinity to extract teams which run into opposition immediately after landing. Aircraft dedicated to covert operations are capable of flying at night and in marginal weather conditions. However, with respect to special operations, they also have some serious disadvantages. The engine and rotor noise and the dust thrown up by the prop wash can identify the LZ to the enemy. They are vulnerable to ground fire, and changes in atmospheric conditions can drastically reduce lift capability.

Drills for "Blind" Drops and Landings

Landing or parachuting onto an unmarked DZ is usually attempted in isolated areas free from hostile forces and in conditions of good visibility (full moon or daylight). Without outside help, the time spent on the drop or landing zone is the second most critical phase of the operation. Actions on landing are divided into assembly, security, and sterilization.

Assembly It is the job of the team commander to ensure that each parachutist know the position of the DZ assembly area. This may be just a particular corner of the DZ or a concealed position 100–200 yards farther afield. High-altitude parachutists and teams carried by aircraft or helicopter will land together. Static-line parachutists may orient themselves by means of the clock system, taking the direction of flight of the insertion aircraft as 12 o'clock. The positions of various landmarks serve as a back-up method of identification. There will be little time available to search for soldiers failing to arrive at the assembly area, but each member of the team will have memorized the position of emergency RVs. A second RV, 5–10 miles from the DZ, might remain "open" for a further four to six hours. Subsequent rendezvous might direct the missing soldier toward the extraction RV or exfiltration route. Within the last few years, technology has provided a means of overcoming assembly problems. When the team leader lands on the DZ, he activates a portable radio homing beacon which emits a weak, high-frequency signal. As the other parachutists land, they activate their personal hand-held radio receivers which pick up the beacon's signals and convert them into an audible "bleep." The signal is strongest when the radio receiver is pointed directly at the beacon and thus provides the rest of the team with a navigational cue to the assembly point and the team commander.

Security Designated parachutists are responsible for ensuring that the area is free of hostile interference and for making the initial response to surprise contact with the enemy. Each team member will have rehearsed his contact drills in the event of an ambush on the DZ. Laying down a fusillade of small-arms fire from a compact defensive position allows the team commander the luxury of choosing to defend the DZ/LZ while calling in an emergency extraction—only really feasible for air-landing operations—or to "shoot and scoot," in the hope of breaking contact with the enemy forces.

Sterilization Sterilization involves removing all traces of the team's presence. This includes the recovery of all parachute items and their burial at the base of bushes or thick undergrowth. Drag marks, heel scuffs, footprints, and impact marks are scrubbed with a leafy tree branch. If equipment or stores are to be left at the insertion point, caches must be concealed and their position noted. This must be done without trampling through ploughed areas or cultivated fields. Individual parachutists are responsible for ensuring that no items of equipment are left behind or lost as a result of placing them on the ground while rolling up parachutes. A cross-country route is taken to the assembly point, avoiding roads and paths that will be used by civilians and enemy patrols.

▄ Pathfinders and Reception Committees

All forms of insertion can benefit from external help, but static-line parachuting and air-landing operations are particularly dependent upon ground teams. These parties perform a number of vital functions which can assist the soldier's entry into enemy-held territory:

1. Selecting a DZ/LZ and clearing it of obstacles.
2. Marking the DZ/LZ with air panels, lights, and radio beacons to provide additional navigation aids and to indicate lines of approach and release or impact points.
3. Providing information on local weather conditions, distinctive landmarks, and aerial obstacles close to the flight path such as towers, pylons, and hills.
4. Acting as forward air controllers to establish an orderly flight and/or landing sequence.
5. Maintaining DZ/LZ security and providing help in moving equipment, establishing caches, and sterilizing the area.

Some or all of these duties can be performed by three different types of ground party:

Mechanical pathfinders Remote-activated beacons and lights offer the most secure help. Three-and-a-half weeks before the launch of Operation Eagle Claw to rescue the American hostages in Tehran, Colonel John T. Carney of the USAF's "special tactics" unit flew a CIA Twin Otter medium aircraft into Iran to investigate the deserted airstrip codenamed Desert One. The first task of Carney's team was to decide whether the old desert runway could accommodate the C-130 tankers. After examining the length and gradient of the strip, the team collected a number of soil samples for analysis. Other members of the team maintained watch on the nearby road, noting that it was heavily used at night by smugglers and commercial traffic. Before leaving, the team implanted radio-controlled lights and navigation beacons. At 2200 hours on the night of the operation, these devices were activated by a radio signal transmitted by the lead aircraft as it approached the strip.

Pathfinder teams Reception duties can be performed by small units of soldiers such as pathfinders or Air Force Special Operations Combat Control Teams. Parties are usually inserted into the area by the most covert means possible. Consequently, most pathfinder units are highly trained HALO parachutists. Pathfinders may also conduct extensive reconnaissance of the area and guide the incoming special mission team to their initial objectives. Unlike their mechanical counterparts, the soldiers are responsive to equipment failure and provide a valuable source of "real-time" intelligence to the planning staff. The subtleties of pathfinder operations are also a fundamental part of resupply and extraction procedures and for convenience will be described below.

Reception committees Indigenous partisan forces can provide reception committees. However, involving a large number of additional poorly trained personnel may be damaging to an otherwise covert operation. One British SAS team (part of Operation Gain), parachuting into France to support the Normandy invasion (1944), were met on the ground by the Germans. The capture and execution of most of these men was ascribed to an informer. Other receptions, notably in Albania, degenerated into a carnival atmosphere with shouting, gunfire, and the plunder of containers.

The primary role of the American Army Special Forces is the training and organization of civilian irregulars. Not surprisingly, they have established standard operating procedures for receptions. The reception party is divided into five groups:

1. The Command Party is composed of the partisan leader, radio operator, messengers, medics, and a Special Forces advisor. The function of this party is to control and coordinate the other reception committee components.

2. The Marking Party distributes the lights or markers. By day, aircraft panels, sheets, or colored strips of cloth are arranged to mark the DZ/LZ. At night, these are substituted with torches, flares, or small fire pits. Some of the markers show wind speed and direction, while others indicate the release point. Security is provided by an authentication signal which may be a particular configuration of panels or a coded light signal. Navigation beacons may be placed in the center of the DZ and directed toward the aircraft's approach path.

3. The Security Party is split into two units. An inner element is positioned around the DZ/LZ and is required to fight holding or delaying actions should the enemy put in a surprise appearance. An outer security element establishes roadblocks or ambushes along rivers and roads running close to the site. Additional partisans may maintain surveillance or mount decoy attacks on local enemy forces. When the personnel or supplies have been recovered, the Security Party deploys into a protective screen to cover the withdrawal to the guerrilla base.

4. During parachute operations the Recovery Party is split into two-man groups and dispersed along the length of the DZ. Each group is assigned to a single parachutist or cargo container, and may position itself under the exit point. This serves as a reference should it become necessary to mount a search for parachutes drifting off the DZ. Once located, one man remains with the bundle or parachutist while the second takes the parachute to the recovery collection point. This man can then lead a detail back to collect injured parachutists or heavy equipment. The Recovery Party is also responsible for sterilizing the DZ, and maintaining a subsequent 48-hour watch on the area for enemy activity.

5. Members of the Command, Recovery and Marking Parties combine to form the Transport Party, moving equipment to distribution points or caches.

A pilot's eye view of a drop zone

The prospective DZ must be examined from the pilot's point of view. The intended flight path must be free of aerial hazards such as hills, and away from towns, night fighter bases, SAM sites, and anti-aircraft batteries. Geographical features that can be seen at night, and thus serve as navigational aids for the low-flying aircraft, are noted and reported.

These include:

- Coastlines with breaking surf or white sandy beaches or river estuaries at least 50 yards wide.
- Waterways more than 30 yards wide which can be seen from the air but are useless as a navigational aid in heavily irrigated areas crisscrossed with rivers or canals. Lakes with a surface area of at least half a square mile provide a good reflective surface but should have a distinctive shape.
- Small well-defined forested areas with an unmistakable shape.
- Straight roads or railways which intersect with other landmarks but are identified most clearly under special conditions. Wet roads are clearly visible in moonlight and railways appear as black lines after a snowfall.

One prominent landmark 5–15 miles from DZ may serve as the final navigational checkpoint or Initial Point (IP). Upon reaching the IP, the pilot will make a turn onto a predetermined compass bearing which will place him over the DZ within a known time. The compass bearing, or "desired track," is bracketed within open quadrants, calculated by the team from the center of the DZ and reported as a series of magnetic azimuths calculated clockwise from magnetic north. The open quadrants provide the pilot with a degree of latitude in choosing his approach route. Outside the quadrants then DZ markers are likely

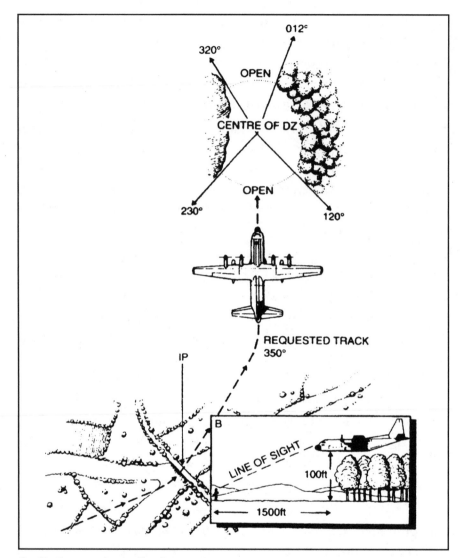

A pilot's eye view of a drop zone

On reaching a prominent landmark or Initial Point (IP) the pilot turns onto a prearranged magnetic bearing (requested track) which will take him over the DZ in a known time. The open quadrants tell the pilot how much latitude he has on the approach. Outside the quadrants, the DZ will be masked (in this instance by hills on the left and woods on the right). Horizontal masking (B) is calculated on the basis of a 15:1 ratio—the release point markers would need to be placed 1,500 ft. from a line of trees 100 ft. in height.

to be masked by surrounding hills or trees and will be invisible to the pilot. The team will also report all aerial obstacles such as radio masts and hills over 300 ft. in height and within a radius of 5 miles of the DZ. High ground over 1,000 ft. should be at least 10 miles away from the DZ. In valleys offering a single line of approach, there must be a turning radius of at least 3 miles on either side of the DZ (1 mile for light aircraft) to allow the pilot to execute a 180° turn.

■ Resupply Operations

A resupply operation that alerts the enemy to the presence of the clandestines forces the team to live with increasing enemy pressure. However, for personnel involved in organizing long-term partisan/ surveillance operations, resupply and its attendant risks become a way of life.

Aerial delivery Supply containers are composed of man-portable packages with carrying straps to facilitate their clearance from the DZ/LZ. Each package is usually waterproofed to permit caching above or below ground or, less commonly, underwater. These may be customized and packed by the team prior to their insertion.

Air-delivery operations are usually single aircraft missions. An aircraft, keeping low to avoid detection, may use the high-speed low-level airdrop system (HSLLADS) where the container, released from a low, fast aircraft, is specially rigged to withstand the shock of the parachute opening at high speed. This system can be used to deliver four 600-lb. containers on a single pass over the DZ. Alternatively, containers can be released for a conventional parachute descent or carefully packed to withstand the impact of being dropped without a parachute (free-drop loads).

Where the enemy has strong low-level air defenses, the team can be supplied using the high-altitude airdrop resupply system (HAARS). This permits pressurized containers to be dropped from a C-130 flying at 150 knots at an altitude of 25,000 ft. After several minutes in free-fall, a time fuse or barometric trigger activates blasting caps which release the parachute retaining devices.

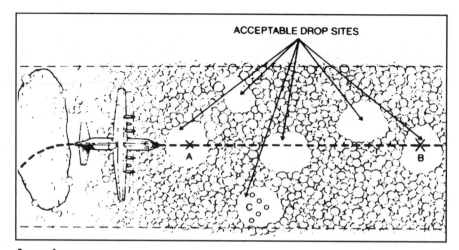

Area drop zones

On reaching an Initial Point, the pilot flies on a prearranged track (A–B) which takes him over a number of clearings, any one of which could serve as a DZ. If the aircraft was detected, the enemy would still be forced to search a wide area of country to find the one clearing selected as a DZ (C). Emergency DZs are a variation on this theme, except that the clearing is unmarked and unmanned and its location is known only to the team and Special Forces Headquarters.

Resupply at point of insertion Additional stores and equipment can be air-landed or dropped at the insertion site and cached. An aircraft dropping parachutists will have to make two passes over the DZ but this still offers the most secure form of resupply.

Emergency and area drop zones An emergency drop zone is chosen before the team is inserted, and its position is kept secret from partisans who may be working with the SAS or other special forces. Emergency resupply procedures are activated after the team misses a prescribed number of scheduled radio contacts. Barring a major communications failure, it is now considered that survivors are evading the enemy. The equipment and stores are dropped "blind" without a reception or identification and navigation panels. The containers will be collected if and when surviving members of the team are able to give their pursuers the slip.

Area drop zones are a variation on this theme. An aircraft makes a predetermined flight on a magnetic bearing between two distant landmarks. Underneath the aircraft's line of flight are a series of open spaces, any one of which could serve as a DZ. The team chooses one of these clearings and lays out marker panels. Once the markings are located, the aircraft releases its cargo in the normal manner. In order to enable the pilot to spot the markers, the flight path is restricted to a maximum length of 15 miles, and the DZ must be within half a mile to the left or right of the aircraft's track. An enemy alerted by the aircraft would be forced to search a corridor representing as much as 30 square miles of countryside.

The small, and possibly irregular-shaped clearings that might be used for emergency and area drops lend themselves to HSLLADS and the free-dropping (no parachute) of containers. Panels marking the release point compensate for the "forward-throw"—the horizontal distance travelled by a container that moves initially at the same velocity and direction as the aircraft. The panels are moved toward the approaching aircraft for a distance equal to the aircraft's altitude.

HALO operations Small, randomly chosen clearings also lend themselves to high-altitude resupply. Under conditions of good ground visibility, markers are used to show the impact point, leaving the pilot to calculate the release point. The panels (daylight) or fire pits (night) are arranged into five markers, placed at 75-ft. intervals in an arrowhead formation pointing into the wind. A simple arrowhead indicates 0–5 knots of wind. Each marker placed along the stem of the arrow indicates an additional 5-knot increment in wind speed. These markers assume an increased importance where the ground team is preparing to receive free-fallers rather than containers. The parachutists, knowing their opening altitude and reading the estimated wind speed and direction from the ground markers, can mentally compute their wind drift after opening. Consequently, the team can "track" to the opening point calculated from the precise information provided by the reception party. Four markers under the arrowhead— 20–25 knots of wind—is an automatic signal to abort or reschedule the operation as parachutists landing in high winds have a significantly increased risk of injury.

Under conditions of poor visibility, navigation beacons and radio communication are used to control the drop. The beacons may be active—sending out continuous signals that are intercepted by the navigation equipment on the approaching aircraft—or passive—responding to a signal from aircraft interrogating the beacon. The signals from passive beacons are less likely to be intercepted by the enemy but provide a more restricted navigation aid.

Low-velocity static-line drops While the DZs employed on most special operations will be small and unmarked, most special operations teams will be trained in pathfinder techniques and able to select and mark larger areas for delivery of assault teams, equipment, and vehicles. A suitable DZ will be remote from enemy forces and screened from curious civilians. Ideally, the prevailing nighttime and early morning weather conditions should be suitable for air operations. Mist, fog, and low clouds may obscure the DZ markers, while high winds may force the pilot to abort the operation. The drop can be made in poor visibility using the All Weather Aerial Delivery System (AWADS), provided the aircraft enjoys instrument meteorological conditions (IMC)—a minimum altitude of 300 ft. and visibility of about half a mile.

The area selected by the team should be free of obstacles such as rocks, trees, fences, pylons, and large animals. Open, flat, or rolling grassland is considered ideal. High pasture above 6,000 ft. results in an increased parachute descent rate. Hillsides with a gradient greater than 30 degrees require a line of approach at right angles to the DZ so that all the parachutes land on the same contour. Frozen or dry swamps or wetlands provide a marginal surface. Water-covered areas can be used in an emergency, provided the depth is not less than 4 ft. and the area is clear of surface and underwater obstructions. The safe minimum water temperature is 50°F, and every effort must be made to recover the parachutists quickly.

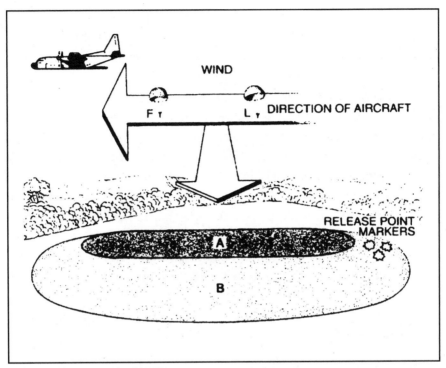

Dispersion and wind drift

This Hercules produces a dispersion pattern calculated as half the aircraft's speed multiplied by the exit time (the elapsed time between the first parachutist jumping (F) and the last parachutists jumping (L)). The dispersion pattern is parallel to the aircraft's flight path (A) and is further complicated by wind drift. In this example, the wind is blowing at right angles to the flight path. The resulting impact points move across the clearing as the wind speed increases (area B). Dispersion and wind drift are cardinal considerations in selecting a DZ for a static-line drop.

The ideal shape of the SZ is circular or square, thus simplifying the pilot's approach. For irregular DZs, the longest axis must parallel the direction of flight to accommodate the dispersion pattern. The length of the dispersion pattern represents the absolute minimum length required for the DZ. A safety factor of 100 yards is usually added to each end. A pathfinder team, selecting a DZ to receive personnel, might choose an area with a minimum size of 300 x 300 yards. Minor mistakes in calculating the wind drift over long, narrow clearings may result in the parachutists being carried away from the DZ.

The "forward throw" of parachute-retarded bundles is naturally less than that experienced by free-dropped containers. The containers experience wind drift for the short period between "forward throw" and impact. The marginal influence of wind drift is compensated for by placing the desired impact point at right angles to, and downwind of, the line of flight.

Before placing the markers on the DZ, the team must calculate the release point and impact points, taking into account:

- Dispersion, calculated in meters as ½ speed of the aircraft (knots) x the elapsed time between the release of the first and last containers or soldiers.

- Wind drift in meters, calculated as aircraft's altitude (hundreds of feet) x wind speed (knots) x a constant (3 or 4 depending upon type of parachute or cargo).

- Forward throw, usually compensated for by moving the release-point marker an additional 100 yards in the direction of the aircraft's approach.

- Mask clearance, to ensure that the pilot's view of the markers is not restricted by rising ground or trees. This is based on a 15:1 ratio such that the DZ markers should be 1,500 ft. away from a line of trees 100 ft. in height. The design of some transport aircraft prevents the pilot from seeing the markers as the aircraft gets close to the DZ (one mile at 1,000 ft.). This is compensated for by placing an additional release-point marker 200 yards to the left or right of the aircraft's track.

Calculating a parachutist's release point

Calculating a high-altitude release point (HARP) for HALO/HAHO parachutists is no easy matter and is usually left to the aircraft's navigator. The wind drift experienced by the soldier in free-fall is calculated by the equation $D = KAV$, where $K = 3$. A is the drop altitude in hundreds of feet, and V is the wind velocity. Allowing for a faster rate of descent at higher altitudes, and the overall weight of equipment carried by the parachutist, a planned release point can be calculated. Once under the canopy, the wind drift is calculated by the same formula, but now K equals the glide ratio of the parachute. For example, $K = 4$ for Ram Air parachutes—a 4:1 ratio representing 4 ft. of horizontal travel for every 1 ft. of descent. However, an accurate release point must also take account of direction and speed of the wind at every 1,000-ft. interval between the release-point altitude and the ground. The wind data can be obtained from the daily meteorological wind forecast or from a radio anemometer released by the aircraft. The averaged data allows the navigator to calculate a more precise release point.

■ Extraction

Extraction is used primarily to recover a team after the completion of their mission. However, the techniques used to recover personnel from behind the lines may be employed to evacuate valuable equipment, prisoners, VIPs, captured documents, downed aircrew or released POWs, and partisan leaders or guides. The type of extraction technique employed will depend upon at least three factors. First, the danger in which the team might find themselves at the end of a mission. Second, the degree of local help available to the team in embarking upon ambitious ventures such as the construction of runways or helicopter landing pads. Third, the availability of aircrew trained and equipped to undertake these missions under a variety of weather conditions.

Extraction procedures should enjoy the same security as insertion and resupply operations, particularly when equipment or documents

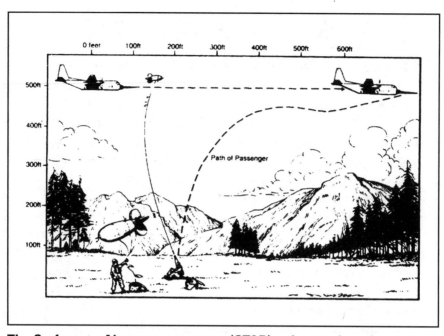

The Surface-to-Air recovery system (STAR) or how to board a moving aircraft

are being recovered and the team is remaining on the ground. The extraction point is always approached with care some time before the prearranged pickup. The team circles the immediate area, spiralling inward toward the extraction point, probing for enemy troops or ambushes. Once the area is deemed "clear," the exfiltration site is watched by a small surveillance party, while the rest of the team establishes a base some distance away. As the aircraft approaches the area, the team commander establishes radio contact and informs the pilot of the approach route, the nature of the terrain, the presence of wounded or sick team members, and recent contacts with the enemy.

Extraction techniques can be divided into the more complicated and dangerous operations that require the aircraft to land and pick up the team and arguably simpler techniques that enable the soldiers to board the aircraft while still in flight. However, the latter techniques are more than a little dramatic.

Surface-to-air recovery (STAR) The Fulton STAR system or "Sky-hook" allows an SAS or any other special forces team to board a specially modified Hercules transport as it passes overhead at 130 mph. On its approach flight, the aircrew drops two waterproofed bags containing the STAR equipment. This includes two fiberglass bottles filled with 650 cubic feet of helium gas, a balloon, 500 ft. of tubular nylon lift-line, protective helmets, coveralls, self-adjusting harnesses, and sheepskin hoods designed to protect the head and neck. Also included is a board with a series of simple instructional cartoons showing how to use the rig.

The first member of the team to be extracted pulls on his coveralls and hood before slipping on his harness which is connected to the balloon by the lift-line. The balloon is then filled with helium and released, and the soldier sits down facing the approaching aircraft.

The C-130 Talon makes a second approach over the clearing. On its nose is a wide Y-shaped fork. The pilot adjusts his airspeed to around 120–150 mph and his altitude to between 370 and 430 ft. His target is the lift-line just below the balloon which is marked with flags or strobe lights. As the aircraft collides with the line, it is guided into the center of the fork and locked tight. The balloon is released and discarded. The passenger is then pulled into the air and winched aboard the aircraft.

STAR is unlikely to be the first choice of extraction for special mission teams, but it has many advantages. The technique can rescue passengers from a clearing too small to accommodate a helicopter. Indeed, a soldier sitting in a small circle of 10-ft. diameter and surrounded by 50-ft. trees can be snatched to safety. Longer, heavy duty lift-lines can accommodate multiple pickups, and STAR can be used under almost any weather conditions.

Mini-STAR This smaller, simplified recovery system is used to recover equipment and documents. A rope connected to the package is suspended between two trees or poles at least 6 ft. off the ground. A helicopter, or light aircraft with a low stall speed, snags the line with a grappling hook trailing below the aircraft.

Air landing Many of the considerations involved in the selection of DZs apply to the choice of aircraft landing zones. Safe operations require a light aircraft strip used for day or night operations to be approximately 1,000 ft. in length and 150 ft. wide, while this is increased to 3,000 ft. x 150 ft. for medium transports. At each end of the runway, an area representing 10 percent of the overall length is cleared as a safety zone. In mountainous terrain above 4,000 ft., further 10 percent increments are needed for every 1,000 ft. of altitude with additional increases for ambient temperatures above 90°F (10 percent) and 100°F (20 percent).

The surface of the runway should be clear of obstructions and smooth and firm, allowing the aircraft to land without its undercarriage being damaged or its wheels becoming bogged. The surface gradient of the land should not exceed 2 percent and the subsoil should be firm to a depth of 2 ft. In northern climates, winter may provide some unusual airfields. Frozen lakes and rivers can serve as runways. Light aircraft will be supported by 8 in. of ice, while an ice-cap three times that thickness will take the weight of a medium-sized transport. Packed snow may also serve as an LZ, but soft or slippery surfaces require a further 7–10 percent increase in length as a safety factor.

Air-landing operations are supported in much the same way as parachute drops. Additional care must be taken to ensure that there are no obstructions such as telephone wires or trees in the approach/takeoff path. The glide/climb ratio for a medium-sized aircraft is approximately 1:40, the aircraft gaining or losing 3 ft. of altitude for every 135 ft. of flight. This, in turn, determines the safe glide path for an aircraft attempting to land or take off at any given airstrip. A medium-sized aircraft forced to clear a 50-ft. obstacle on its approach would need a further 2,000 ft. to land safely. The glide/climb ratio for light aircraft is 1:20.

Three sets of panels or lights show the pilot the initial touchdown point. The third marker indicates the very last point at which the aircraft can land safely. Navigation and timing become crucial in air-landing operations. The runway lights are usually switched on two minutes before the expected time of arrival and remain displayed for a further four minutes or until the aircraft has landed. Security for the ground team is ensured by the aircraft appearing at the right time and on the correct approach track. If the aircraft appears suspicious, the landing lights are extinguished. Conversely, if the signal light is flashing the wrong code of the day, or no signal is in evidence, the pilot will abort the landing.

Helicopter extraction A team awaiting extraction may be fortunate in finding themselves in open, flat countryside that lends itself to rotary-wing operations. Under other conditions, the construction of a helicopter LZ may require considerable thought and effort. Vertical takeoffs and landings are difficult for heavily laden helicopters. Packed with soldiers and equipment, the aircraft noses into the air in the same way as a fixed-wing aircraft. Ideally, the surface of the LZ must be clear of obstacles, firm enough to support the helicopter's weight, and with no more than a 15 percent slope. Landing pads can be constructed on hillsides by cutting and filling the slope to create a smooth platform. Similar rubble and log platforms can be built in swamps and marshes.

The overall dimensions of the LZ will vary with the size and airlift capability of the helicopter, encompassing circular areas with diameters of 80–165 ft. The inner hard pad, or platform, must accommodate the spread of the aircraft's landing gear. This is surrounded by an area also cleared to ground level and free of loose objects such as rocks that might be whipped into the air by the prop wash. Beyond this, the vegetation is cleared to below 3 ft. in height to provide horizontal clearance for an aircraft landing or taking off. In clearing obstacles from the flight path, the helicopter's climb/glide ratio is considered to be 1:5 or to require 300 ft. to clear a 60-ft. obstacle such as a line of trees.

The size of the LZ may be increased by as much as 40 percent for night operations. It may be necessary also to take into account the density altitude in planning LZs. Density altitude is a function of altitude, temperature, and humidity. High, hot, dry conditions reduce a

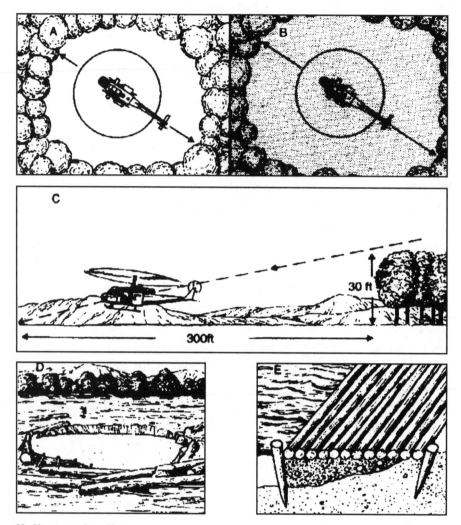

Helicopter landing zones

A medium-sized helicopter needs a clearing 35 meters in diameter for day operations (A) and a 50-meter diameter area for night operations (B).

In selecting a potential LZ the ground party assesses obstacles using a 1:10
ratio to calculate clearances for landing and takeoff—an aircraft will need 300 ft. to
land safely after passing over a 30 ft.-high treeline (C). In difficult territory a landing
pad will also need to be constructed to take the weight of the helicopter. In mountainous terrain, trees are cut down and soil excavated to produce a flat pad (D). In
swamp areas, gravel and timber are used to build a raised landing platform (E).

Calling for a resupply mission

Having chosen a suitable area, the team sends a radio signal reporting the drop zone. This data usually includes:

1. Team identification code.
2. Military grid coordinates of the center of the DZ.
3. Open quadrants.
4. Magnetic compass bearing (azimuth) of desired aircraft track.
5. Obstacles and other hazards to aircraft.
6. Navigational reference points.
7. Initial Points.
8. Date and time of drop using Greenwich Mean Time (ZULU Time).
9. Equipment or stores required.
10. Alternative DZ—used in an emergency and usually manned by a skeleton team.

Once the DZ report is processed, Special Forces headquarters sends a confirmation, usually by a blind transmission broadcast at a prearranged time. The confirmation message includes:

1. Codename of DZ identifying the mission.
2. Aircraft track or approach to DZ.
3. Date and time of drop.
4. Number of cargo containers or personnel—assisting the reception in recovery and calculation of dispersion.
5. Drop altitude—assisting the ground team in calculating release point and wind drift.
6. Date and time of drop at alternative DZ, if its use should become necessary.

helicopter's lift capabilities and require a proportionate increase in the size of the LZ. The thin, turbulent air around mountains also reduces lift capability. High cross- or tailwinds will necessitate an approach and departure route facing into the wind.

Carefully planned helicopter LZs represent an ideal. In many instances it is possible for the helicopter to extract a team without landing. In Southeast Asia the Americans were faced with recovering teams from thick jungle and in continuous contact with Communist forces. The team requiring emergency extraction might find themselves in unbroken jungle or on the side of a heavily forested hill. Even when large clearings were available to serve as helicopter LZs, these might be ambushed by an enemy hoping to use the Special Forces team as bait for the larger prey. Consequently, much thought went into the design of extraction techniques that would enable a helicopter hovering above the jungle canopy to remove the team from the midst of a fierce firefight, more than 100 ft. below.

The troop ladder allowed the team to climb up to the waiting helicopter. Rucksacks were attached to the lower rungs and, in dire emergency, the men could hook onto the ladder by their safety rigs. In this way the team could be pulled clear of the trees and carried slung underneath the aircraft, until the pilot found a safe area to land and take the soldiers on board.

As normally used, the ladder method of extraction was slow and soldiers attempting to climb to safety presented easy targets for enemy marksmen. Members of the Military Assistance Command Vietnam (MACV) Recondo School, tasked with training soldiers for LRRP missions, attempted to overcome this problem by designing the Stabilized Tactical Airborne Body Operations (STABO) rig. STABO was a modification of the earlier McGuire Hanson and Palmer rings, essentially nylon-webbing saddles constructed to carry the solider and his equipment suspended beneath the aircraft. However, a team in danger of being overrun would have little time to configure an extraction harness dropped to them by the aircrew. The STABO rig was designed to resolve this problem by replacing the standard issue web suspenders on the soldier's Load Bearing Equipment or the yoke and belt that

A UH-60 Blackhawk helicopter extracts a four-man patrol using STABO.

Each man is wearing a STABO rig and is connected to the line dropped by the helicopter by D-rings on the shoulders of each rig. While being winched aboard, the outside men stretch their arms to counteract the natural tendency to spin in the air.

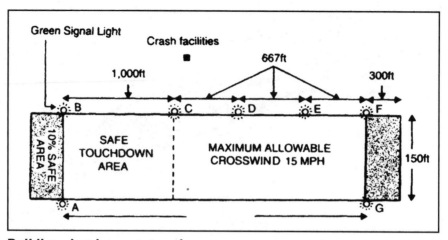

Building airstrips: construction

As the pilot approaches the end of the runway in darkness, he sees two green lights (A and B) which mark the beginning of the safe touchdown area. To allow for an undershoot, a 20 percent safety zone is cleared in front of the green signal lights. The next light is white (C) and is placed a third of the way along the runway. It marks the end of the safe touchdown area. If the pilot lands beyond the white marker light, he is faced with aborting the landing or attempting to survive the resulting crash. Additional white lights (D and E) are placed at 667 ft. intervals, until the aircraft reaches the end of the airstrip and two red signal lamps (F and G). Temporary parking areas, which hold the aircraft while it is being loaded or unloaded, lie to the right-hand side. These are marked by blue or amber lights. The command and control party and crash facilities are located on the other side of the runway.

carry ammunition pouches and water bottles. The STABO rig was worn throughout the operation and was snapped onto the suspension rope quickly and easily, using two D-rings sewn to the shoulders of the rig.

Once each soldier was connected to his own suspension rope, several aircraft, or a helicopter with a large lift capacity, were needed to extract the entire team simultaneously. The pilot had to gain height to pull his passengers out of the jungle canopy before moving forward; then he had to avoid dragging his charges through trees or bouncing them across the LZ. Slung below the aircraft, the soldiers

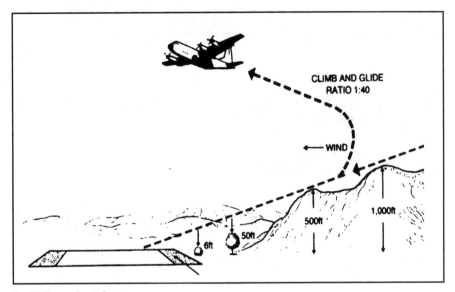

Building airstrips

Takeoff and landing clearances for medium transport aircraft.

were connected by a safety rope in case one of the individual ropes snapped. Stability was maintained by interlocking arms and legs. The men at each end could stretch out their arms to overcome the natural tendency to spin in the slipstream.

Special Procedures Insertion/Extraction (SPIE) was a similar system developed by the US Navy for its Sea-Air-Land (SEAL) commandos. This had the advantage of using a single rope along which a series of rings were spliced at 5-ft. intervals. The design of the system prevented the men colliding with one another and left their hands free to fire their weapons at the opposition below.

CHAPTER 4

Waterborne Operations

A WINDING COASTLINE, with covers and natural harbors, offers the other major opportunity for covert insertion of SAS and other special mission teams. One of the more enduring beach landing sites (BLS) was "Sea View" on the Albanian coast, south of the small town of Valona. Beyond the narrow inlet and rocky shore there is a ravine several hundred feet above the sea, the walls of which have eroded to form a number of caves. The area was first discovered by Colonel Sir N.L.D. "Billy" McLean, and SOE officer dispatched to organize resistance to the Italian and German armies of occupation. By the time the young actor, Anthony Quayle, arrived in January 1944 to begin his tour of duty for SOE, the damp lice- and scorpion-ridden caverns were also home to American OSS and British MI6 intelligence officers. "Sea View" outlived World War II, becoming the primary insertion site for agents dispatched by MI6 and the CIA in an attempt to overthrow Enver Hoxha's postwar Communist regime.

"Sea View" exemplified the problems associated with maritime operations. Attempts to land agents or supplies from SOE's fleet of fishing boats were thwarted by the weather, which frequently obscured the small signal torch intended to provide both a navigational aid and a means of authenticating the security of the BLS. In the absence of detailed beach reconnaissance, some of the skippers were loath to venture too close to shore. This made the task of picking up agents and seriously ill personnel extremely difficult. Pursued by the enemy and with food, gas, and radio batteries exhausted, "Sea View" often became untenable for the agents. Extracts from Sir Anthony Quayle's operations underscore the clandestines' dependence upon regular support sorties:

March 26: Signal from Bari agreeing I come out and make personal report. Told to stand by for sortie. No date given, and radio contact all to hell through lack of petrol.

March 27: No reply to my urgent signals, so decide to cross over to Sea View and await sortie. Snow worse. Four feet everywhere, and deeper in drifts. Ice on summit. . . . Flashed but no sortie.

March 30: Learnt that boat HAD come previous night, but to wrong beach. HQ confused to the last.

. . . Conditions were perfect that night. I lay on the cliff above the creek signaling out to sea—but no boat came. I did not have the strength to climb back into the cave, so I slept on the headland in the rain. In the dawn I woke up vomiting.

Sick with malaria and jaundice, Quayle was finally evacuated on April 3, 1944.

The long distances between an SAS or any other special forces base and the target area or BLS often necessitate a variety of transport. A team may be delivered to the operational area (primary delivery) by the fastest means available but will then choose a more covert form of transport to insert onto the target or landing area (secondary delivery). For example, an aircraft might carry the team to a rendezvous with a submarine, which then transports the team through the operational area to a drop-off point close to the enemy coast.

■ Primary Delivery

A sea plane might provide the ideal means of delivering a team to a submarine rendezvous but maritime air-landing operations require optimum conditions, with low crosswinds and wave height, and an air/water temperature high enough to avoid ice formation which might endanger the aircraft. A more reliable means of insertion involves dropping the team and their equipment by static-line parachutes. Approaching the rendezvous at wave-top level to avoid radar detection, the aircraft reaches the Initial Point and turns toward the predetermined DZ. The submarine may release flares or radio beacons to mark the DZ, and, if submerged, may transmit an infrared authentication signal through the periscope. In the absence of surface signals the navigator will use the on-board navigation equipment to calculate the release point, whereupon the aircraft will rise to the drop height (500–2,000 ft.), first releasing the team's equipment, packed into containers or assembled onto parachute-rigged pallets, before dispatching the team.

After checking his canopy for malfunctions, the parachutist, clad in a swimmer's dry suit, releases his individual waterproofed equipment container. Hanging below him on a suspension rope, the container holds his rucksack or Bergen and vital equipment, such as weapon and underwater breathing apparatus, sealed inside buoyant waterproof bags. While still in the air, he may don his swimmer's fins before maneuvering the steerable 'chute toward the recovery vessel or the team's boats. As the parachutist approaches the water, he grasps the liftwebs and releases himself from the parachute harness, dropping into the water just before impact to avoid being enveloped by the canopy.

Assembly, retrieval of equipment, and subsequent sterilization, crucial to any operation, are made more difficult by the waves, tide, and currents. Linked into pairs by buddy lines, the team members load their inflatables with stores and equipment, before cutting away the pallets and allowing them to sink, along with other extraneous items such as parachutes, equipment straps, and damaged equipment.

The team is dispatched to the area of operations using the quickest available means of transport (primary boats).

A range of vehicles, such as submarines and boats, take the party close to the beach or target, where a more covert means of transportation (surface or underwater swimming, mini-submersibles, canoes, or small boats) is selected for the final approach (secondary delivery).

MISSION PLANNING MATRIX				
Method	**Maximum Range One Way** (miles)	**Maximum Sustained Speed** (miles)	**Equipment Carried**	**Secrecy Afforded**
Small Boat	Limited only by amount of fuel carried (1.7–6.8 km/gal dependent on load)	21.0 at max. load with motor; 2.3 at max. load with paddles	Up to 2,500 lbs. total wt per boat	Poor to fair
Under-water (SCUBA)	0.93 open circuit; 1.9 closed circuit (0.3 miles when towing a bundle)	3.7–4.3 without equipment	Individual equipment only (1 bundle per person)	Excellent
Surface swimming	6.2 w/o bundle	4.3–5.0 without equipment	Individual equipment only (1 bundle per person)	Good

MISSION PLANNING MATRIX (continued)				
Sterilization of BLS	**Method to Drop-off Point by Service**			**Special Training Required**
	Navy	**AF**	**Army**	
May be difficult and time consuming	Patrol boat Amphibious aircraft Submarine	Static-line parachuting	Helicopter drop	Minimal
Depends on availability of cover	Patrol boat Amphibious aircraft Submarine	Static-line Military free-fall	Helicopter cast	Extensive
Easy	Patrol boat Amphibious aircraft Helicopter cast Submarine	Static-line Military free-fall	Helicopter cast	Minimal

More than 50 percent of the team's equipment may be duplicated as a hedge against loss or damage, but the wide-scale dispersal and loss of stores packages dropped into the sea can mean the end of the operation. Troops inserting by HALO or HAHO parachute drop are severely limited in the amount of equipment that can be carried safely in their personal equipment containers. They are thus dependent upon resupply drops or prepositioned equipment caches.

If the submarine commander decides to surface despite the risk of radar detection by patrolling ships and aircraft, a skilled aircrew can drop the men and their equipment close to the boat. Entering a submerged submarine is more difficult. Dropped upstream of the submerged craft, the men assemble their stores and don their diving equipment, before connecting themselves to a long rope. After forming a line in the water, the outside divers activate transponder beacons, producing a signal that is picked up by the submarine's sonar. Running at periscope depth and aiming for a point midway between the two signals, the submarine's periscope snags the swimmers' rope and allows the team to drift astern. As the vessel comes to a stop, the swimmers haul themselves, hand over hand, to the periscope. A guide rope is attached from the periscope to the "lockout" chamber to aid the swimmers in their descent. Reducing the buoyancy of the stores containers enables them to sink to the deck of the submarine, where they are stored in stowage boxes between the deck casing and the pressure hull. With their stores and equipment safe, the team enters the submarine through the lockout chamber. A surface swimmer team can also be recovered by a submerged submarine using small air tanks and SCUBA demand regulators, attached at intervals along a vertical rope which runs from the lockout chamber to the periscope housing or a small buoy released to float on the surface.

■ Secondary Delivery and Recovery

Transport to the BLS or target depends upon a range of factors, including distance, weather and sea conditions, enemy surveillance, the nature of the operation, and the amount of equipment required.

Penetration by combat swimmers using underwater breathing apparatus offers the most secure form of insertion and is one of the methods of choice for entering heavily defended rivers and harbors. However, it requires a high level of training, and its operational range is restricted (1 mile open circuit, 1.9 miles closed circuit and 0.3 miles towing equipment bundle). Surface swimming requires less training and still offers an unobtrusive means of approaching the enemy coast. Again this is limited by range (1.3 miles) and the amount of equipment that can be transported. Both swimming techniques leave the operators vulnerable to tides, currents, and adverse weather. Swimmers can be free-dropped closer to the coast by helicopter (helocasting) or small boat, but these are relatively high-profile techniques only suitable for use against a technologically unsophisticated enemy.

Not surprisingly, a range of underwater vehicles has been developed to provide a highly reliable means of inserting and extracting swimmers. The first basic type is the two-man "chariot" or "wet"-swimmer delivery vehicle (SDV). The divers sit astride the SDV clad in their dry suits and underwater breathing apparatus. Equipped with sophisticated navigation, depth, and acoustic transponder instruments, the operational range is limited by the diver's air and the craft's battery power supply. Larger four- and six-man vehicles can carry a larger payload including additional air and a large battery unit which can be used to recharge the diver's electrically heated undersuits—vital for operations in cold water. The current American Mark Eight SDV carries four SEALs, a pilot, and copilot. Unfortunately, the design of the craft forces its passengers to travel crouched in a depression along the vessel's hull. It is claimed that a long ride is so demanding physically that SEAL teams must recuperate on the shore for several hours before beginning their mission.

Much more ideal is the "dry" SDV, or mini-submarine, similar to the commercial craft used in the deep oil and gas fields. Designed for operations in the colder latitudes, the "dry" SDV keeps the divers safe and warm. It has an operational range of hundreds of miles and mission duration of several days, and it can dive deep to avoid enemy antisubmarine defenses and attack craft.

Both types of vehicle can be carried to the operational area by "mother" submarines. They can be cached on the sea floor or river bottom close to the target, while the divers complete their tasks, which may take them far inland. Upon the swimmer's return, the SDV is located by means of an underwater beacon. A second beacon is dropped by the parent submarine at a prearranged rendezvous. On reaching this point, the SDV makes a prearranged change of course to approach the waiting boat, guided by a third beacon on the submarine which transmits at a different frequency. This somewhat convoluted procedure is by way of a security check, to ensure the safety of the parent craft, should a swimmer team and their equipment fall into enemy hands. An enemy commander who captured the team, their SDV, and its acoustic transponder receiver would still need to know the new magnetic bearing at the prearranged RV and the new frequency of the submarine's beacon, in order to locate and destroy the mother craft. Quite apart from their use on reconnaissance and sabotage missions, SDVs also provide a covert means of conducting beach resupply operations for the SAS or other special forces operating in the interior of a country.

The operation of other insertion vehicles requires far less training. Rubber inflatable boats, such as Geminis and Zodiacs, and rigid- and semirigid-hulled raider craft are used to transport swimmers to their drop-off point, or land teams and their stores on the coast. Propelled by high-powered outboard or marine diesel engines, these craft are limited only by the amount of fuel carried and are capable of travelling at high speeds. Larger American boats, such as the Medium SEAL Support Craft and the Seafox, can accommodate a team and their equipment while serving as a heavily armed and highly mobile support weapons platform. However, these boats are noisy and offer a relatively high-profile radar silhouette. Should the engine fail, they are slow and maneuver poorly.

The other common insertion vehicle, the canoe, has none of these disadvantages. Capable of being dismantled and dropped by parachute, it is limited only by its size and the stamina of its two-man crew.

A remarkable British-built boat was designed to combine the advantages of a "wet"-SDV and a high-powered surface craft. On the surface, the Subskimmer-80 is a fast, rigid-hulled inflatable powered by a 80-hp outboard motor. As the team approaches the coast, the engine is sealed and the air sucked out of the hull, allowing the boat to sink. Once submerged, the craft is powered by electrical thrusters, giving it an operational range of 6 miles at 2½ knots.

The journey in to the beach can be the most critical part of the operation. Heavy swell and surf may threaten to capsize the team's craft with the resulting loss of personnel and equipment. At an early stage in the operation, the survivors could find themselves in the sea or cast ashore, no longer an effective military force, and in need of urgent recovery.

Boat drills are designed to avoid this eventuality. Items of equipment, which have been waterproofed with grease or wrapped in plastic, are secured to the boat to prevent them being lost in the event of a capsize. These are distributed evenly along the bottom of the boat to maintain a low center of gravity. Sharp and pointed items of equipment are padded to ensure that they do not penetrate the rubber-skinned hull. Paddles are wrapped to avoid noise and secured by cords to the boat. Lines are also attached to each side of the boat to be used for recovering a member of the team thrown overboard or for righting the boat after a capsize. Team members wear camouflaged life jackets and individual weapons are connected to each man by a sling or lanyard while a second, longer cord secures the weapon to the boat. If the party is using more than one boat, visual contact is maintained throughout the journey. Hand signals and the simple expedient of following the lead boat avoid the need for radio communications.

As the boats approach the first line of surf, speed is reduced sufficiently to maintain their position relative to the beach while scout swimmers are detached to check the shoreline for enemy sentries. Once ashore, the scouts part company to check the beach for 50 yards in each direction. If the beach is clear, a prearranged recognition signal is flashed. The scouts maintain covering fire and security positions until the landing is completed and the equipment un-loaded. A secure cache may need to be found for the boat and any excess stores and equipment before the landing area is sterilized and the team begins the next phase of their infiltration overland.

At the end of a mission, not all SAS or other special forces teams seeking extraction from an enemy coast will be lucky enough to have a parent vessel waiting to pick them up. Swimmers can be recovered by air, using STAR or the various helicopter extraction systems. The Chinook can hover just above the water with its loading ramp sub-merged, enabling a team and their inflatable to be winched into the loading bay. The raised flight deck prevents thousands of gallons of water pouring into the cockpit. During takeoff, the water is allowed to escape through the rear of the aircraft and through drain holes in the fuselage.

Underwater Operations

Underwater swimmers may be used to conduct covert reconnaissance of enemy harbors or beach defenses. Equally, swimmer teams may be used to attack enemy shipping, underwater obstacles, or coastal targets heavily defended from the land but open to a seaborne assault. As a total swim of about one mile is considered feasible on a combat mission, the diver is dropped off as close as possible to the target, either by canoe, with one man staying with the boat, or by SDV, which is left moored on the bottom.

Open SCUBA equipment is unsuitable for military operations. Quite apart from the cloud of bubbles formed from the expired air, it is noisy and only 5 percent of the air is actually breathed, the rest escaping into the water. By contrast, closed-circuit rebreather equipment, such as the Emerson apparatus, is very efficient. The re-breather removes exhaled carbon dioxide and recharges the remaining nitrogen gas (which forms the bulk of air) with pulsed oxygen. Such economical use of oxygen ensures that a 12.7 cubic foot cylinder lasts for four hours or more. The main disadvantage of oxygen rebreathing equipment is that it limits the diver to shallow water—pure oxygen

Taking the war into the enemy's harbors

becomes toxic at pressures above two atmospheres (a depth of 30 ft.)—
and the equipment itself is not designed to withstand high pressures.
However, this is an advantage to the combat swimmer as the gas
supply lasts longer on shallow dives and some swimmer detection
systems have difficulty in locating intruders in shallow water. Moreover, it will be easier to make a free ascent in shallow water in the
event of equipment failure.

On their swim in to the target, the divers have the additional
problem of carrying their equipment and explosives, usually magnetic or "limpet" mines. Some mines weigh around 30 lbs. and are
constructed of synthetic plastics to give them neutral buoyancy,
others need to be carried in a "buoyancy bag," or air bladder, which
is partly inflated to make the load weightless under water. The
diver may also carry an "attack board"—a piece of light plastic with
the fluorescent dials of a watch, depth gauge, and compass arranged

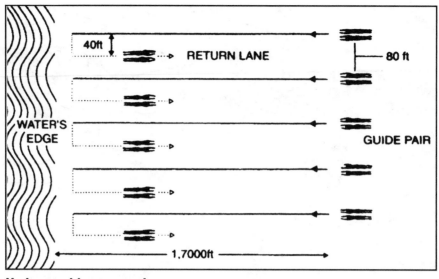

40ft

RETURN LANE

80 ft

WATER'S EDGE

GUIDE PAIR

1,7000ft

Hydrographic reconnaissance

Swimmer pairs are dropped into the sea 80 ft. apart with a designated guide pair in the center. When the pairs are in position, the guide pair signals the swimmers to move toward the beach and start taking soundings and bottom samples.

in a highly visible triangle, designed to simplify the problems associated with diving in conditions of zero visibility.

Entering the harbor, the diver may determine the direction of any currents by the position of the ships relative to their anchor chains. Starting his attack run up-current allows the diver to drift with the flow from target to target, avoiding any revealing movements that will betray his presence by creating phosphorescent swirls in the water. In the darkness, a nearby ship betrays its presence by an increased noise level, compass deviations, and a "blacker than black" shadow under the boat's hull. The placement of the limpet charges depends on the type of ship and hull configuration and the location of critical compartments within the ship (e.g., engine room, sonar domes, screws, and rudder). If the boat is preparing to sail, many of these areas are dangerous to the swimmers who may be pulled into the screws or underwater suction openings along the chine of the hull (intersection between the sides and bottom of the ship). During

---

Leaving the submarine

Once inside enemy waters, the parent submarine is placed in considerable peril. This is heightened as the special forces teams prepare to disembark at the drop-off point. A range of techniques have been refined to ensure that disembarkation is carried out as quickly and as unobtrusively as possible. Where the threat is minimal, the sub may surface to allow the boats to be inflated and either slid over the side or positioned on the deck to await a "wet" launch as the submarine submerges beneath them. Alternatively, the boat may partly surface with its decks awash, enabling the team to enter the water from the conning tower. As the submarine submerges at dead-slow, to avoid the propellers injuring the swimmers, the team assembles their equipment and inflates their boats in the water. The most covert means of disembarkation involves personnel leaving a submerged submarine through the lockout chamber. This technique, which is the optimum method of releasing divers for free-swimming or SDV insertions, can also be used to launch boat teams. A pair of naval divers removes the boats from the stowage compartments and inflates them on the surface, while the rest of the team makes a free ascent to the surface with their equipment.

---

training, these areas are closed down, but on a combat dive the mission will take priority and it is left to the team leader to make a tactical decision.

▨ Beach Reconnaissance

The detailed reconnaissance and survey of prospective coastal landing sites is a major task of maritime special forces. The BLS may be intended for assault landings by marines or other conventional forces (e.g., the Falklands War and the US invasion of Grenada). The reconnaissance party will determine whether the slope of the beach and the water depth is suitable for landing craft. They will also identify the presence of natural and man-made obstacles, observe the local sea conditions, and pinpoint enemy defenses and potential helicopter LZs in the immediate area behind the beach.

A comprehensive survey of a landing site may require a hydrographic survey, a beach survey, and a surf report. A hydrographic survey, which is usually conducted at night by scout swimmers, is designed to gather specific information about the beach and the adjoining seabed, including gradients, beach and seabed composition, underwater obstacles, and the type and severity of surf breaking on the foreshore.

As the pairs of scout swimmers swim slowly toward the beach, they are kept on their predetermined course by guide swimmers employing a compass or navigating with reference to a beach landmark. When a lead line, lowered to the seabed, indicates a depth of 21 ft., the scout swimmers signal to the guide pair to stop. The depth is recorded on a slate, and the guide pair estimates the distance to the high-water mark. The depth is measured at further 80-ft. intervals, with bottom samples taken at the 18-, 12- and 6-ft. soundings. When diving to the bottom to obtain a sample, the swimmer avoids splashing by executing a jack-knife dive, thrusting himself straight down and only using his fins when he is several feet below the surface. Care is also taken to avoid raising the line and slate above the water during soundings, standing in the shallows, or allowing the moonlight to reflect off the swimmers' face masks.

The positions of all man-made defenses and natural underwater obstacles (reefs, sandbars, rocks, and kelp) are also noted as are inshore currents running parallel to the beach. The latter are measured by observing the movement and direction of an object as it is allowed to drift with the current over a one-minute period. The distance in feet, divided by a factor of 100, gives the approximate speed of the current in knots. At the water's edge, the scout swimmers may crawl ashore to investigate the composition and gradient of the foreshore (area between the extreme low-water mark and the upper limit of the breaking waves). This data will determine the type and number of military vehicles which can be offloaded from beached landing craft. Returning to the water, the swimmers move a set distance along the beach, before swimming out to sea where another series of soundings and samples are taken.

Combat beach reconnaissance

A. A swimmer and one of the boat party measure the gradient of the beach around the high-water mark. Combat-swimmers will have explored the adjacent seabed during a night hydrographic recce.

B. One of the boat party, holding a stopwatch and notebook, completes a surf report.

C. Two "boat keepers" provide security for the survey and defend the inflatable: the team's only means of escape.

D. Cartographers and surveyors chart the hinterland behind the beach, The resulting maps and photographs will show roads, enemy positions, and potential helicopter LZs (amphibious landing) or potential escape and evasion routes, egress points, areas to cache material, and degree of isolation (covert landing).

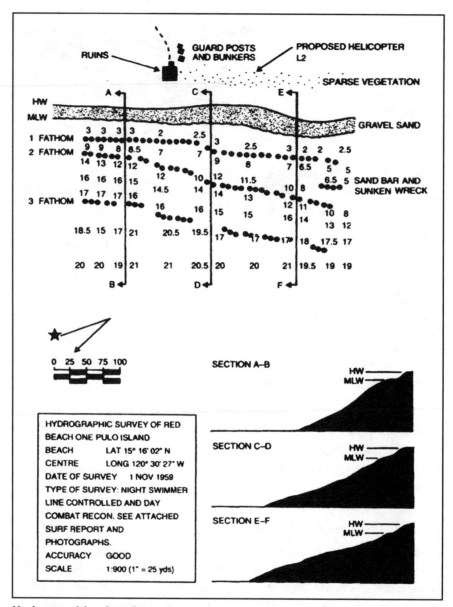

Hydrographic sketch

The end product of a beach reconnaissance, the hydrographic sketch shows the beach hinterland and the soundings along the adjoining seabed. The inclination of the seabed below the high water (HW) and mid low water (MLW) marks is of interest to marine units intending a beach landing with amphibious vehicles. Three sections along the beach are shown.

One pair of scout swimmers may be detailed to make a surf report. Removing their face masks to avoid inadvertent reflections, the swimmers watch the beach for signs of human activity. When it is deemed safe, fins are removed and the scouts move close to the center of the BLS where they can watch the waves break on the shoreline. Throughout a ten-minute period, the scout swimmers record each wave, noting the average and maximum wave heights, the period of time between each wave, and the angle at which the surf hits the beach. Each wave is also placed into one of three categories:

Spilling The wave becomes unstable at crest and gently spills down the face.

Plunging The wave crest advances faster than the base of the wave, the crest falling into a trough and causing the air trapped inside the breaker to be released explosively.

Surging Found on steep beaches, the base of the wave advances faster than the crest, with the result that the breaker surges up the beach. Much of the water is sucked back into the sea as the next wave approaches.

The scouts also note the characteristics of the shore indicated by the different surf patterns. Half of the waves approaching a shoreline break when the water depth is between one to two wave heights. The remainder break as the water depth becomes less than the wave height. Consequently, a steep seabed allows the waves to break directly onto or close to the beach, producing a violent shoreward rush of water if the wave is higher than 3–4 ft. Dangerous surf conditions can be accentuated by offshore sandbars, deeper than two wave heights, which can cause waves to peak or produce multiple breaker lines. In contrast, reefs, shoals, islands, currents, a rocky seabed, and a gently sloping beach can disrupt wave patterns, reducing surf.

However, calm water, natural coves, and gently sloping beaches, ideal for landing, often allow kelp and seaweed to accumulate. Kelp and weed barriers in offshore waters or in the tidal zone can impede the progress of small boats and swimmers toward the shore. These areas are avoided, if possible.

Finding the beach landing site

In daylight, the drop-off point is likely to be at least 2 miles offshore as this represents the limit of horizontal visibility for an observer on the beach at a height of 3 ft. above the surface of the water. In practice it could be as much as 20 miles out to sea and in a carefully chosen radar blind spot.

Currents, strongest at full moon and running between the drop-off point and the beach, may carry the boat or swimmers along the coast and away from the BLS, endangering the operation. (A one-knot current will carry a weighted bottle 100 ft. in one minute. When attempting to navigate distances in excess of 1,500 ft., a 0.2 knot current is considered critical.) This forces the navigator to use offset navigation to compensate for speed and direction of local currents, details of which are found in the National Ocean Survey current tables. Multiplying the time required for an uncompensated passage by the speed of the current, and knowing the current's direction or "set," allows the navigator to plot a compensated track "up current" of the BLS. Throughout the journey the boat's passage may be reassessed continually using a combination of dead reckoning, celestial observation, and shoreline silhouette.

A team intending to conduct an extensive beach survey might arrive at first light, hoping to complete the reconnaissance and return before the local population leave their homes. An American Naval Special Warfare "recon" team would consist of a team commander, "boat keeper," cartographer, and at least two swimmers for every 25 yards of beach to by surveyed. The area to be examined stretches from the foreshore to the hinterland, 5 miles behind the beach. The local geography and geology are noted, together with man-made structures, potential routes, and beach exits. Notes, sketches, and soil samples are complemented with photographs showing individual features or beach panoramas. The final product of this exhaustive reconnaissance is a detailed map or hydrographic sketch and a wealth of additional information that will enable a full assessment of a particular site for boat landings. Natural hazards can be avoided and, where necessary, underwater defenses identified for demolition.

Cleared channels can then be marked with acoustic underwater beacons. Operations launched without such detailed reconnaissance may end in failure and the death of the special mission team. The South Korean authorities have collected a virtual museum of Communist infiltration craft, including a three-man "dry"-SDV captured in 1965 after the retreating tide left it stranded on mudflats in the estuary of the Han and Imjin rivers. The failures of other covert maritime operations were briefly mentioned in chapter 1.

■ Riverine Operations

Rivers provide access to the interior of enemy-held territory. During the Vietnam War, American special forces teams and their allies used the tributaries in the Mekong Delta to launch raids, ambushes, and combat rescue operations deep inside Vietcong sanctuary areas. Some rivers, thousands of miles long, can provide access to a number of neighboring countries—the might Mekong River also passed through Cambodia and Laos which were theaters of fighting during the Vietnam War.

Riverine operations suffer from several disadvantages which limit their use to counterinsurgency operations. Some areas of the waterway may enjoy little concealment. If the boats are seen by the enemy, they may be fired upon or, worse, being restricted to the river, may fall prey to an ambush carefully prepared at a place and time of the enemy's choosing. Outboard motors are noisy and erode the essential elements of security and concealment. The alternative, paddling or rowing the boats by night, is slow and a well-concealed lying-up position has to be found along the bank before first light.

The team's relatively slow progress increases mission duration and the amount of stores needed to support the operation. However, there are some advantages in using boats, as they can transport large quantities of weapons and equipment and gain access to areas of jungle virtually impenetrable to ground patrols. In this sense, small boats offer some of the benefits associated with light trucks and armed attack vehicles.

Like those of the ground patrol, many of the tactics of riverine movement are concerned with concealment and surviving, if not avoiding, ambushes. Two or more boats can provide mutual support using the same tactics as those employed by motorized patrols. Long distances can be covered by continuous movement with the boats maintaining moderate speed, the lead boat stopping to investigate potentially dangerous areas. This is the fastest but least secure form of movement. If an ambush is sprung, the boats may not be well positioned to bring the combined weight of their automatic weapons to bear and attempts to land troops on the bank to outflank the ambush may be thwarted-by the lack of a suitable landing site.

Somewhat slower but more secure methods are required when the river ahead is concealed by islands and densely foliated, winding banks. Movement by alternate bounds involves the two boats rotating the point position. At a bend in the river, the crew of one boat goes ashore and takes up positions covering the waterway, while the point boat moves farther upriver and sets up its own fire position on the bank. If the area is clear, the crew of the point craft signals the other boat forward. This boat passes the scout boat and moves into the lead position. The disadvantage of the technique is that the men in the second boat are given little time to observe the river ahead before they pass the stationary scout boat. Although even slower, moving by successive bounds avoids rotating the lead position as the second craft joins the scout boat. Together the crews observe the river ahead before the crew of the second boat takes over the position and the lead boat moves forward to a new position farther along the river.

Planning covert beach landings

The utmost care is required for covert missions that lack the air and naval gunfire support enjoyed by conventional operations, and as much consideration is given to the selection of water landing sites as to choosing DZs and LZs for air operations. American planners employ the process of "reverse planning" in landing site assessment. Essentially, this is a step by step backward visualization of an operation, starting with the safe arrival of a team or cargo at an inland operational base.

The technique may reveal that an otherwise ideal site is made untenable by barriers between the coast and the area of operations. Such barriers might include heavily patrolled roads, a large hostile civilian population, areas offering little concealment, adverse terrain such as swamps or mountains, or concentrations of enemy troops. The area immediately behind the BLS itself must offer cover for personnel as they process and cache stores, and also provide concealed avenues and exits for evasion should the landing become compromised. Ideally, the landing site itself should be protected from the prevailing winds, free of natural hazards, and composed of a material that lends itself to sterilization—although it may be impossible to obliterate totally tracks and footprints from a sandy beach at night.

Inadequate sterilization, in the guise of divers' masks, explosives, plastic-wrapped food, and poorly concealed equipment caches containing underwater breathing apparatus and radio transmitters, has, in the past, provided durable evidence of Soviet incursions along the Swedish coast. Similar finds have betrayed the activities of North Korean teams on the ROK's coastline, prompting a search for the teams or agents who might have landed. Quite apart from the resulting state of heightened alert, which makes it difficult for the team or agent to carry out their tasks, the unsuspecting intruders may return to their cache or landing site and fall into a well-prepared ambush.

A waterborne force may use its high-speed boats to raid an inland target, but this requires the element of surprise, a waterway broad enough to allow the assault craft to take evading action, and friendly artillery or mortar fire to cover the withdrawal. Generally, small boat operations are used to support a large ground raiding force by dropping the troops at their line of departure, positioning small blocking forces or support weapons, or placing security patrols on the flanks of the raiders.

Mounting ambushes from small boats has benefits as the exfiltration transport is already on hand to evacuate the wounded and ferry the team to safety. A crucial consideration is the time required for

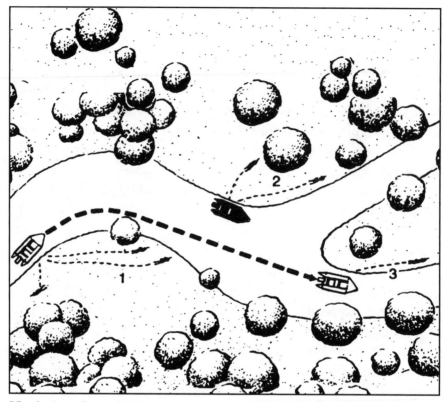

Moving up rivers by "alternate bounds"

Using small boats to move through enemy territory requires the same fieldcraft as land patrols using vehicles. One boat stops and its crew moves into a temporary surveillance position to observe the river ahead (1). Covered by the team on the bank, a second craft moves into forward or scout position to establish an observation post on the bank where the river forks (2). The first craft now alternates as lead boat, moving forward to establish an overwatch position beyond the fork (3). The danger with this technique is that it does not allow the soldiers in the rear boat to observe the river ahead before they move into the scout position.

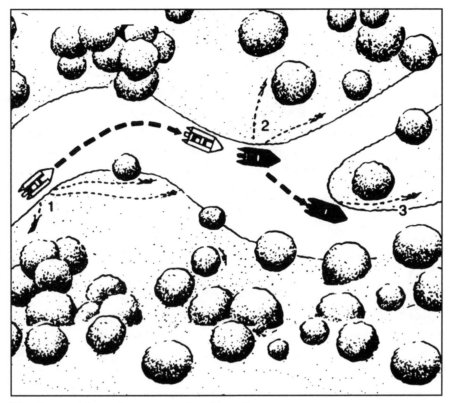

Moving up rivers by successive bounds

Although slower, movement by successive bounds allows each boat to maintain its position in the column. It uses a dedicated forward scout element like a foot patrol. Here, covered by the observation post on the bank (1), the scout craft moves to the fork in the river. When the area is cleared and deemed safe, the second boat in the column joins the scout boat and the two crews observe the river ahead (2). Leaving the crew of the second boat in the overwatch position and covered by their weapons, the scout craft once again moves forward (3).

the operation, which includes the waiting time at an ambush site. During this period, changes in the direction and the level of the river flow may occur, due to tides, weather, or local irrigation projects, leaving boats stranded and effectively blocking the withdrawal route. Another problem is to provide security for the boats and their waiting crewmen. Assuming a "worst case scenario"—that the enemy has spotted the boats—the team commander may leave a small security group close to the disembarkation point, to maintain surveillance and lay a smaller ambush. The crewmen and the security group also cover the main force as they withdraw back to the boats.

CHAPTER 5

Operating behind the Lines

ONCE THE INSERTION PHASE has been completed successfully, the team is ready to infiltrate into their operational area. Preparation for this phase of the mission is no less important than for the insertion. The route will be planned with meticulous care, using skills that become second nature to the maritime navigator. Direction, speed, and time become dynamic factors that enable the team to arrive at the right place at the right time. There are no accolades for crossing miles of wild country in conditions of zero visibility and arriving ten minutes late at an extraction or agent rendezvous.

Difficult terrain may minimize the possibility of contact with local civilians and enemy patrols, offering concealment and unrestricted movement, and hindering the enemy's security measures. With care, speed becomes part of the art of stealth. A large, alert, hostile force is unlikely to find the proverbial "needle" that slips through the "haystack" in a single night. Nevertheless, the terrain and climate exact their own price.

It is obvious that a 5,000-ft. mountain range cannot be negotiated at the same speed as a comparable stretch of flat ground simply by drawing a line across a map and expending a little additional effort.

Bogs, boulder fields, thick forest, soft snow, mist, and heavy rain will all combine to disrupt the route plan. To these obstacles must be added physiological constraints. Rations are limited and the team may survive on one full meal a day, but the hard manual work involved in carrying a heavy pack for 6 miles over a 3,000-ft. peak will consume approximately 3,000 kilocalories of energy and one-third of a gallon of water. When a car runs out of gas, it stops; when a human being runs out of fuel, he loses the ability to maintain body heat and risks developing exhaustion and hypothermia.

▬ The "Art of the Possible"

In 1892, the Scottish climber, Naismith, proposed a basic formula to help civilian mountaineers and hill walkers plan expeditions. He advocated an allowance of 3 mph plus half an hour for ever 1,000 ft. of climbing. Naismith's rule was later corrected for fitness levels and integrated into informative graphs for Mountain Leadership students. While providing an aid for the Mountain Leader planning an expedition, the graphs and tables also served to warn him of the impossible: distances and times that would take his party beyond their endurance. For example, the very fit walker was defined as someone able to climb 1,000 ft. in a horizontal distance of 2,500 ft. in 15 minutes or less. A party composed of such individuals would be expected to cover a 40-mile trek, involving 1,000 ft. of climbing, in just over 8 hours. An additional allowance (50 percent of the journey time) might be added if the party were carrying heavy rucksacks, or moving at night, increasing the time required to complete their journey to around 13 hours. Overall, the work required of the walkers would be equivalent to an energy input of 9,000 kilocalories; Mountain Leadership books recommend that walkers attempting such a feat should consume a series of meals that would provide about 4,000 kilocalories. This is the equivalent of two American C-Ration packs or four LRRP Ration Packs per day.

While mission planning has to take account of the same considerations, the SAS and all the world's top special forces units recruit the handful of individuals who, under constant training, become superbly conditioned athletes, enabling them to surpass Naismith's expectations. For example, the North Korean "Blue House" team was expected to carry 60 lbs. of sand across a 40-mile mountainous course in just six and a half hours. Herein lies the rationale for the professional Soviet Spetsnaz's recruitment of Olympic-grade athletes and the design of British SAS selection. Despite carrying heavy rucksacks and other equipment, such individuals will compensate for delays caused by difficult ground or weather conditions by moving fast and even running for long distances. Because they are well conditioned, they withstand the hardships of bad weather, insufficient food, and arduous manual work much better than the average civilian hill walker. Nevertheless, these operations exact their toll in terms of physical well-being. During the Borneo conflict Australian SAS patrols recorded weight losses of 6–8 lbs. after 12-day patrols in the jungle. After Vietnam, some American Special Operations personnel attributed the onset of chronic illness to the physical deprivation and inadequate diets experienced on missions.

In daylight and on open mountainous terrain, teams drawn from professional units can easily cover 40–60 miles each day carrying 50–100 lbs. of equipment. Like the North Koreans, some Western teams will accomplish this in 8–10 hours, leaving ample time for rest and recuperation. This punishing pace can be kept up for days or even weeks.

Each day's journey is split into multiple legs, minimizing the possibility of a serious navigation error and introducing random changes in direction to confuse search parties should the team be spotted. The team commander will memorize the terrain, noting landmarks, areas of concealment for halts, possible escape routes and rallying areas in the event of a contact, water sources, potential ambush sites, and those parts of the route that may be overlooked by an enemy observation post on high ground. The team will move more slowly when passing through thick scrub or climbing the sides of hills, but this time can be made up by running downhill and along the flat. If the team falls behind time, the pace can be forced during the last hours of daylight.

■ Tactical Movement

Camouflage and deception start with route selection, forcing the team commander to find a compromise between speed and concealment. Undulating ground, streambeds, and hedgerows provide concealment from prying eyes, while thick woods and forest offer protection from night-vision, thermal imaging, and portable radar equipment. In thick vegetation or on rough ground, noise, reduced visibility, and difficulty in navigating may weigh in favor of a less restrictive route such as a local path or beaten track. If an alternative route is not available, the area is crossed slowly, in good visibility, to reduce noise and risk of injury. One foot is moved at a time, the soldier's weight being shifted to the rear leg. Twigs and stones are pushed out of the way with the toe of the lead foot, before the heel is placed on the ground, gradually rolling the weight along the outside of the foot and lowering the sole slowly onto the ground.

Paths or roads serve civilian traffic and represent the main lines of communication for military forces poorly supplied with maps. They are the obvious sites for security force ambushes and roadblocks. Where roads serve as navigation markers, the team might walk on a parallel course 100–200 yards to one side (known to the Royal Marines as "handrailing"). Hills are crossed by contouring around the sides rather than skylining the patrol on the tops. New Zealand SAS patrols, moving through heavily used sections of the Ho Chi Minh Trail on the Vietnamese border, timed their activities to coincide with those of the enemy and villagers. By moving throughout the morning, resting in the early afternoon and continuing their journey until last light, the patrol minimized the chance of walking into a resting enemy force or being caught in a night ambush.

In more hostile areas, the team may move when the inhabitants are resting or inactive and lie up and sleep when enemy civilians and soldiers are active. This may mean travelling by night. Darkness, however, brings its own problems. Movement is slower and navigation more difficult. Shape, color, and distance are distorted, with light-colored objects appearing to be closer than they really are,

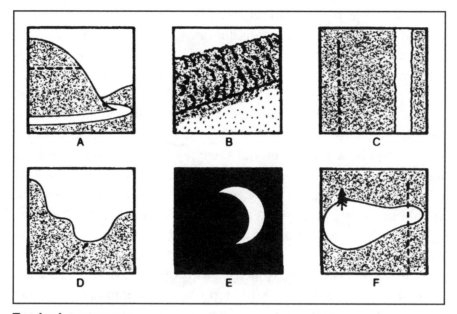

Tactical movement

The essential lessons taught to the SAS and all the world's top Special Forces units are shown in this series of illustrations:

A. Contour hills at a point two-thirds up the slope. This avoids paths and tracks in the valleys and prevents the team from being silhouetted on the tops.

B. Use available cover (e.g., walk along the hedgerows rather than across an open field).

C. Avoid tracks if possible. If a highway serves as an essential landmark, it can be followed some distance away ("handrailing").

D. Use dead ground such as gullies and streambeds.

E. Night movement is slow but safer.

F. Cross open ground at the narrowest point.

while dark objects seem farther away. Sounds seem louder and carry farther. Moonlight may provide illumination; however, the soldiers must stop frequently to check their background to ensure that they are not silhouetted against the sky or casting long, moving shadows.

In potentially dangerous areas, speed is balanced with listening, observation, tracking, and counter-tracking. The bounding overwatch technique involves slow, careful movement. The lead scout moves forward to check the route ahead, while the team covers him and waits. After a period of painstaking observation, the scout motions the team forward. Once the new position is occupied, he moves ahead once more. If the patrol wishes to step up the pace, they may have to spend a quarter or a third of their time stopping regularly to watch and listen. British patrols in Borneo—finding themselves in thick jungle—occasionally dispensed with the services of a lead scout walking 20 yards ahead, instead stopping for 10 minutes every half hour to listen and 10 minutes every hour to rest. The first indication of a nearby Indonesian patrol could be the startled alarm response of the wildlife, followed by an unnatural silence as the animals and birds watched the intruders pass through their territory. A careful study of the local wildlife and their habits is essential to prevent false contacts that will betray the presence of the team. In Vietnam, the sudden appearance of monkeys, climbing out of the jungle canopy to feed at dusk, often surprised American soldiers who mistook them for VC sappers launching an attack and opened fire.

In these and similar surroundings, the first telltale signs of an enemy presence may be the swish of feet moving through long grass, the sound of branches catching on equipment, or the crack of breaking twigs. Secure within his rear areas, the enemy's fieldcraft may lapse, with cooking fires, poorly concealed latrines, litter, and groups of noisy soldiers indicating not only a hostile presence but also dispositions and numbers.

In Borneo (1962–65), patrols restricted meals to a series of snacks eaten at the rest stops, usually chocolate, raisins, and tea, and a main meal cooked at the previous rest stop. The soldier left on guard had his meal cooked for him and was relieved by the man who finished his meal first. The patrol then walked for another 30–60 minutes, clearing the cooking area and the smells that might betray their presence to enemy trackers, before selecting a concealed site for a temporary overnight stop.

The overnight stop had to offer concealment from the ground and air, a single approach route and an escape lane in the event of the hide being discovered. Ideally, the site would also be close to a source of water, yet not so close that enemy soldiers and civilians using the stream or river were likely to spot the patrol. Once the area was cleared, sleeping positions selected, and, if necessary, a shelter built, boots were left on and rucksacks packed for a rapid move. As darkness fell, at least one sentry was left on watch to listen for the telltale sounds of an enemy patrol tracking the team. The sentry and his sleeping comrades were connected to one another by a communication cord tied to each man's wrist. If an enemy patrol came too close, a sharp tug alerted the patrol commander, who led the men down the prearranged escape route. In the event of a surprise attack, a line of Claymore mines covering the approach would be detonated to catch the enemy in a deadly fusillade of steel balls, both delaying and discouraging pursuit.

Blending into the surroundings to avoid being seen entails more than wearing a disruptive-pattern camouflage suit. Carefully applied local vegetation, strips of sacking, and scrim nets further disrupt shape without creating rustling noises. Two-tone camouflage paint or burnt cork is used to shade exposed skin. Particular attention is paid to disrupting the outline of cheekbones, nose, and chin. Large blotches are recommended for deciduous forests; vertical slashes for coniferous forests; broad slashes in jungle; thin slashes in desert; a wide blotch in barren snow; and very thin slashes in grasslands.

Shiny personal objects, such as watches and rings, are removed or covered, and the metal surfaces on the soldier's weapon and equipment are dulled. Noise discipline is strictly observed, communication being maintained by well-rehearsed hand signals. Other sources of potential noise are eliminated by taping down loose equipment, removing nonessential items from the pockets, and padding equipment in the rucksack and webbing pouches. Uniforms are fitted carefully to ensure that they do not rustle or snag on foliage.

Many Malaysian, Indonesian, and Vietnamese guerrillas owe their lives to the fact that they smelled the British and American troops lying in ambush to kill them. A variety of odors can betray the team's presence, persisting on still, moist, or cold air and leaving easily identifiable signs for the enemy tracker long after the patrol has left. Carried on the wind, cigarette smoke can be detected for up to a quarter of a mile. In Malaysia, it was not unknown for British troops, smelling the cigarette smoke from a guerrilla camp, to ambush and assault the wrong area of jungle. In the still, moist air of the forests, air currents often carried the smoke on circuitous routes, leaving a strong trace on everything with which it came in contact. The heavy smoker is also tainted with the smell of smoke and aromatic tars. Worse still, he may have developed a highly audible smoker's cough. Some commanding officers excluded smokers from reconnaissance patrols in Malaysia and Borneo. In a special unit, smoking can be an automatic disqualification.

Soaps, other toilet articles, and insect repellent all leave a distinctive smell, immediately obvious to the nonuser. The same is true of onion, garlic, and spices, used to make the rations more palatable. At rest stops, latrine facilities and cooking stoves leave telltale smells. If necessary, food is eaten cold or cooked on an odorless fuel source such as pressurized gas. Human waste, contained in plastic bags, is buried, weighed down and dropped into deep water, or carried in the rucksack for the duration of the mission.

▄ Obstacles and Other Areas of Danger

Particular care is required when crossing tracks, clearings, and rivers or when meeting resupply drops or local agents. Where possible, obstacles such as clearings, buildings, and track junctions are given a wide berth. A careful surveillance is placed on roads and tracks before they are crossed. Ideally, the lead scout moves first, covered by the team commander and a flank scout, while the rest of the team maintains all-round defense. Once the lead scout is safely across, the remaining team members cross in groups, or individually, with watching and listening intervals between crossings.

Clearings are crossed at their narrowest point after a lengthy period of observation. A variety of patrol formations may be used to cross broad areas of open ground, the principal considerations being command and control and the most effective positioning of the team's firepower, particularly the support weapons such as machine guns. Double and single file are easy for the team commander to control with hand signals, and ideal for moving along the edge of woods or hedgerows, but are vulnerable to a contact from the front. Spearhead or "wedge" and arrowhead or "T" formations concentrate the team's firepower to the front but are difficult to control. A diamond formation may be used to cross open ground at night, providing closely packed all-round firepower. Extended line, normally used by infantry sections assaulting enemy positions, is also difficult to control and vulnerable on the rear and flanks. However, the team commander may use it to concentrate observation and firepower to the front when moving toward a hill or ridge line or to reduce track signs on soft or boggy ground.

Deep, fast-flowing rivers represent a dual hazard, carrying the possibility of men being swept away and drowned, or ambushed by enemy troops on the opposite bank. When preparing for possible conflict with the former Soviet Union in Central Europe, NATO military planners noted that NATO reconnaissance or special mission teams travelling east would have to face a series of formidable water obstacles running approximately north–south, with, on average, one 300-ft.-wide obstacle every 60–90 miles, and 1,000-ft.-wide rivers every 150–180 miles.

Approaching a water obstacle, the team halts and dispatches the lead scout to reconnoiter the crossing point, probing in both directions along the bank for signs of enemy activity. He will then examine the feasibility of crossing the obstacle, checking that it is not too wide or too fast, or the water so cold that it produces cramps. He will also note entry and exit points and concealed "dead" ground on the far

---

Offset navigation

Pinpoint navigation is required to reach a particular point, say on a track running across the team's front. Poor visibility, and the need to make best use of the ground, may result in the team veering off course. The men reach the track but not their objective, forcing them to make a decision as to whether it now lies to their left or right. Using offset navigation, a deliberate deviation is introduced to the left or right of the intended line of march. Each degree of offset results in a deviation of 55 ft. for every 100 yards of travel. Once the target area is reached the team make a 90° turn toward their objective.

---

bank. The team then moves to the crossing point and places the far bank under observation.

Narrow streams and rivers can be crossed one man at a time. The lead scout goes first, entering the water and then moving some way along the bank before crossing, to confuse onlookers as to the exit point on the other bank. A concealed point some way downstream can be reached by drifting with the current. Rucksacks, and particularly those with their contents sealed inside plastic bags, will float. Otherwise, kits can be wrapped inside a poncho raft and the personal weapon strapped to the side ready for immediate action.

Team members run the risk of being scattered or even drowned by currents in fast-flowing rivers. A security rope slung between both banks can make the crossing less hazardous but presents a problem in getting the first man and rope across to the other bank. The task will be allotted to the lead scout or the team's strongest swimmer. A bend in the river may provide the opportunity to employ a pendulum technique. Ropes are attached to both ends of the swimmer's rucksack or poncho raft or, where additional buoyancy is required, to a small log, with a third line securing the soldier. The swimmer enters the water up-current of the proposed landing site, and the other team members alternately tug back and forth on the lines securing the raft,

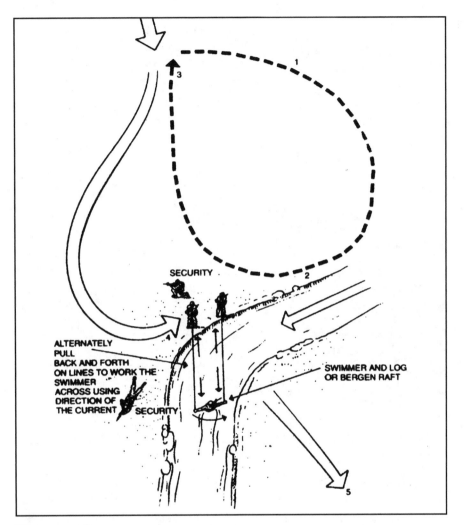

River crossings

Approaching the river, the team leader sends scouts to recce the crossing point (1). Moving in a wide loop, the scouts clear the riverbank (2) looking for signs of enemy activity before returning to make their report (3). The team then approaches the river using a different route in case the scouts were spotted (4). A bend in a fast-flowing river enables the soldiers to use the current to get the first man and safety line across. The men waiting their turn to cross maintain security around the crossing point. As team members are ferried across, security is also maintained on the opposite bank. When the last man has crossed, the team continues their mission (5).

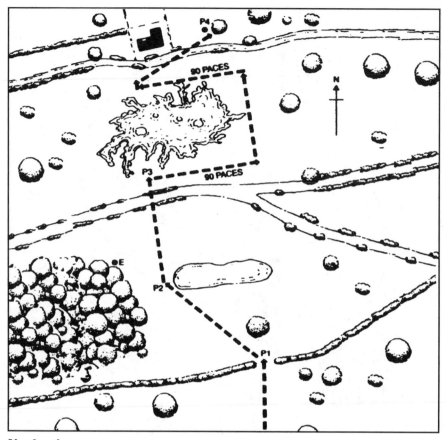

Navigation

A team leader prepares to move at night or under conditions of zero visibility. The move is split into a series of legs with RVs at obvious geographical features (P1, P2 and P3). At each of these points a compass bearing is taken to the next RV (x degrees). The reverse bearing is also taken (x - 180 degrees), as the previous RV will serve as a rallying point if any of the soldiers becomes lost. The route avoids obvious danger areas, and an RV is chosen at the corner of the wood (E) in the event of the team being separated after a contact with the enemy. When the team reaches the marsh, the area is bypassed, a pace count enabling them to return to their original bearing on the other side. On the final leg to the deserted building on the other side of the stream, use is made of offset navigation: a deliberate deviation in the route is introduced to the east of the building. On reaching the other side of the stream, the team makes a 90-degree turn to move westerly along the bank until the outer fence line is reached. Scouts then recce the final RV.

until the current pulls the swimmer into the far bank. The security rope is then secured diagonally across the river, so that the other members of the team can cross by using the current rather than attempting to swim against it. A pulley system, with a double loop of rope, may be used as an additional safety measure, allowing the passengers to be pulled across. The rope is retrieved easily once the last man has crossed.

Larger bodies of water, such as the great European rivers, pose a more formidable challenge that yields best to small inflatable boats.

Tracking

For the lead scout out in front of the team, the first evidence of an enemy presence may be slight man-made disturbances to the environment. These small clues are known as "sign," and spotting them is akin to solving those visual puzzles where the reader is presented with two near-identical pictures and asked to spot the differences. Comparison of the two pictures reveals that certain features seem out of place or do not match. One of the life-saving lessons taught to American Special Forces personnel beginning their tour in Vietnam was that felled brush and wilting foliage might be old camouflage concealing an enemy ambush site or encampment.

Confirming and correctly interpreting sign requires good detective work. The tracker will classify sign into top sign (above knee height) or ground sign (below knee height) and permanent sign or temporary sign. The latter is ultimately obliterated by sunlight, wind, rain, frost, and snow but is useful for determining the age of a track. An old enemy campsite may provide an interesting mixture of ground sign. Human waste finally decays, but the degree of decomposition and the numbers of flies and beetles, together with their immature forms, may provide an estimate of age. Ration cans, cigarette ends, scraps of cloth, equipment, and old fireplaces persist for much longer, but all gradually weather and age. Rust can form on metal within 12 hours, and cloth and paper is flattened by rain. Paper bleaches in sunlight, first turning yellow, within about three days, and then white.

Such "clues" can occasionally be used to turn the tables on the enemy. Communist guerrillas operating in northern Malaysia were usually extremely careful about concealing camps and overnight Lying Up Positions (LUPs) but were sometimes known to scatter empty British rations tins around their abandoned encampment. Security force patrols, passing through the area, took one look at the rubbish and attributed it, incorrectly, to an untidy Commonwealth army or Malaysian police unit.

A lead scout studies some old footprints on the trail ahead and then returns to report to the team commander that "A party of ten enemy soldiers and two civilians passed along the track two days ago. Two of the soldiers and the two civilians were carrying heavy packs. A third soldier was suffering from a wound in the lower half of the body. The troops had little or no combat training and were oblivious to the possibility of our presence in the area." It sounds like the script from a Hollywood B-grade war movie, and yet it is possible to derive all this information from a set of footprints.

Tracks or footprints are the best type of ground sign. Although often incomplete, they provide positive identification of the presence of other people and the direction of travel. They are most obvious when a shadow is cast across them; consequently, the best times for tracking are early morning and evening when the sun is low. As the sun begins to climb across the sky, faint tracks become harder to spot. However, tracks moving directly toward a low sun can also be difficult to see and have to be followed from the side, where the shadows cast by the prints are more obvious.

The number of people in the group is calculated by using the valid assumption that the stride length of most human beings falls within narrowly defined limits. The first reference point sought by the tracker is a clear set of footprints or "key prints." These are usually left by the last person in the group. Two successive prints are chosen and a small marker is placed in line with the back of the heel of the rear key print. A second marker is then placed next to the instep of the front print. Although the stride length is usually measured from the heel of the rear print to the heel of the front footprint, this

Patrol positions and their responsibilities

Throughout the march the team members must move in a military formation. They are the interlopers and are vastly outnumbered by the opposition. Survival depends upon seeing and avoiding the enemy before they themselves are seen. The patrol structure itself is geared toward stealth and the need to guard against unpleasant surprises.

In most instances, the patrol will travel in single file with 5–10 yards between each man. The lead soldier in an American patrol is the front scout or point man. His task is to watch for enemy patrols or any suspicious tracks that may mark their presence in the immediate vicinity. In anticipation of surprise contact, the point covers the arc of fire to the front of the patrol and is also responsible for maintaining the correct route of march or compass bearing, while making best tactical use of the ground. Behind the point is the team leader, who interacts with and provides covering fire for him, while selecting the route and checking the direction of march against the compass bearing.

The third position is manned by the first flank scout and team sniper, covering the team leader to the front and an arc of fire to the left and right of the patrol. The first flank scout also assists in maintaining a navigation check. The second flank scout, who is also the team weapons specialist, covers a complementary arc of fire to the other side of the patrol. He may also maintain a pace count to the next navigation reference point, thus providing a means of measuring distance in poor visibility or on a featureless terrain. The two flank scouts are each equipped with one of the team's light support weapons such as a grenade launcher and light machine gun. The fifth slot is manned by the assistant team leader, a second decision-maker who covers the rear scout and supervises counter-tracking activities. As the assistant team leader may find himself in command of the patrol, he maintains a careful note of the team's position and route. The last man in the patrol is the rear scout and team demolition specialist. He covers the rear of the patrol and is responsible for spotting enemy trackers and obliterating the patrol's tracks.

Team Position and Covering Arc of Fire	Title	Duties
	Lead Scout	• Navigation, best use of ground, tracker and patrol's "ears and eyes" in the front.
	Team Leader	• Primary decision maker. Selects route and compass bearings. Provides covering fire for head scout.
	First Flank Scout	• Support weapon and team radio operator. Checks navigation.
	Second Flank Scout	• Support weapon and team weapons specialist. Maintains pace count at night or in zero visibility.
	Assistant Team Leader	• Second decision maker. Checks route and navigation and supervises counter-tracking activities of rear scout.
	Rear Scout	• Counter-tracking and watching for enemy combat trackers at rear of patrol. Team demolition specialist.

The duties and patrol positions of a six-man special mission team

technique allows the additional half print from heel to instep to compensate for any person in the group with a slightly longer stride.

An imaginary box can now be drawn using both sides of the track or road and lines passing through the front and back markers. On average, each individual making the tracks will have left one print inside the imaginary box. Therefore, counting the key print only once, the number of prints and partial prints between the two markers equals the number of people making the tracks. This estimate is good for parties of fewer than eighteen people. Tracks on soft ground may not provide a clear set of "key prints," but an estimate can still be made by taking a cross section of the trail 36 in. in length. Now the sides of the road or track and the two lines 36 in. apart, form the sides of an imaginary box. Each print or partial print within this box is counted and the total divided by two in order to provide an estimate of the number of people making the tracks.

Weathering may indicate the age of the prints, the persistence of which depend upon soil composition and climate. When the tracks are made, small animals and leaves are squashed into the surface, but leaves and debris blown or falling into existing tracks are not crushed or pressed into the soil. Moisture binds the soil on the edges or a recent print, producing sharp edges that are highlighted by shadow. Sunlight and dry air will crumble the soil and soften and smooth the edges of the print. The sharp edges of a print are also destroyed by rain, which may break up the surface and puddle in the bottom. Heavy or persistent rain completely obliterates spoor. A well-defined track discovered on soft ground is likely to have been made after recent rainfall. The tracker will keep a mental note of the time of the last rain and will know, from experience, how quickly prints deteriorate after exposure to the morning sun.

Top sign

The next time you are out in the country, watch how parties of walkers move through thick scrub, often thoughtlessly pushing branches and thorns out of their path and then releasing them under tension to flick back into the face of the person behind. Each time

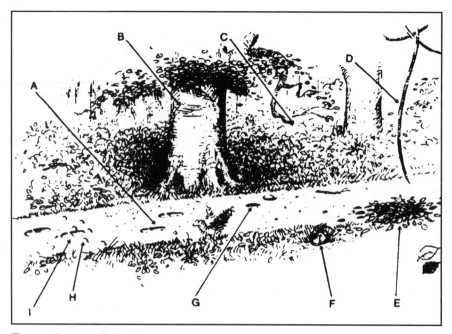

Top and ground sign

A. Footprints not only confirm the presence of other people in the immediate area, they also provide a wealth of information about the individuals who made the tracks.

B. Scars on a tree where it has been carelessly rubbed by equipment or where a soldier has leaned his rucksack against it to rest.

C. A branch of the same tree broken in the direction of travel.

D. Climbers and vines pulled free as the party pushed through the foliage.

E. Pile of fallen leaves dispersed in the direction of travel, exposing the black undersides where they are beginning to rot.

F. Discarded can from ration pack.

G. Stone kicked out of its natural depression in the ground.

H & I. Animal tracks (H) superimposed over the party's footprints (I). Small animals such as deer go in search of water at dawn. Knowledge of the local wildlife may enable the tracker to calculate when the tracks were made (e.g., the previous night).

this is done, small fractures or breaks leave little messages which can be understood by the experienced tracker. In really thick bush, the branches and vines may get caught as they are pushed out of a person's path. This leaves a small "road sign" which points to the actual line of march and which advertises itself to the tracker who notices the dull, lighter green undersides of leaves on tangled branches hastily pushed aside. If the direction taken by the party is unclear, the tree can be shaken. This causes the displaced branches to spring back and move in the opposite direction to the line of march.

Some types of broken foliage wilt and die quickly in the heat of the day. Finding a broken branch, which has not yet died, may indicate that it was broken after sunset on the previous day. Bruises and fractures on trees change color slowly and are sealed finally by sap or resins, the speed of the repair being governed by the type of plant and climate. Freshly broken twigs may retain the smell of sap for three to four hours, and the fractured end may remain the same color for up to five hours before darkening. A more precise time-scale can be obtained by breaking a fresh branch and watching the flow of sap and color changes. Scraps of cloth from uniforms may be left on thorns to bleach in the sun. Broken spiderwebs, clearly visible in the early morning dew and well above ground level, probably indicate the passage of a man.

Ground sign

In Vietnam, the Americans were amazed when rehabilitated VC sappers demonstrated how they could pass into a rice field without crushing the stems or leaving other types of top sign. This was done by carefully and methodically moving stalks out of the way, a few at a time, so that the crop literally enclosed them. like fish in water. They did, however, leave ground sign. An ex-Green Beret and Vietnam veteran, asked by a journalist what sort of techniques needed to be used to avoid leaving tracks, replied, "You would have to learn to fly."

Mud from the soles of boots may be scuffed onto rocks, fallen logs and tree roots. This can be prevented by covering the boot tread with cloth or cardboard, but soil fragments may still be left on the rocks.

Rocks embedded in the soil may also appear to offer an attractive series of "stepping stones" to avoid leaving prints on soft ground. However, the combined weight of a man and his rucksack forces soil out from beneath rocks, forming a zone of crumbled soil around the base.

Long grass will lie after being trodden down and will point in the direction of travel. Man is one of the few animals whose foot will break a stick in two places. Dead leaves splinter when trodden on and leaves decaying on the forest floor tend to pile up in the direction of travel, exposing their black undersides. An experienced tracker, confronted with suspected spoor, will look for an overall pattern in the leaves, taking care to replace leaves and twigs displaced by the wind. Each leaf is examined in turn for the presence of a "straight edge" made by the side of a boot Underneath the leaf litter, the remains of crushed soil animals, such as beetles and worms, may help to confirm the spoor.

Other disturbances to small animal life provide rough timescales. Worm casts are excreted at night and remain soft and moist until dried by the sun, when they become hard and brittle. A powdered worm cast on a fresh track was probably crushed sometime between one hour after sunrise and the time the track was found. A broken but otherwise intact cast was probably crushed between its formation and one hour after sunrise.

One trick to avoid tracker teams and dogs is to move for some distance along a watercourse. However, prints and scuff marks may still be left in the streams and shallow rivers and particularly at the party's entry and exit points. A recent crossing may result in mud being stirred up and otherwise dirty rocks and banks being splashed. Much can remain suspended in still water for hours, while running water may disperse the sediment, only to reveal footprints in the stream bed. Steep banks may show scuff marks and broken vegetation where the party scrambled up the side, using trees and bushes as handholds.

Speed and load can also be determined from the tracks. The runner leaves prints that emphasize the ball of the foot and toes. Skid marks and dirt sprayed onto vegetation along the side of the trail may be present on soft ground. A soldier carrying heavy equipment will

Reading footprints

A fresh print in moist soil appears sharp (A). As the print dries and the soil crumbles, the print becomes faint and indistinct (B). The leaves and other debris lodged in the print are clearly not crushed and have fallen or blown onto the track after it was made. The rate of weathering, which depends on the soil and climate, can enable a tracker to determine the age of the prints.

A clear set of key prints allows the tracker to determine a box, based on the average stride length (C). Counting the key prints only once reveals the number of people making the tracks. An eight-man party made the prints in this example.

produce deep prints, with the maximum pressure again being exerted by the front of the foot. The stride may be shorter, and there may be top sign where the pack or load has snagged on foliage and been pulled free, or has scraped and chipped bark from trees. An injured soldier may leave a blood spoor or, in favoring one leg consistently, leave a left or right print with a deeper impression. Wounded or exhausted soldiers may fall behind and be forced to run occasionally to catch up with the party.

Prints faithfully record the design of the undersides of the shoe or boot. Most soldiers wear standard-issue equipment, with older types of gear issued to reserve or rear echelon units. Prints made by unusual military boots may identify a commando unit, but high-grade combat units usually signal their presence by the care taken to avoid leaving tracks. The most obvious ploy involves taping cardboard over the undersides of the boots or wrapping footwear in cloth. Such devices send a clear warning to the tracker: a party that takes care to erase their tracks will probably also employ potentially lethal counter-tracking strategies.

Counter-Tracking

The enemy will undoubtedly deploy its own specialist trackers, responsible for locating intruders crossing its borders and security within its rear areas. A combat tracker team (CTT) is a specialized four-man patrol composed of a commander, tracker, and two flank scouts who also assist in following trails. Specialists in reconnaissance, tracking, and close-quarter battle, they provide a formidable adversary to the special mission team. In Vietnam, some Communist CTTs were deployed specifically to locate and destroy American long-range patrols, the two teams becoming locked into a deadly cycle of tracking and counter-tracking, ambush and counter-ambush.

Counter-tracking is the art of covering your own tracks and deceiving and confusing enemy trackers. The best counter-tracker is the experienced tracker who has learned from the mistakes of others. Counter-tracking techniques can be divided into active and passive. Passive techniques, good route planning and well-honed fieldcraft, are part of the SAS or any other special mission team's overall camouflage. Essentially they center around careful concealment of waste and rubbish, checking camouflage against background, observing noise and light discipline, selecting ground least likely to leave tracks, and avoiding breakage or crushing of vegetation or leaving scuff marks on rocks and trees.

Active counter-tracking is a deliberate attempt to confuse and elude trackers who might have picked up the team's trail. In open ground, moving toward a setting or rising sun forces the tracker to follow the spoor from the side and track diagonally into the sun. As

Covering the trail

The rear scout and assistant team leader obliterate the patrol's tracks and cover the brushmarks with debris.

the sun rises or dusk falls, the tracks become increasingly difficult to follow. Multiple and false trails are designed to mislead the enemy as to team size and intentions. The team's tracks can be mixed with animal spoor or the direction concealed by phoney trail signs made by breaking foliage in the opposite direction of travel or walking backwards. However, the last ploy will not fool an experienced tracker who will note the wider and shorter stride length, deeper heel prints, and dirt and stones kicked up by the heel in the actual direction of travel.

In his book, *A Cross Eyed View*, jungle warfare expert John Cross recalls that Communist guerrillas frequently walked backwards over soft ground to confuse the security forces. As this rarely fooled the Gurkha trackers, one guerrilla band came up with a more ingenious ploy. During the Malaysian campaign, the mountainous jungle in the north of the country was home to a large population of tigers. Occasionally, a big cat would turn "man-eater" or would be trapped inside a

---

Passive counter-tracking

All team members have a role to play in leaving as little trace of their passing on the landscape as possible. The lead scout selects the ground, where possible using logs or rocks to cross streams, and avoiding paths and soft ground, which leave tracks, in favor of rock and hard surfaces. The team commander introduces random changes of direction into the route plan, matches patrol formations with the type of country being crossed and chooses the less obvious route to be followed. In areas of soft ground, he may split the team into several parties to minimize tracks and mislead those trying to interpret them. Finally, the assistant team commander will supervise the rear scout in obliterating the team's tracks by sweeping brushwood across the trail. In areas where there are large game animals, feet cut from a carcass can be used to obliterate tracks. All team members may attempt to minimize the track by walking in one another's footprints, walking on the toes or sides of the feet to minimize prints, and walking astride or along the edges of paths.

---

security force cordon, greatly adding to the danger of these jungle operations. One band of guerrillas presumably shot and killed a big tiger and then used one or more of its paws to leave pug marks on the trail behind them. This job was left to the last guerrilla in the party, who also swept the track clean of footprints. However, he made a careless mistake. In turning around to leave the paw marks, he forgot to reverse the paw. The resulting track appeared to move away from the guerrillas toward a very cautious Gurkha patrol moving along the same path, some distance behind. The soldiers soon realized that not only had they failed to encounter the tiger, but also, as they moved farther up the trail, that the "older" tracks were becoming increasingly fresh. Discounting the possibility that they had picked up the trail of a tiger walking backwards, they soon saw through the subterfuge and began to hunt their human quarry.

Counter-tracking techniques, aimed at deceiving the enemy, become futile once the trackers and accompanying hunter/killer force

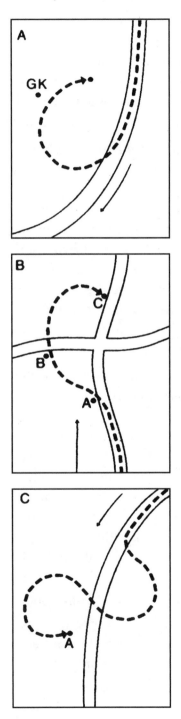

(A) Active counter-tracking: the fishhook

The team leaves the track and circles back in the shape of a fishhook. Rucksacks are left with gatekeepers who guard an escape and evasion corridor (GK). The rest of the team sets up a temporary surveillance position overlooking the trail and behind a screen of Claymore mines. If enemy trackers put in an appearance, the mechanical ambush will force the survivors to probe more cautiously; meanwhile, the team changes course.

(B) Active counter-tracking: the forward hook

The forward hook is used to avoid danger areas such as villages and track junctions and to by-pass potential ambush sites. The team leaves the trail (A) and sets up an overwatch position overlooking the danger area (B). If the area is safe, the team circles back to the track and sets up another temporary surveillance position behind a mechanical ambush to catch any trackers attempting to pick up the team's trail which was lost at (A).

(C) Active counter-tracking: the "S"-shaped hook

The last stratagem developed during the Vietnam War, the double or "S"-shaped hook is designed to sweep both sides of a trail for enemy ambushes before the team sets up an overwatch position and their own ambush (A).

make visual contact with the team. How can a team check that, despite all their efforts, they are not being tracked by the enemy? And if the enemy is in pursuit, what sort of techniques can the SOF use to ensure that they are in a position always to shoot first? These problems were solved by three evasive patrol movements used by American and Australian patrols in Vietnam:

Button hook In this simple maneuver, also known as the "fishhook," the patrol left their line of march and used the cover of the jungle to double back to an "overwatch" position, so that the soldiers could observe the trail behind them. From their concealed OP, the patrol was well placed to confirm that they were being pursued and to mount an ambush. Frequently, a "mechanical ambush" was employed, using booby traps or Claymore mines fitted with delayed-action fuses. Even if the trackers survived the encounter, they were forced to slow their pace in order to probe for more ambushes. Meanwhile, the team, well clear of the ambush site, changed direction and moved fast, beginning active counter-tracking again to break contact.

Forward hook When approaching a track junction or another potentially dangerous obstacle, a patrol would sometimes employ the "forward hook," whereby they moved to the left or right of their line of march on a semicircular track and halted at a point where the danger area could be watched from a safe distance. If the area was quiet, the patrol would move again, skirting the danger area while circling back toward their line of march. Rejoining their original track, they then chose a second temporary surveillance position overlooking the trail. The object of this "overwatch" position was to spot enemy trackers painstakingly searching for the spoor that was lost at the point where the team began their "forward hook."

Double hook This technique involved a half figure eight, which again provided two "overwatch" positions. After sweeping the bush on both sides of the trail, the soldiers doubled back to watch for trackers. The forward and double hooks were designed not only to elude pursuit but to avoid blocking forces that might by lying in ambush to the team's front.

▉ Contact Drills

If, despite all precautions, the lead scout is surprised by an enemy force, or the team walks into the "killing ground" of an ambush, he who thinks, shoots, and moves first has the best chance of survival. The most important rule is that the small patrol or team must seek to break the contact and disappear back into the landscape, with the minimum of casualties. In response, the experienced enemy will attempt to outflank and encircle the smaller force of prevent their escape. The well-rehearsed escape routines are known as "contact drills." These are divided into three phases: immediate action drills, delaying actions, and evasion.

A contact to the front is met by the scout who lays down a brief burst of suppressive fire, while the other team members cover arcs of fire on the flanks. After firing, the scout withdraws to the rear of the team, and the team leader opens fire to the front. The sequence is repeated as the men move to the rear in successive bounds, either individually or in pairs. Eventually the flank scouts bring their machine guns and light support weapons into play, as the assistant team leader and rear scout prepare explosive charges or Claymore mines to delay pursuit. This backwards "rippling" movement is continued until contact is finally broken. The reverse technique is used in the event of a contact to the rear.

A contact to the side is met initially by one of the flank scouts, whose support weapon provides security for the rest of the team withdrawing from the contact. This delaying action allows the other team members to retreat a short distance and construct a screen of Claymore mines. As the scouts rejoin the team, the soldiers continue to move away from the contact. In twos and threes, the soldiers move to the rear in short bounds, while the other members of the team lay down covering fire. However, if the team finds themselves caught in the "killing ground" of an ambush, casualties may be minimized by breaking through and reforming behind the enemy positions.

At night the team's personal weapons may help the enemy pinpoint its position. In contrast, fragmentation and white phosphorus

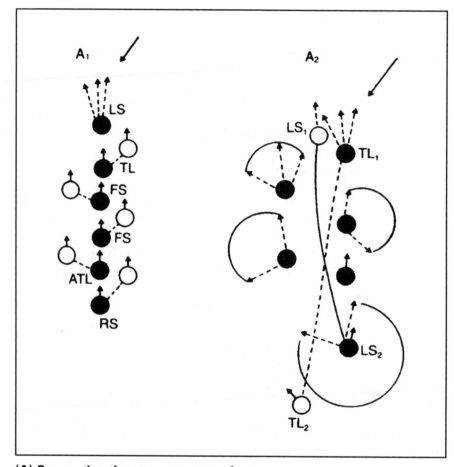

(A) On meeting the enemy, contact front

The lead scout bears the brunt of a surprise contact to the front. He who shoots first usually survives the firefight. At the first burst of gunfire, the rest of the team moves into defensive positions to protect their flanks. This creates a corridor along the center of the team (A1). The lead scout "shoots and scoots" to the rear of the patrol (LS2). The team leader then opens fire before moving back to the rear of the patrol (TL2). This rippling "fire and movement" continues until all of the team falls back behind the assistant team leader and the rear scout who, by this time, have laid out a screen of protective Claymore mines (A2).

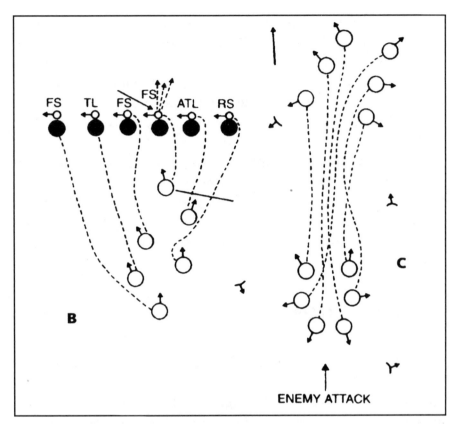

(B) On meeting the enemy, contact flank

A surprise contact on the flank is met by the flank scouts who carry the support weapons such as machine guns and grenade launchers. The rest of the team moves to the opposite flank and lays down suppressive fire while preparing a protective screen of Claymore mines. In a full-blown ambush, with enemy on both sides of the trail or the other flank blocked by obstacles, the team attempts to fight their way through the enemy positions and reform behind them.

(C) On meeting the enemy, contact at an overnight rest stop

Overnight rest stops of lying-up positions are screened by Claymore mines, leaving a narrow escape and evasion corridor. If an enemy patrol appears to investigate the area too closely (they may be following the team's tracks), the sentry tugs a communications cord which is connected to the team leader's wrist and, in turn, to the rest of the patrol. Moving silently, the team activates the delayed-action Claymore screen and departs along the escape and evasion corridor.

grenades can panic the enemy and delay pursuit without giving away the position of the withdrawing team. During these brief actions, soldiers are at risk of becoming separated from the team, particularly the lead scout who may be seriously wounded in the initial exchange of fire. Left to their own devices, the men will attempt to make their way to one of a series of RVs. For Commonwealth patrols in Borneo, the first RV, designed to reunite the lost soldier with his team, was the Patrol RV—usually a prearranged geographical feature or grid reference, which was kept open for four hours after the contact. Missing this RV meant a longer walk to the Troop RV, usually the last overnight rest stop, which was manned for a further 12 hours. If this, too, was missed, the man would have to find his own way to either the Border RV (insertion LZ) or to the War RV (the nearest security force position).

■ Communications

Whereas in high-threat situations, partisan couriers and agents operating their own radios, and even animals such as homing pigeons, may be used, the most secure and reliable means of communication is provided by the team radio. The signaler, who has trained extensively in radio telegraphy, is capable of sending and receiving Morse code at speeds of between twelve and eighteen words per minute. He must be able to service his equipment under field conditions and, using his knowledge of aerial construction, overcome difficulties posed by terrain and climate.

Radios for clandestine forces must be light and capable of providing trouble-free service for long periods. Some modern military transmitters are designed to provide more than 1,000 hours' fault-free service. However, as this figure can decline sharply under field conditions, the design of the set must lend itself to servicing by its trained operator. The British PRC-320 can employ a simple whip aerial to send voice ground-wave transmissions to other patrols and aircraft up to a distance of 60 miles and long-range continuous wave (CW) Morse signals using a sky-wave antenna. British and American forces have evaluated Thorn EMI Electronics' PRC-319 transmitter. Small (8 in. high, 8¼ in. wide, and 4 in. deep) and light (4.8 lbs.), the communications package consists of a powerful 50-watt transmitter with data, CW Morse, and voice facilities, an electronic message unit, battery, and one to two aerial tuners. Able to transmit over a wide frequency spectrum (1.5–40 MHz), the set can store ten pairs of channels in a protected memory and has an integral burst-message capability for covert communications (see below).

A variety of factors serve to determine the operational range of a radio set:

Frequency Since the 1980s, most long-range man-pack transmitters for the use of the SAS and other special forces have employed the high frequency (HF) portion of the electromagnetic spectrum between 3 to 30 megahertz. This takes advantage of sky-wave propagation to transmit signals for hundreds of miles by bouncing the radio waves off the ionosphere—a belt of electrically charged gas particles 30–300 miles above the Earth's surface. The problem with HF transmission is that it is easily intercepted by security forces and the signal must be modified further to maintain transmission security. Transmitters employing Very High Frequency (30–300 MHz) and Ultra High Frequency (300–3,000 MHz) propagate signals by ground waves (the sky-wave component passing through the ionosphere and being lost into space). They are consequently limited to line of sight transmission. Longer distances can be spanned by automatic ground relay stations, set up by signals support personnel, or flying relay stations, if friendly forces have control of the airspace.

Power output Man-pack transmitters are powered by portable high-power batteries. Battery power is conserved by HF transmission, which allows long-range propagation at low power settings, and Morse code which, apart from offering a convenient binary code for transmitting information, provides a very power-efficient signal. If a team is involved in long-term operations, the batteries can be recharged with a lightweight hand-cranked generator.

Aerial construction Antenna construction will determine the power and nature of the emission. Efficient transmission requires the aerial to be "grounded," allowing a component of the emission to pass into the earth (counterpoise). Ideally, the aerial length should equal or exceed the transmission wavelength, but this may be impractical and half- or quarter-wave aerials may be employed. Simple formulas enable the signaler to calculate his aerial length:

$$\text{full wave} = 936/f$$
$$\tfrac{1}{2}\text{ wave} = 468/f$$
$$\tfrac{1}{4}\text{ wave} = 234/f$$

(where f is the operating frequency in megacycles)

Within these constraints, aerials come in a great variety of shapes and sizes depending on the nature of the signal desired (ground- or sky-wave), signal direction (omnidirectional 360° transmission or highly directional), the operating frequency, signal modulation, and terrain and climate. The simple quarter-wave aerial is usually erected vertically and produces an omnidirectional signal, making it useful for inter-team communications when the exact location of the other patrols is uncertain. Normally used when a ground-wave is desired, it makes use of sky-waves with FM radios. the typical half-wave antenna is a doublet or dipole aerial composed of two quarter-wave aerials connected by a coaxial cable. Constructed vertically, it produces an omnidirectional signal, while in the horizontal position it becomes bidirectional, broadcasting at 90° to the wire. A variant, the slant-wire antenna, has one quarter-wave aerial connected to a support at an angle of 30°–60° and a second aerial, or counterpoise, positioned horizontally, just above the ground, pointing away from the slanting wire. This system, which radiates both ground- and sky-waves in the direction of the counterpoise, is used for long-range communications.

Climate and terrain These can both have an adverse effect on radio transmission. Radio waves are absorbed or screened by moist jungle foliage and surrounding hills, reducing the operational range from

40–90 percent. Aerials need to be sited well clear of dense foliage, in clearings or above the tree canopy. Communications in desert areas can be excellent, but poor electrical grounding can reduce the operational range unless the aerial is located near subterranean water or oases. Polar regions are plagued by magnetic storms and other disturbances in the ionosphere, blocking some frequencies for days or even weeks, and introducing static which reduces the clarity of the signal. Batteries are depleted by the cold, while snowfalls can produce shorts and grounds that disable the transmitter.

■ Radio Security

Much of this chapter has concentrated on the special mission team's efforts to eradicate all evidence of their intrusion into hostile territory and the enemy's attempts to spot the inevitable traces left by their passage. A different sort of cat-and-mouse game takes place in the ether, between the team radio operator and the opposition's signals and electronic warfare operators.

Interception of clandestine radio signals provides an escalating yield of valuable intelligence:

1. Mere detection of the signal alerts the enemy to the presence behind its lines of a clandestine party. Overall security is tightened and, by counting illicit transmissions, the security apparatus builds up a picture of the size and organization of the threat.

2. The signals can be jammed electronically, threatening to sever the clandestine's links with their support elements.

3. Mobile and static stations equipped with radio detection-finding equipment (DF) can attempt to triangulate the operator and his transmitter. A security net is then thrown around the transmitter's approximately location. The net tightens progressively with each intercepted broadcast. A mobile transmitter (e.g., man-pack or vehicle-mounted radio) is met by roadblocks and roving patrols carrying their own DF apparatus.

4. The signal intercepts are routinely passed to specialist cryptoanalysts who attempt to decipher the code, using supercomputers programed to break codes. Cryptoanalysis employs techniques that range from the identification of commonly occurring letters and words to advanced mathematical investigations. The ability to read an enemy's signal traffic not only endangers their current operations but may adversely affect future missions.

The physical risk to the team is dependent partly upon the enemy's response time. If the time required to mount a security operation exceeds mission duration, or if the response always places the enemy behind the team, the risk is minimal. However, an examination of former front line Russian ground-based electronic intercept and DF capabilities demonstrates that the response time can be very short. During a routine sweep of the VHF band, a Russian communications intelligence (COMINT) operator detects a clandestine radio transmission and initiates a response:

- 10 seconds—an alert has been flashed to the radio DF-net control stations (NCS) and the COMINT analysis unit.

- 20–25 seconds—the Russians response can continue even if the radio goes off the air.

- 55 seconds—the NCS network has acquired several bearings. The information is passed to the plotting and analysis section.

- 115 seconds—plotting and planning correlates NCS data with COMINT, map analysis, and other collateral information.

- 2–3 minutes—jamming, artillery air strikes, and search and destroy missions are in progress.

During the Falklands War, one British team may have been compromised by Argentine direction-finding equipment. Throughout the conflict, Argentine positions on the hills and in the settlements were watched by British Special Forces teams. Captain John Hamilton's SAS patrol managed to establish themselves within 2,500 yards of the Argentine garrison at Port Howard. The patrol had been transmitting detailed and accurate reports to the Task Force Headquarters when, on

June 10, Hamilton and his signaller discovered that they were surrounded by enemy soldiers. As the SAS men opened fire on the enemy,
hoping to fight their way out of the encirclement, Hamilton was hit
in the back but continued to provide covering fire that allowed his
signaller to escape. There was no escape for Captain Hamilton who
was killed soon after, his unselfish heroism earning him a posthumous
Military Cross.

Transmission security This is the first line of defense against the
enemy's electronic warfare specialists. An operator contemplating a
"continuous wave" or standard radio telegraphic Morse transmission
will use a bidirectional aerial and the lowest possible power settings.
Activating the set only when required, the operator might employ
simple "Crack" or "Q" Codes to send short routine situation reports,
such as "I am well" or "Meeting resupply drop as arranged." Near the
coast, the experienced operator may disguise longer transmissions
among the routine maritime traffic. (Note, however, that in 1993,
maritime Morse code was discontinued in favor of automatic communications systems.) If, by chance, the signal is intercepted and
jammed, the operator will switch to the first of a prearranged series of
alternative or antijam (A/J) frequencies.

The "burst" transmitter was designed to compress messages,
which are sent as a very short pulses of Morse, to avoid interception
and radio location. The message is typed into the transmission *en clair*
and then encoded and transmitted as a high-speed burst. Messages
are loaded into the equipment, using a keyboard, and displayed
for checking on a small liquid crystal screen. The message is then
scrambled or encrypted before being transmitted through the radio,
in a short one- to two-second pulse, by depressing a single key.

Modern DF-equipment can nevertheless detect and intercept
pulsed transmissions in seconds. Determining the magnetic bearing
of the signal, and using the Doppler effect to measure the angular ele-
vation of the sky-waves, takes slightly longer, but makes it possible for
a single station to locate a transmitter with an accuracy of 10 percent
of the overall distance.

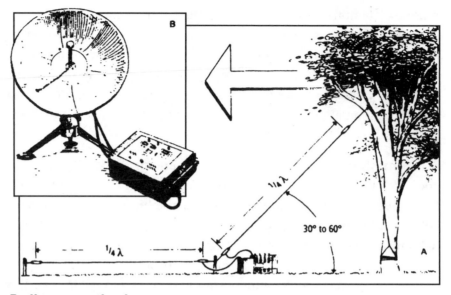

Radio communications

Aerial construction is the key to long-range radio communications "behind the lines." A slant-wave antenna uses two pieces of wire. One piece is slanted down from the antenna support (a tree) at an angle of 30 to 60 degrees to the transmitter. The other wire is used as a counterpoise just above the ground and laid out from the transmitter away from the slanting wire. Maximum transmission occurs in the direction of the slanting wire and counterpoise (A). A more secure technique uses a satellite ground terminal which beams the message up to a military communications satellite (B).

In the 1980s, military frequency-hopping sets became available. The "hopper" seeks to avoid detection by switching frequencies rapidly during transmission, ensuring that only a fragment of the message is broadcast on any particular frequency. The prearranged frequency changes are followed by the base station but not, it is hoped, by the COMINT eavesdropper, who might be faced with ten such hops every second. In theory, the rapidly changing signal is difficult to detect, intercept, or locate. Technology has met this challenge by producing "hopper traps" which can detect a signal that remains on frequency for only three milliseconds and continues to follow it through 1,000 frequency changes per second. Meanwhile, DF elements employing the Doppler effect can use a ten-millisecond fragment to locate the transmitter with an accuracy of one degree of the compass.

The principle of the third type of covert communications system is to send a highly directional signal into the sky to be intercepted by some sort of flying platform. During World War II, OSS case officers were flown over Germany and spoke with their agents, standing in darkened fields below, using the Joan Eleanor radio telephone. This device, invented by an RCA engineer, Steve Simpson, had its own lifelong batteries, was totally secure, and provided "real-time" communications. This enabled instant clarification of the message in minutes, rather than days, as had been the practice with radio communications. The conversation was taped, the message *en clair*, avoiding the usual errors introduced during decoding and encoding.

In the 1980s, man-pack satellite communications became available for the use of the SAS and other special forces. Now the message is transmitted into space to be intercepted by a different type of flying platform: the military communications satellite (SATCOM). The signal can be relayed instantly to a line of sight ground station or stored for later transmission as the satellite orbits over a friendly country. Providing stock-in-trade two-way communications during the Gulf War, the low-powered, highly directional pulsed signal from a satellite could be received only in a small area around the Special Forces team, making Iraqi interception almost impossible. Current equipment such as the "X-Band Special Applications Terminal," fits the transmitter, keyboard, and parabolic antennae into two large suitcases.

Communications satellites are prime targets in a total war situation, and it is unlikely that the surviving satellites would be assigned to SAS or other special forces operations. In order to retain the security offered by skyward transmission, astronomical bodies can be used as inert relays. A signal can be bounced off the moon using half a kilowatt of power, but it would be intercepted immediately by a myriad scientific, civilian, and military receivers.

During the 1960s, the British military and the American Navy experimented with meteor shower communications. It was discovered that the ionized trails of meteors entering the Earth's atmosphere reflected electromagnetic energy in the VHF range, providing a brief communications path every three to four minutes for pulsed transmissions. The operational range is approximately 60–400 miles between any two points on the Earth's surface.

Since the 1970s, the US Weather Service has employed meteor shower communications to feed meteorological information back from remote recording stations. These scattered slave stations, powered by solar panels, record and store weather indices such as wind velocity, temperature, and barometric pressures. When a computer-driven search by the master station, in an area of the sky enjoying an annual meteor shower, detects a "meteor scar" in the ionosphere, the coordinates are burst transmitted to the slave stations with orders to transmit their stored data. A military master station could transmit instructions continuously from its remote, secure location. The signals from the clandestine slave stations would be available only for interception within a small, very narrow ellipse approximately 8 x 20 miles in size.

Crypto-security Until recently, the one-time code pad, invented during World War II, offered the most secure means of encoding messages. The code had provided a method of transposing words to a set of prearranged random number of blocks which were employed only once and were almost impossible to break (see chapter 9). Modern transmitters can be set to encode signals, based on a daily code, which is electronically inscribed onto key cards.

Physical security This is the radio operator's third defense against detection. It embraces routine security, to keep radios, codes, frequencies, and transmission procedures secret, together with security in the field. The commonsense rules for field security include moving the radio between transmissions, sterilizing the radio sites, posting guards during transmission, taking care to conceal the aerial, and ensuring that cryptographic materials do not fall into enemy hands if the team is captured. If the team is conducting extended operations in a particular area, it may be necessary to place the radio site under surveillance before and after transmission, and to avoid obvious transmission sites, such as high ground, in favor of concealed ground on slopes and in valleys.

Agent meetings

Meeting agents, to gain valuable information or replace damaged equipment, poses a security problem for the soldiers in that the agent network may have been penetrated by the enemy's security apparatus. Whenever possible, the team will arrive at the RV the night before contact is to be made. The next day is spent in a lying-up position close enough to the RV to keep it under surveillance and to spot enemy troops moving into the area to lay an ambush. As dusk approaches, one man moves out of the hide and circles the area slowly, gradually spiralling in toward the RV point. Once the area has been thoroughly screened for signs of an ambush, the soldier positions himself close to the contact point and waits for the RV to open.

The actual meeting is a one-way transaction guarded by a two-way security check. The appearance of the agent and soldier at the right place and time, and the exchange of prearranged passwords, establish the validity of the contact. The agent may provide food and equipment or impart intelligence about the terrain, the civilian population and their customs, and the locations, strength, and habits of the local garrison. The soldier, for his part, is not expected to provide any military information. Requests for such information will result in the agent being treated with deep suspicion, and the contact will abruptly be brought to an end.

CHAPTER 6

The Mission

MODERN COVERT INSERTION TECHNOLOGY and the soldier's superlative training are combined within the single aim of infiltrating the special mission team into their operational area. Once there, they are expected to justify the expenditure of resources and effort by carrying out a small number of specific missions which conventional units could accomplish, if at all, only with great difficulty.

Taking the war into the enemy's camp

While a single team may be sent behind the lines on a reconnaissance mission or on a special operation, it is more usual to insert a squadron or troop to wage war within a defined operational area. A small advance party normally enters the area first, to identify a small, well-concealed and secure forward operational base (FOB). A prospective FOB must be close to both a source of water and suitable DZs/LZs or beaches to provide access for insertion, extraction, and resupply missions. The advance team will serve as a reception party for the rest of the force, which will radiate throughout the operational area. If the host country enjoys a Resistance organization, the FOB may serve as the headquarters of the guerrilla army. Raids and ambushes provoke an intense reaction. The British SAS experience in France suggests that, under enemy pressure, the FOB will need to be moved continuously and, in a heavily populated country with a hostile population and an efficient security apparatus, that operating bases may have to be discarded altogether.

Most SAS and other SF units are organized to allow the primary operating modules to be combined into larger offensive forces. The British 22nd Special Air Service Regiment deploys four fighting, or "Sabre," Squadrons, each of which is subdivided into four sixteen-man troops. Every troop has four independent patrols, each consisting of four cross-trained specialists. An American Special Forces Group (Airborne) consists of three or more operational or "line" companies, themselves composed of an administrative detachment and an operational "C" detachment. In the field, the "C" detachment commands and controls three "B" detachments, each of which commands four operational "A" detachments. The twelve-man "A" detachment is the basic operational or training team of the US Army's Special Forces. The American SF specialty is training local forces and leading them on operations ultimately designed to seize control of their Guerrilla Warfare Operational Area (GWOA).

A Russian Spetsnaz Brigade is deployed in an operational area about 30 miles ahead of its own forces. Deploying during the transition to war, the brigade places 50 percent of its seven-man groups within the area of operations, holding another 10 percent in reserve, while the remaining 40 percent prepare and train for operations. Each front is allocated about sixty groups which are responsible for reconnaissance or diversionary and sabotage missions. On sabotage operations each group is allocated one target per day and a maximum of three targets per mission. The first strike echelon (composed of three armies) seeking to attack along a 200-mile corridor, would use twelve teams to assist the main thrust, with another four groups conducting diversionary operations on the flanks. Some of these teams would be engaged in reconnaissance, collecting intelligence to be used for locating targets for Spetsnaz groups with the second strike echelon. Another thirty-six groups are assigned to the strategic front level (with an operational depth of 600 miles). Half of these groups would conduct operations in the direction of the main thrust.

◼ Long-Range Surveillance and Reconnaissance

Long-range reconnaissance and surveillance are about gathering intelligence deep behind enemy lines. The information gleaned enables planners to predict the enemy's intentions and provides the opportunity to destroy key units and installations, before they have even entered the conflict.

The first modern American Long-Range Reconnaissance Patrols (LRRPs) were deployed by the Provisional Reconnaissance Companies, formed in the early 1960s to support the US Army in Germany. The long-range patrol will keep on the move, potential targets being watched from short-term surveillance positions or investigated by circling the objective as close as local cover will allow (close target reconnaissance). Former Soviet LRRP Companies were deployed in an area of 350 sq. miles with each group or team being responsible for covering 10–15 sq. miles within the Company area.

In the American Army, the long-term surveillance of a major target, from a static OP, falls to dedicated units such as the Long-Range Surveillance Companies and Detachments assigned to Military Intelligence Brigades or divisional armored divisions. The subjects of extended surveillance are important targets such as major military formations and roads, railways, docks, airfields, or natural avenues likely to be used by advancing enemy forces. While the basic techniques used by both types of intelligence gatherers are similar, the long-range surveillance unit may employ a wider range of electronic devices to collect information.

The value of the information gleaned from such observations can be immense. For example, the type and volume of rail or road traffic travelling toward the front may indicate the time and place of the next offensive and, additionally, the overall effectiveness of friendly air strikes against the enemy's lines of communication (LOC). An unusual increase in activity may signify a unit preparing to move into

Covert surveillance

A sturdy long-term hide used by long-range surveillance troops (A) and a tempo-rary overwatch position that might be used by a long-range reconnaissance patrol (B).

battle. A team watching an enemy airbase may send a timely warning about an impending air strike. If the aircraft using the base pose a particular threat, the surveillance team may be able to orchestrate an air or ground attack, timed to optimize damage. British SAS surveillance teams attempted to do this inside Argentina during the Falklands War. The prospective targets were the Super Etendard aircraft and their Exocet missiles which were so effectively harrying the British Taskforce. Extended surveillance was necessary as the Argentine air force moved the aircraft between airfields constantly as a security measure.

Watching the enemy

An observer makes a brief scan of the terrain looking for enemy activity. Rather than sweeping across the countryside, the observer stops very briefly at a series of points between the OP and the horizon. A more detailed search follows, systematically examining the terrain from one side to the other in overlapping strips. The search starts with the area close to the OP and slowly moves toward the horizon. Again, rather than just scanning the ground, the observer stops at each point, constantly alert for movement, man-made structures, sound, reflections, and inadequate camouflage.

The construction of the OP will depend upon how long it is to be used. The LRRP may move into a well-chosen position at night. After checking the immediate area, a soldier is left on guard while the rest of the team prepares the hide. Working behind a black hessian screen, they clear an area and protect it with a camouflaged, waterproofed covering—a defense against both the weather and detection by enemy aircraft. They then camouflage the hide, taking care to avoid disturbing or cutting the local undergrowth and foliage. A basic four-man OP might have the living area laid out in the shape of a cross, each man occupying one of its arms, with a kit well in the center. A sentry and observer/radio operator remain on duty, while the third man sleeps and the fourth rests or attends to personal needs. The soldiers rotate counterclockwise through the positions at hourly intervals, ensuring that the observer is replaced before fatigue lowers his efficiency.

The cross-shaped OP provides all-round observation, is easy to construct and offers a number of potential escape routes. Other OP designs depend upon terrain and cover. Square OPs can be built under large bushes and, with the soldiers lying head to foot, provide all-round defense. Rectangular designs take advantage of straight lines such as walls and fence lines. The men are arranged in pairs, with two resting while an observer/radio operator and an observer/sentry share surveillance. Long-term surveillance positions consist of underground bunkers, sturdily built with reinforced roofs constructed from sandbags, wire mesh, and corrugated iron, supported by internal uprights and covered in an outer shell of unobtrusive turf. Stay-behind teams have the best opportunity of constructing well-built and sited OPs with the help of local engineer units.

Regardless of the type of OP, it will need to be near a source of water and offer unrestricted observation and radio communications. While providing a number of concealed escape and exit routes, it must be positioned away from road, tracks, buildings, or any other areas likely to increase the probability of accidental discovery. Well camouflaged, and sited in an inaccessible position apt to be avoided by routine foot patrols, the OP site also must be situated away from the skyline or any unusual geographical feature likely to interest a

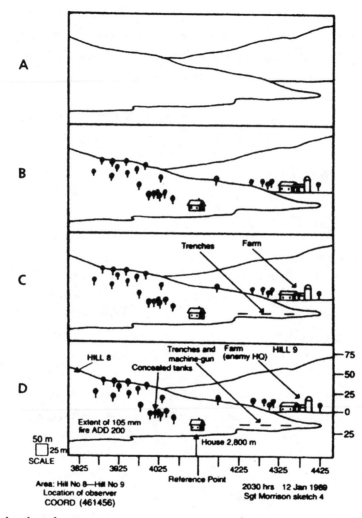

Terrain sketch

Four stages in the drawing of a detailed terrain sketch. The outlines of geographical features, such as hills and valleys, are drawn (A). Prominent features such as buildings, woods, railways, and the like are superimposed on the landscape (B). One feature is taken as a central reference point. The range and compass bearing of key features and enemy positions are added (C). Scales are added showing altitude and bearings and notes are made showing ongoing friendly operations and enemy activity (D). A terrain sketch is an invaluable aid to the precise reporting of intelligence and the determination of the positions of targets for fire-support operations.

bored sentry. If a suitable site for a team OP is not available, several smaller OPs may be used or a temporary site found and a team base established some distance away, allowing the OP to be occupied in shifts. Often, however, the team is forced to work with the operational terrain.

An eight-man American Special Forces team, one of many, was inserted into southern Iraq in February 1991, to maintain surveillance on Highway Eight. On both sides of the road, the area was parcelled into small farms and irrigated by numerous canals which in turn were fed by the Euphrates River. After caching an emergency radio along their escape and evasion corridor, the team constructed two four-man hides in the soft soil of a canal bank. The two hides were on either side of the canal, about 150 yards apart and some 300 yards from the highway. The OPs were completed by first light but as the sun rose, an unforeseen and potentially lethal problem became apparent. The area quickly became a hive of activity, with women gathering firewood, men herding livestock, and groups of children roaming through the fields between the highway and the OPs. Finally, the inevitable happened as two children, curious about the overnight appearance of a small hole in the side of the canal bank, actually peered into the hide's observation port, saw the soldiers, and ran off screaming.

Electronic ears and eyes

The team's intelligence-gathering activities can extend far beyond the visual range of the OP. A range of electronic equipment may be used to monitor roads or dead ground or to ensure continuing surveillance in areas of low visibility or high threat. Unattended Ground Sensors (UGS) were used by the Americans in Vietnam to monitor traffic along the myriad Communist infiltration routes that made up the Ho Chi Minh Trail. Disguised as trees or bushes, the sensors were dropped by aircraft or left by LRRPs which had infiltrated the trail structure. The signals from these devices were passed to circling aircraft and on to monitoring stations in Thailand and Vietnam. Ultimately, they were used to select targets for air strikes. In the post-Vietnam

Remote surveillance equipment

A. Audio Unit DT-383/GSQ: integral microphone detects noises with the same sensitivity and frequency range as the human ear. After three consecutive activations within 30 seconds, a 15-second alarm is transmitted down a landline. A photo-cell unit can be set to turn off the device in the daytime.

B. Disposable Seismic Intrusion Detector An/GSQ-160: Emits a continuous radio frequency signal and senses changes in the reflected energy caused by vehicles or personnel up to 120 ft. Useful in sand or swamp areas where seismic devices lack sensitivity. It can even survive immersion due to heavy rain or tidal flooding and can be adjusted to switch on at dusk. The device is designed to be recovered at the end of the mission.

C. Electromagnetic Intrusion Detector (EMID) An/GSQ-160. This device radiates a continuous radio signal on two frequencies and senses changes in the reflected energy, which results from movement.

D. Air Delivered Non-Recoverable Seismic Intrusion Detector An/GSQ-176. Camouflaged to look like small trees, these devices were dropped in their thousands during the Vietnam War. They transmitted a radio alarm signal to circling aircraft or signals intelligence base. The immediate area was then targeted for artillery or air strikes.

E. Miniature Seismic Intrusion Detector An/GSQ-154: Equipped with a logic unit and external geophone to minimize background signals. The unit issues a radio alarm signal when it detects intrusion by vehicles (up to 300 ft.) or ground troops (up to 90 ft.).

era, UGS technology proliferated, with sensors falling into several different categories:

Magnetic or remote electromagnetic sensors (REMS) Magnetic sensors can detect objects composed of iron-bearing (ferrous) metals such as small arms, vehicles, artillery pieces, tanks, and other military hardware, all of which distort the Earth's magnetic field. Sensors such as the lightweight, Magnetic Intrusion Detector (MAGID) Model T4, DT-516/GSQ detect vehicles at 60–80 ft. and humans at 10–15 ft. They can be used to defend the team's perimeter or to monitor roads and tracks during surveillance or ambush operations. Magnetic sensors operate over a relatively short distance but can transmit their signal back to the team some 1,000–2,000 yards away. Other magnetic perimeter intrusion systems employ a cable, buried 1–2 ft. underground, which totally encloses the team OP, providing an early warning of enemy troops in the immediate vicinity.

Seismic sensors These detect vibrations and work on the same principle as the commercial equipment used to record earthquakes or underground atomic weapons tests. Again, these can be used to protect the team's OP or to gather intelligence. The Disposable Seismic Intrusion Detector AN/GSQ-159 detected soldiers at 30 yards and vehicles at a range of 100 yards, remaining active for 7–60 days until its batteries expired. The US Army's Patrol Seismic Intrusion Device (PSID) registers movement at a range of 130 yards and can be monitored from a position 2,000 yards away. All seismic sensors suffer from background "clutter" resulting from natural vibrations and movement in the Earth.

Acoustic sensors These are basically microphones, capable of detecting sounds within the range of the human ear, linked to small integral FM radio transmitters. The US Army's Acoustic Buoy was designed to be suspended from trees and could detect sounds over a distance of 300–400 yards.

Disturbance sensors These transmit a sweeping radio alarm signal when moved or stepped on. The American Army's Noiseless Button

Bomblets (NBB) were camouflaged to look like stones, twigs, or other debris and were activated by movement as slight as ½₂ in. Other devices employ a long, extremely thin wire which acts as an electrical circuit. When a vehicle or soldier breaks the wire, a monitor notes the interruption of the electrical current and transmits a radio alarm signal.

Infrared sensors Widely used as commercial and domestic anti-intrusion devices, infrared sensors can be designed to operate in an active or passive mode. These instruments are likely to be used to defend team base perimeters, rather than for remote intelligence collecting. The passive sensor uses the "thermostat principle" to monitor a quadrant of ground, approximately 100° in width and 50 ft. deep. It is capable of registering the body heat of an intruder entering this space. The active IR-sensor uses an IR-light source to create an invisible fence between a series of pairs of emitters and receivers which can be separated up to distances of 1,000 yards. It is activated by an intruder interrupting the beam.

Using a network of different types of UGS, a team can monitor those parts of the operational area that are out of the line of sight of the surveillance OP. These mechanical slaves also act as "force multipliers," helping to gather a volume of data greatly exceeding the intelligence-gathering capabilities of the surveillance team alone. Additionally, they can be used to stand guard on the team's perimeter.

The team commander radioed immediately for an emergency helicopter extraction and moved his team out of the hides and along the canal bank. Perhaps not surprisingly, the Iraqi farmers seemed to dismiss the children's story about soldiers in the ground and the team was left alone. The helicopter extraction was cancelled but, as the hides were now compromised, the team moved to a high point on the canal bank. Over the next four hours, they continued to report on the road traffic, much of it travelling north, away from the fighting in Kuwait.

At around midday, the team was spotted again. This time a group of children led by a shepherd came along the canal and actually walked right up to the team. After an exchange of pleasantries in Arabic—the team was not prepared to kill unarmed civilians and, anyway, the area was still crawling with farmers—they were allowed to leave. When the man was seen to leave the children with a neighbor and drive into town, the team radioed for another emergency extraction and combat aircraft to provide close air support. Unbeknown to the team, however, the ground war was now in progress and all available aircraft were heavily committed.

Very soon, some 100–200 Iraqi troops, travelling in a variety of trucks and buses, pulled up on the highway opposite the canal, where they were joined by civilian paramilitaries and Bedouin farmers sporting antique rifles. The team stuffed all their classified radio equipment into one rucksack and activated a preset charge of C4 plastic explosive with a 60-second fuse. Sparing the LST-5 SATCOM radio, the other items of team and individual equipment were packed into the remaining rucksacks and thrown onto the explosive charge. The Special Forces then moved along the canal to set up a defensive position.

The main assault came across the open ground between the highway and the canal, while other smaller parties moved toward the canal on the team's flanks. To the front, the Iraqis found themselves facing superior marksmen. Although each team member only carried a double basic load of 5.56mm ammunition (420 rounds), most were highly trained snipers and easily outclassed the Iraqis at a range of 500 yards. Meanwhile, the flanking attacks were broken up by a 40mm high-explosive grenades from the M203 carried by the team weapons specialist.

This was the first of many assaults before F-16 Falcons put in a welcome appearance 45 minutes later. With more enemy troops arriving every minute, the Iraqi vehicles became the first target for the F-16's cluster bombs. Having reduced the vehicles to burning, twisted metal, the American aircraft turned their attention to the advancing infantry who were now within 200 yards of the team's position. The team directed the third air strike onto the canal itself, scattering high explosive and incendiary bomblets over the few Iraqis who had managed to reach the ditch and who were attempting to outflank the team. Two team members then cleared the burning canal, which now resembled a butcher's shop, eliminating survivors and gathering up their Kalashnikov rifles and ammunition.

With evening approaching, the team continued to select targets for the solitary F-16 which remained on station high above the road. The men knew, however, that they could not direct close air support in the dark. As night fell, the team commander decided to divide his Green Berets into small groups and attempt to slip through the pre-planned escape and evasion corridor into the open desert. Using their night-vision goggles to negotiate the canal, the men had just reached open country when the F-16 pilot radioed the only message they wanted to hear: "Your birds [two MH-60 Blackhawk helicopters] are 12 minutes out." The team commander, Chief Warrant Officer Richard Balwanz, was awarded America's second highest decoration for valor, the Silver Star. The other members of the team were awarded the Bronze Star.

Not all surveillance and reconnaissance missions entail a technically simple road watch. Some teams may be asked to cover a wide swath of countryside, collecting precise and accurate records on the times and locations of enemy units entering and leaving the area. A simple technique must be used to record this information (size, activity, location, unit, time, equipment), which will work when the observer is tired or when several events are occurring simultaneously in his area. A detailed picture map of the terrain can be employed as a useful template to record information. Firstly, a detailed sketch is made of the countryside, noting the heights of hills and the position of dead ground hidden from the observer's view. Secondly, major reference points such as villages, towns, roads, railways, woods, lines of trees, and fences are superimposed on the drawing. Working with the local map, the observer's sketch is then given a scale, a series of magnetic bearings running across the top of the drawing, and a series of semicircular lines that provide the range of landmarks with reference to the OP. Finally, the positions of enemy units are superimposed on the drawing.

Concealed within the OP, the observer may use tried and tested techniques in watching the countryside. Firstly, he may scan the ground for 30 seconds, looking for signs of movement or enemy activity. A more detailed systematic search follows, first with the naked eye and then binoculars. Starting close to the hide and moving toward the horizon and back again in overlapping 50-yard strips, the observer sweeps across the terrain from one side of his visual field to the other. At each spot, the soldier pauses, noting any changes from his last observation, alert for new man-made structures, movement, camouflage nets, reflections, noise, or other signs of human occupation. Each time the enemy is found, he makes notes in his log and on the terrain sketch. Polaroid photographs may be taken to complement the terrain sketch. A recent innovation of some military significance has been the design of still and video cameras which can transmit their photographs in digital form over a satellite communications link.

During the hours of darkness, observation is limited by the prevailing weather conditions and the amount of natural ambient light. Image intensifiers or "starlight scopes" amplify the low-level background light. Their effective range can vary from 150–2,000 yards and their "passive" mode of operation cannot be detected by the enemy. However, their value is greatly reduced by cloud cover, rain, fog, or smoke, all of which reduce light levels. In contrast, thermal imagers use an infrared beam to probe into the darkness, penetrating fog, smoke, and the dark inner recesses of woods and buildings. The effective range can vary between 400–4,000 yards; however, the beam is highly visible to enemy infrared collectors.

Night observation without STANO (surveillance, target acquisition, and night observation) equipment varies not only with local light conditions but also with the observer's night-vision faculty. Night vision is determined genetically but can be degraded further by eye disease, vitamin A deficiency, smoking, and alcohol intake. One manual suggests scanning objects quickly with abrupt, irregular movements, stopping only momentarily at each point in the visual field. Objects subjected to further scrutiny are then examined by focusing on a point, about 10° from the center of the object, so that the image falls on the rod region of the retina—the cells at the back of the eye most responsive to low light intensities.

Another night-time problem is that the brain translates poorly lit features into moving objects, so that an army of shadows, trees, and bushes appears to be stalking the unfortunate observer. Faced with an apparently moving shape, the observer glances away for 10–20 seconds and then returns the gaze at the suspicious object. If after repeating this exercise several times, the relative position of the shape has not changed, it is most probably a trick of the light.

If the team is positioned to call in air or artillery strikes, it becomes necessary to determine the precise range of targets. The team may carry a small lightweight battery-powered laser range finder such as the US Army's AN/GVS-5. Held like a pair of binoculars, the device indicates the range of an object in meters. It also provides a horizontal scale in mils—used for determining distances between objects—and a vertical scale showing altitude. Measuring angles in mils allows the military a useful and simple method of relating angles to distance: an angle of one mil equals one meter at a range of 1,000 m; two meters at 2,000 m; three meters at 3.000 m, and so on. Consequently, two objects at a range of 4,000 m and separated by an angle of 10 miles are 40 m apart.

A cruder technique, however, can be used to measure the angles, and thus distances, between targets. With a fully extended arm, the observer's hand determines angles, with one finger approximating 30 mils; three fingers 100 mils; four fingers 125 mils; spread hand 300 mils; and clenched fist 180 miles.

■ Air and Artillery Fire Support Operations

The end result of intelligence gathering may be the targeting of massed enemy formations, fuel dumps, headquarters units, or lines of communication (e.g., road junctions, bridges, and railway lines) for friendly artillery or air strikes. Close to friendly lines, artillery is capable of providing powerful, highly accurate fire, in all weather, day or night. Ranges vary from 6–9 miles for 105mm Howitzers to 12 miles for the MM107SP 175mm Howitzer and 20–70 miles for various battlefield rocket and missile systems. Similarly, as with the American team in Iraq, close air or artillery support may be required to get the team out of trouble.

The professionals in this game are the Forward Air/Artillery Control (FAC) teams. Using intelligence derived from reconnaissance/ surveillance missions, they infiltrate an area with the registration points of a number of known targets. Once in a position to overlook the target, the team opens radio communications and, using their prearranged call sign, issues the warning order: "Fire Mission." The artillery battery is then given the location of the target (e.g., Grid 345670 Direction 0450), and the target description (e.g., fuel dump), which will enable the battery to choose the most appropriate type of ammunition and fuse action. Finally, the observer chooses his method of fire control: "Adjust Fire" (observer will adjust the barrage until it falls onto the target); "Fire for Effect" (no adjustment necessary); "At My Command" (observer wishes to control time of delivery of artillery fire); "Cannot Observe" (target present at location but not visible).

If the observer is adjusting the artillery fire, a ranging single smoke round may be fired into the center of the target zone. The observer then makes the lateral correction—measuring the angle in mils between the target and the smoke, translating this into meters and multiplying it by the known distance between the observer and the target. For example, if the angle is 150 mils and the target observer distance is 2,000 m, a command is sent "Left" or "Right 300" (a mil is equivalent to two meters at 2,000 m; therefore $2 \times 150 = 300$ m). The observer now uses the falling shells to bracket the target for range. If the shells are falling short, the observer might provide the correction "Add 400." If this now results in the rounds overshooting, the observer may split the bracket by making the adjustment "Drop 200." The bracket continues to be split and the command "Fire for Effect" is given when heavy artillery shells (8 in. or 175mm) are falling within 100 m of the target or lighter ordnance is falling within 50 m. When

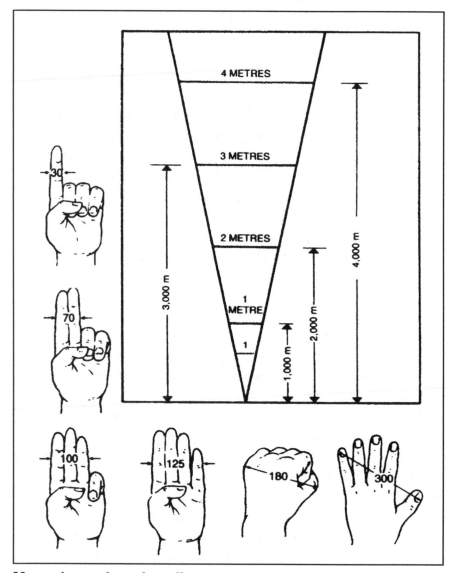

Measuring angles using mils

This is a useful method for relating angles to distance. It is of particular use to the SAS and other special forces parties in defining targets and controlling air and artillery strikes. There are 6,400 mils in a circle. One mil equals an angular distance of one meter at a range of 1,000 meters. Rough estimates of angles in mils can be obtained by using the fingers and knuckles of a hand with the arm fully extended.

Using geometry to penetrate heavily guarded installations

In high-threat situations, where enemy sensors may detect the beam from a laser range finder, or where a target is so heavily guarded that close reconnaissance becomes impossible, a little knowledge and simple arithmetic may hold the answer. Some targets will be so well guarded as to make close reconnaissance suicidal. For the team faced with providing a detailed description of such installations, simple schoolroom geometry can provide heights and distances. The distance between a particular object and a remote observer can be determined by constructing a simple triangle. A team member faced with, say a high-security fence, who wishes to determine the distance between the fence and a building inside the compound, takes an initial compass bearing on his target (say 20°) before moving parallel to the building until the angle between the observer and the building is increased by 45° (a compass bearing of 65°). The distance between the two compass readings equals the distance between the building and the fence. To minimize error, the observer may repeat the technique, moving back in the opposite direction until he obtains a difference of 45° on his compass, a bearing of 315° (360°− 45° = 315°). The distance between the building and fence is now found by dividing the total distance between the two outside compass readings by two.

The heights of buildings, radio towers, bridges, chimneys, and the like, can be estimated by similar methods. For example, the height of a radio tower ("X" feet) inside a heavily defended enemy headquarters can be measured by using ratio and proportion. Holding a rule or scale at arm's length, the observer measures the length of the tower ("a" inches), the distance between the scale and the observer's eye ("b" inches), and then uses his map to measure the distance to the radio tower ("Y" feet). Substituting into the formula $a/b = X/Y$, the height of the tower $(X) = a \times Y/b$.

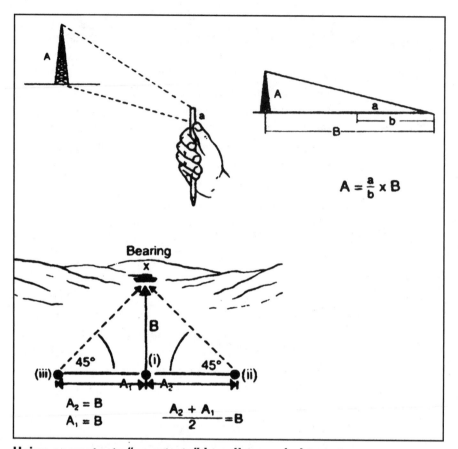

$$A = \frac{a}{b} \times B$$

$A_2 = B$
$A_1 = B$

$$\frac{A_2 + A_1}{2} = B$$

Using geometry to "penetrate" heavily guarded targets

The observer takes an initial bearing (Bearing X) at enemy tanks on the far side of open ground (A). In order to determine the range (distance B) to call in an air strike, the observer moves along a line parallel to the target until the bearing is increased or decreased by 45 degrees (points ii and iii). Distances A1 and A2 equal distance B (the initial distance between the observer and the tanks). Error is minimized by measuring both A1 and A2 and dividing by two.

Similarly, ratio and proportion yield the height of a radio antenna (height "A"). The distance between the observer and the radio tower is found from the method above or is calculated from a map. This is distance "B." Holding a pencil at arm's length, the apparent height of the tower (height "a") is measured on the pencil in inches. Finally, the distance between the observer's eye and the pencil is measured in inches (distance "b"). Solving the simple equation a/b x B = A provides an approximate value for the height of the radio antenna.

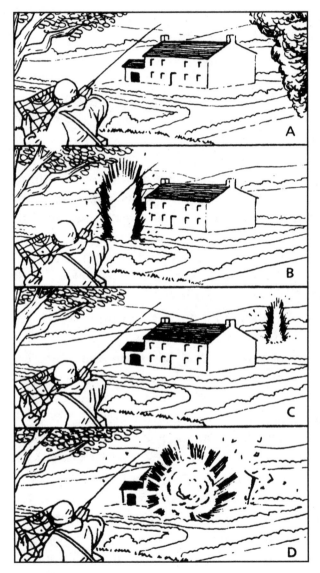

Fire support operations

To identify whether the enemy has set up headquarters in an apparently deserted civilian building, the forward artillery controller calls for a smoke round (A) and makes a lateral correction using the angle between the round and the target (in mils) and the known range (in meters). The first ranging round falls short (B), and the FAC corrects the range, with the result that the next shell over-shoots the target (C). The increase is now halved ("splitting the bracket"), and the next shell is on target (D). The observer now calls his fire mission ("fire for effect").

the observer is satisfied with the results, he calls "End of Mission" and reports the results, e.g., "Target Destroyed."

Air interdiction or close air support missions may also be controlled by an observer on the ground. Maintaining voice contact with the lead pilot or the Battlefield Command and Control Center aircraft, the team's observer provides information on the type of target and the presence of enemy defenses around the target area. If the team has been unable to get sufficiently close to the target to place laser or homing beacons, they may identify their own position with an FM radio beacon, thus providing the pilots with a landmark by which the target's direction and distance can be referenced. If beacons are not available, the team may pop a smoke grenade, but security requires that this is only identified by the pilot. For example, the team will report deploying smoke and air panels, and the pilot replies, "Roger, I have green smoke and two red panels aligned east-west." The lead pilot is now talked onto the target by means of a clock referencing system. The nose of the aircraft is taken as 12 o'clock and the tail as 6 o'clock. Altitude is reported as "High" (above the aircraft) and "Low" (below the aircraft). Consequently, target directions might be given as "3 o'clock Low." more precise directions being meaningless to the pilot watching the ground racing by underneath.

Recommending the direction of attack is difficult for the non-flyer, which is why this task is usually left to Special Operations Combat Control Teams (USAF) or Forward Air Controllers (RAF). The US Air Force devotes a whole manual, *AFM 3-5, Special Air Warfare Tactics*, to this and similar flying techniques. Concealed enemy positions in woods and forests are attacked at a steep dive angle so that the pilot can see his target, releasing his ordnance high and pulling out of the dive with sufficient altitude to escape the weapons' blast. Targets on open ground are attacked by means of shallow dive angles, allowing a lower and more accurate attack. The observer will "spot" the exploding munitions, providing corrections for the next aircraft on the "taxi-line." Once again the observer may employ a clock reference system, controlling the strike with commands like "Go Dry" (make the pass without releasing ordnance), "Break It Off" (emergency call to stop air attack) or "Hold High and Dry" (term used to halt the attack and hold the aircraft at a high circling altitude). The observer's job is made more difficult when the target is defended, forcing the aircraft to split the ground fire by rolling into attack from different directions at the same time.

■ Training Indigenous Forces

In a conventional war, small parties of SAS or other special forces may arm, train, and organize local Resistance forces (unconventional warfare). The many clandestine groups operating with the French Resistance during the 1944 Normandy invasion forced the German Army to divert eight divisions from the fighting, during one of the most crucial battles of World War II. In postwar counterinsurgency conflicts, Special Forces organized local people into irregular militia to defend their villages against the incursions of Communist guerrillas. These irregular militia exerted an effect out of all proportion to the handful of Special Forces instructors who trained and led them, while civil aid projects improved the people's lot by building roads, schools, hospitals, and wells, as well as encouraging village government and national political parties which represented minority interests. Overall, these programs redressed many of the grievances and inequalities that fanned the flames of revolution.

The primary role of the American Special Forces is still the training of indigenous forces. During the Gulf War, the 5th Special Forces Group attached training teams to every Coalition Arab battalion, providing instruction in personal and small unit skills such as navigation, reconnaissance, and close air support operations. During combat, the Green Berets acted as FACs, calling in circling attack aircraft and coordinating combat support requirements. After the conflict, the 5th SFG helped train the reconstructed Kuwaiti forces.

Most of the irregular forces which the Green Berets are asked to train already have a command structure and basic military skills. However, Special Forces instructors are expected to raise an underground army under any conditions. But how do you turn several

Training guerrillas

The essential skills taught to partisan troops by the American Special Forces Master Program. From left to right and in order of instruction: navigation, field hygiene, battlefield first aid, weapons training, marksmanship, patrolling and small unit tactics, raids and ambushes, demolition and sabotage, intelligence gathering and analysis, air operations, propaganda and motivation, and leadership and tactical skills.

hundred poorly educated farmers into a guerrilla force? One answer is to use an American Special Forces 30-day Master Training Program.

The first twenty-four instructional hours on the Master Program are spent introducing maps and compasses and teaching navigation. The students have to memorize common map symbols, mentally transform contour lines into hills and valleys, and relate six-figure map references to exact positions on the map. The students are then taught to use the compass and protractor (or an integrated compass/ protractor system such as the *Silva* compass) to transform a line between two points on the map into a magnetic bearing that will take them from A to B. To minimize the risk of getting lost *en route*, the journey is split into multiple short legs which take them from one landmark or rendezvous (RV) to the next. At each RV the new compass bearing is obtained, but the opposite bearing (i.e., $X - 80°$) is also calculated and memorized to allow the party to retrace their steps to the previous RV, should the men become lost. In combat, the previous RV is an obvious rallying point (emergency RV) if the party become separated after an ambush or firefight.

As time is always of the essence in small group warfare, a team cannot afford to get lost. The students are taught to take back bearings from several prominent features in order to triangulate or "fix" their position. A position fix from back bearings may not be possible at night or in featureless terrain, but the group can keep track of their progress by counting the number of paces they take. This is usually left to one man in the group, who may use a piece of knotted string to mark off each 100 paces. The individual's average stride length is then multiplied by the pace count.

Navigation is a practical skill and 20 hours are allotted to field exercises, just less than half at night, culminating in conducted group and, finally, solitary navigation walks. These provide an opportunity to test the students and reinforce classroom lessons. One lesson that is stressed continuously is that the guerrilla soldier must commit everything to memory. No marks must be left on the map; bearings and map references are never written down. Should the group walk into an ambush, the enemy must be left guessing as to their route and mission.

The next six-hour teaching block is devoted to combat medicine and field sanitation. Here the emphasis is on preventive medicine as it is easier to teach a soldier to keep himself healthy than attempt to treat an outbreak of dysentery. The budding guerrilla must become self-reliant, taking his own water from the paddy field and river and ensuring that it is filtered and boiled before filling his canteen. In the Far East, many particularly nasty diseases are spread by contaminating food and water with human waste. Excreta and food waste need to be buried away from the camp. They should be well concealed to avoid the attentions of animals and enemy scouts.

Personal hygiene is important, to avoid serious diseases and the buildup of dirt and sweat which attract disease-carrying parasites such as lice. On the other hand, washing too frequently may remove natural oils and skin bacteria that act as a barrier to more dangerous organisms. In order to avoid the fragrance of commercial soap, which advertises its user, animal fats can be saponified by boiling with wood ash (the fat and the alkali in ash combine to form a simple soap). Washing with soap can also help keep uniforms clean and parasite-free.

Casualties present the guerrilla commander with a stark choice. They can be killed, to prevent them giving useful information to the enemy, or they can be carried to safety and treated by the guerrilla doctor or Special Forces medic. Morale dictates the second choice, but this leaves the problem of keeping casualties alive until medical aid can be reached. The majority of casualties who are still alive an hour after being wounded have a good chance of survival, and this is where battlefield first aid proves important.

Bleeding has to be stopped, and students are taught to apply field or pressure dressings in cases of open chest, head, and abdominal wounds. If the wound cavity is tightly packed, the dressing absorbs blood and expands to exert pressure on the ruptured blood vessels, preventing further bleeding. The Rhodesian SAS used to carry tampons in their medical kits as these are admirably suited to packing wounds. If the patient is to be moved, it may be necessary to immobilize broken limbs with splints or bandages.

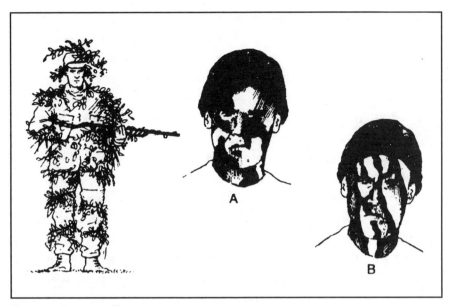

Personal camouflage

The ability to remain unseen is a vital asset to the irregular fighter. Camouflage cream applied to exposed areas of skin can be applied in blotches (A) to blend with a snowscape or deciduous forest or in slashes (B) when in areas of coniferous forest, desert, and jungle.

The student is also taught to recognize the weak, rapid pulse and clammy skin of the patient in shock. Shock is a common killer on the battlefield. A patient with shock due to blood loss can be stabilized with a plasma expander, such as an isotonic fluid containing the blood protein albumin, which restores blood volume. The skilled medic can introduce this through a vein in the patient's hand or wrist, but during the Falklands War many lives were saved by ordinary soldiers trained in rectal infusion. In this simple technique, a tube is introduced through the rectum and into that part of the patient's lower bowel which quickly absorbs the fluid.

Some casualties may be in great pain and most will carry the standard 10–15 mg self-injecting morphine ampoule, but the budding medic must learn which patients can be given morphine and which cannot. Morphine is usually given to soldiers with serious injuries, such as amputations or projectile wounds to the limbs or abdomen, but not to patients with head or chest injuries, as one side effect of morphine is to depress breathing. Once administered, the time and morphine dose are written on the soldier's forehead or on a card attached to his uniform—an overdose of morphine can kill. When the students have assimilated this first aid, it is rigorously tested on simulated night-combat exercises.

Once the students have shown themselves to be self-reliant and can find their way around the bush, the next forty-five instructional hours are spent on individual tactical skills. Here the novice is taught about camouflage and the human characteristics of shape, shine, silhouette, smell and sound which can betray a soldier to the most common battlefield sensor—the human eye. Skin is dulled and its shape disrupted with camouflage cream. Fresh vegetation is used to break up the shape of the head, shoulders, and equipment load. Sound is reduced by packing equipment tightly and taping down loose straps and fittings. When moving through the bush, a few basic field signs replace verbal instructions. Most importantly, the soldier is taught to note constantly how he blends into his surroundings.

The Special Forces instructors are well versed in the lessons of the past. An American pilot, returning from a bombing mission during the Korean War, reported long columns of North Korean commandos far behind the United Nations' lines. The commandos had simplified their personal camouflage, with each man cutting down a small tree and wedging the stump into his personal equipment. Although this was a great idea in theory, as proved by the fact that the "forest" had managed to cross enemy lines, it was ruined when the commandos heard the American aircraft—and promptly sat down in the middle of a road! The North Vietnamese Army regulars were more canny, drawing on their experiences of fighting the French. Individual units were prepared for guerrilla operations in South Vietnam as they travelled down the Ho Chi Minh Trail. Each soldier sewed bands, cut from old tire tubes, and other attachments to his uniform, to hold camouflage materials. When the foliage died or they moved into an area with different vegetation, the material was simply changed.

Locomotion techniques match movement to cover and terrain. Close to the enemy, but in good cover, a soldier may use a high crawl, moving on his knees and elbows with his weapon cradled on the tops of his arms. In poor cover, the soldier is taught to use the slower low crawl, pressing his body against the ground as he alternately pushes his arms and legs forward. Finally, the students are taught to move in patrol formation, watching for the enemy, moving into all-round defense during temporary halts and using the buddy system to maintain watch and yet ensure that everybody eats during cooking stops.

The students are now ready for a 70-hour instructional period in the field, learning how to set up a secure patrol base with perimeter defenses, Claymore mines, and safe corridors that serve as entry and exit points for patrols. Student patrols are sent out on raiding and ambush tasks. At night there is the added difficulty of maintaining the spacing between each member of the patrol, while ensuring that the men stay together. A white patch sewn into the back of a man's collar can serve as a marker at night. During the day it is hidden by the folded-down collar. As insurance, each man turns around frequently to check the man behind him. At this stage the Master Program also introduces the students to a wide range of US and indigenous small arms and support weapons. Many may never have seen a weapon before, and the instructor's first task is to convince them to keep their weapons to hand at all times. The second problem is to ensure that the students keep their personal weapon clean, rust-free, and well oiled despite the damp, dirty conditions in which they may find themselves. Human nature is such that the tired student coming in from the field will drop his weapon on his bedroll and assign its cleaning and maintenance a lower priority than washing, eating, and sleeping. This phase of the course is only allotted thirty-eight instructional hours, and Special Forces know form experience that such bad habits are discouraged most effectively by punitive punishments. Candidates for the Australian SAS who are found without their weapon spend their precious free time running around Swanbourne barracks, holding their weapon over their head, chanting "I must not leave my rifle."

Ammunition will always be in short supply, and the students are coached in marksmanship. A firm, comfortable weapon position, breath control, and a fluid trigger squeeze may, in combat, enable an attack to be broken at a range where enemy fire is still ineffective. Darkness is the guerrillas' natural ally, but night shooting requires further self-discipline and concentration. In Malaysia, British soldiers who walked into a night ambush and survived often did so as a result of the Communist insurgents' habit of firing over the heads of their poorly lit targets. Once the shooting starts, a jammed rifle can prove lethal. The students have to learn how to clear the chamber or adjust the gas regulator to get the weapon firing again. In a long firefight, magazines need to be changed and the weapon recocked, but this is when the enemy will move forward. Such lethal vulnerability is avoided by ensuring that the first two rounds loaded in the magazine are tracer. These will be the last two bullets fired. When the first tracer appears, the second tracer round is automatically chambered and ready to be fired. The magazine is now changed, while the soldier still has a loaded weapon. When the second tracer is fired, the first bullet from the new magazine is chambered without the need to recock the weapon.

No less important is the siting of support weapons, to decimate enemy forces caught in the killing ground of an ambush or to provide covering fire for a raid. A machine gun may assume great importance in the contact drills of a guerrilla patrol which is itself caught in an ambush. The standard contact drill for a small patrol is to break contact and evade the enemy, with the minimum of casualties. At the first sign of an enemy to the front of a guerrilla patrol, the lead scout sprays the area with automatic fire and then moves through the patrol and takes up a firing position 30–50 yards behind the last man. Other team members perform the same action, either singly or in pairs. The machine gun is usually carried by the last man and can be brought into play if the enemy seeks to maintain contact. The machine gun can buy sufficient time for the other team members to prime delayed-action Claymore mines.

Up to this point the Master Program has taught basic infantry skills adapted to small group warfare. The rest of the course covers the more unusual skills taught only to commando and guerrilla forces. The first eight hours of this second half of the course are spent learning intelligence collection. Information about the enemy can be gathered from field observations, from talking to villagers, or from documents taken from the bodies of enemy soldiers killed in action. The interrogation of prisoners may also yield a harvest of intelligence about enemy strengths and dispositions. Simple facts are often vitally important. Letters may reveal that guerrilla operations have reduced enemy morale to a point where many are deserting or might defect, if given the opportunity. An increase in traffic along a previously quiet road might mean the presence of a new headquarters or supply depot. The presence of elite unit tags on the uniform of a dead enemy soldier may mean that the enemy is planning another counterinsurgency drive.

Thirty-one instructional hours are allotted to the vital task of laying out drop zones and beach landing sites. Particular attention is paid to securing the area and calculating the positions of the markers to ensure that the supplies land on the right clearing or beach. Without constant resupply drops, weapons and ammunition must be taken from the enemy, and food must be provided by local villagers.

The last teaching block, of 29 hours, covers demolitions and sabotage, with the emphasis on turning common chemicals and un-exploded enemy munitions into demolition charges and booby traps. The training ends with 105 hours of squad and platoon tests. These assess and reinforce all the subject material taught on the program.

The Master Program has several aims. First, it serves as a selection course since many candidates will find that they do not have the mental and physical attributes for guerrilla warfare. Those who fail the course may be better suited to work as couriers or intelligence gatherers. Alternatively, they may find a role in one of the many support tasks at base camp. Second, it teaches basic guerrilla warfare, fostering team work and esprit de corps among the rank and file.

Some graduates who excel in a particular course area will be selected for an "A" Team specialty such as medic or weapons specialist. Third, it gives the Green Beret instructors the opportunity to identify potential leaders and instructors from all-around star graduates. The former become indigenous officers and NCOs in the guerrilla army, while the instructors seed further programs to produce additional trained guerrillas, leaders, and teachers. In this way, the irregular force grows quickly.

■ Sabotage

Explosives greatly increase the potential for sabotage. The American Special Forces handbook, *FM 31-20*, details the black art of constructing bombs and booby traps, using commercial chemicals and fertilizers. A simple bomb can be given a deadly shrapnel effect by packing the explosives with nails, stones, or broken glass. However, military explosives are used mainly for demolition tasks and fall into two categories: high explosives and low or incendiary explosives.

Upon detonation, high explosives are converted instantaneously to heat and gas, with the production of a high-pressure, high-speed shock wave which, properly harnessed, can be highly destructive. Nevertheless, as the explosive charges may have to be dropped by aircraft and then carried into the target, compounds such as TNT or C3/C4 plastic explosive must be inert and safe to handle. In order for them to explode, a sequence of events must take place.

A detonator or blasting cap is embedded in the primary charge. When this explodes, it produces a shock wave that sets off the main charge. Sometimes, however, the primary explosive is so stable that the detonator on its own may not be sufficient. In this instance, a hole is made in the primary charge and filled with a wad of more volatile explosive or "primer." The detonator, usually initiated by a fuse or an electrical circuit, now explodes the primer, which initiates the main charge. Finally, the fuse must be ignited or the electrical circuit closed, to begin once more the sequence of events that culminates in the explosion.

Charges Military explosives come in all shapes and sizes, each being designed for a specific task. Simple slab explosive must be positioned carefully to cut steel or reinforced concrete. The demolitions man is taught simple formulas relating the thickness of the target to be breached to the number of pounds of plastic explosive required for the job. A long length of explosive ("ribbon charge") can produce a fissure in concrete or slice through a steel beam. A "saddle charge" funnels the shock waves to produce a cross fracture, while a "diamond charge" cuts at right angles to the explosives. Shaped charges concentrate the shock waves onto a small target area to produce a linear tubular fracture. Military shaped charges, such as the "beehive," funnel and concentrate the shock wave by way of a narrow aperture, but simple household objects such as cups, bowls, and wine bottles can also be used to funnel or "shape" the explosive force. The simultaneous activation of diametrically opposed charges—"counterforce"—produces two shock waves that meet inside the target to cause internal destruction.

Buildings can be destroyed by dust initiators that produce two distinct explosions. The main charge is enclosed by a "cover charge" of wheat flour, gasoline, or coal dust, which is dispersed or vaporized by the first explosion before igniting and saturating the atmosphere inside the building with burning material in a second explosion.

Sabotage: imagination and training

The small commando or guerrilla force cannot risk incurring casualties in armed clashes with the enemy. Mines and booby traps provide another means of demoralizing and hurting the enemy, without risking costly battles. These and other fragmentation weapons, such as grenades and shells, accounted for just under half of all American deaths in Vietnam during 1965–70. Referred to as "expedient interdiction techniques," booby traps, mines, and snipers can deny the enemy certain lines of communication, forcing him to undertake additional security measures. This type of warfare makes the best use of the limited resources of a small guerrilla force.

Techniques are limited only by imagination and training. Pressure or remote-activated Claymore mines might be left along the route taken by regular patrols or around the perimeter of enemy bases. Spetsnaz groups favor jumping mines, which propel a canister of projectiles and explosive high into the air, killing or maiming many people in addition to the poor unfortunate who actually treads on the pressure plate. Other mines can wipe out the crew of a military vehicle and subsequently force the convoy to move at snail's pace, while it probes for other booby traps. These gains can be consolidated by roving sniper teams, who alternate duties periodically and can operate for long periods in the field. Enemy troops evacuating their wounded and probing for other booby traps are harassed by the sniper who eliminates key personnel such as officers, NCOs, radio operators, and engineers. A few well-placed bullets from a roving sniper team may also damage or destroy radar, signals, and telecommunications equipment. Mortars are another powerful interdiction weapon. Vietcong mortar teams shelled America and Australian bases intermittently from the safety of the jungle. Garrisons were forced to deploy routine patrols to search for the mortar-baseplate marks, in the hope of later targeting the guerrillas with counter-battery fire.

The war in Southeast Asia also taught the Americans that a range of primitive animal traps could be adapted as antipersonnel devices. Concealed pits, lined with punji stakes and smeared with pig excrement, were capable of inflicting deep leg wounds, with the attendant risk of blood poisoning. Logs, armed with rows of lethal spikes, were turned into deadfall traps by hoisting them into the tree canopy and suspending them with a simple by precarious trip wire. Mantraps, designed to impede the enemy, were constructed from sharpened bamboo or hardwood spikes mounted on scaffolding and concealed in the foliage. Activated by a trip wire, using gravity or a tightly wound spring band for momentum, these devices impaled the unlucky soldier who stumbled upon them.

Equally simple and cost-effective sabotage techniques were conceived for urban operations by World War II Allied clandestine organizations. Sand or finely ground Carborundum powder poured into the axle grease chambers brought French railway cars to a grinding halt. An even simpler expedient was that of jumbling the car destination cards at the siding office, thus ensuring that the week's trains were made up from the wrong cars. Dropping a handful of sugar into a gas tank proved unreliable, but demerara treacle did cause vehicle engines to seize. Sugar had a marked effect when thrown into the concrete being mixed by German engineers building the coastal defenses in France: the resulting chemistry ensured that the fortifications partly dissolved in the rain. Logs and coal bricks, hollowed out and filled with plastic explosive rigged to a detonator and match-head fuse, were left to be shovelled into factory furnaces. Similar devices, inserted into dead rats, reputedly accounted for nine steam boilers in Belgian factories. The discovery of doctored rodents in a crashed British aircraft resulted in the institution of elaborate measures to dispose of dead animals, thus wasting further production time.

Demolition, however, involves more than choosing the right charge for the job. The saboteur must be clear about his aims and use his knowledge to produce maximum damage and inconvenience to an enemy. While a slab of explosive might obliterate a single aircraft, a series of smaller charges, strategically placed on the undercarriage, cockpit, or wings could disable an entire squadron. The destruction of the control tower or fuel stocks, or cratering of the runway, may deprive the enemy of aircraft for a few vital hours. A section of railway track is replaced easily and quickly by teams of tracklayers. The destruction of track at multiple points, the demolition of a railway bridge or the derailment of a train at a steep curve, inside a tunnel, or on a bridge, will maximize the havoc and greatly delay repairs. Well aware of this, the enemy usually guards vital points such as railway bridges and tunnels. Trains may be preceded by advance guard armored trains or inspection cars. Consequently, full-scale attacks on airfields and railways may take the form of well-planned and rehearsed raids or ambushes.

Faced with a target such as a bridge, the demolitions expert must identify the weakest points which can be cut with explosives to topple or destabilize the structure. Cutting the load-bearing piers may require an inordinate amount of explosive, but charges laid carefully on the roadway, close to the ends of a cantilever bridge, can cause the collapse of the suspended span. Equally, the destruction of the pylon-carrying towers on a suspension bridge or the girder arms of continuous span-tuss bridge will cause instability and collapse.

Initiator systems The long, patient wait is over, and the enemy troop train is approaching. Charges have been laid on the railway bridge. The saboteurs will wait until the engine and most of the carriages are on the bridge before the charges are exploded. This gives the saboteurs only a few vital seconds to detonate their charges, which must explode simultaneously to produce the correct pattern of explosions that will topple the bridge.

Most war films show saboteurs using an electrical system to fire their charges. An electrical initiator is basically a circuit that connects a battery to the detonators. The electrical blasting cap contains a thin wire bridge, similar to the filament in a lightbulb, which becomes hot enough to ignite a small charge in the base of the cap when an electrical current is passed through the wire. Although the electrical connections may be waterproofed by means of grease, they are still susceptible to mechanical damage, and a short circuit or a break in the circuit wire disables the entire system. During the war in Europe, German engineers would prepare road bridges for demolition and then wait for the first Allied tanks to nose across before firing the charges. At least two key bridges in Holland and Germany fell into Allied hands when the initiator system failed at the last moment.

Another problem with electrical initiators is random frequency hazard (RFH), where a radio transmission near the demolitions circuit detonates the charge prematurely.

Detonation cord provides an alternative firing system. "Det cord" is an instantaneous fuse consisting of reinforced cable with a small high-explosive core. As the fuse itself consists of explosive, it is ignited by a detonator and primer. The cord then literally explodes at a rate of around 20,000 ft. per second, until it reaches the blasting cap or detonator—a thin cardboard or metal tube containing guncotton or some other explosive. Detonation cord has other uses. Some manuals recommend connecting a length of "det cord" to a grenade, which is then thrown into a minefield to blow a foot-wide corridor through the mines.

Occasionally, the demolition team may wish to make their escape before the charges go off. This may be achieved with safety fuse—a flexible plastic-coated cable containing a black powder core surrounded by fiber wrapping. Similar to the delayed action fuses used commercially in quarries and civil development, the cord burns at a standard rate (4 in. every 12–16 seconds) until it reaches the explosive in the blasting cap.

Low explosives These are employed to start fires in buildings, stores, oil depots, or ammunition dumps. Incendiary devices are easy to ignite, burn with an intense heat, and are difficult to extinguish. They use a fuse consisting of a mixture of chemicals, called the "first-fire mixture," which ignite easily and slowly reach a combustion temperature sufficient to kindle the main charge or "main-fire mixture." By the time the incendiary device is consumed, the target should be a roaring inferno.

Booby traps Explosives can also be fashioned into extremely effective booby traps. Quite apart from harassing the enemy, booby traps are usefully employed along the team's exfiltration route. If the enemy is close behind, or actually in contact with the team, precious time cannot be wasted in the design of cunning traps. With this in mind, the American Special Forces are issued with the M2A1 and M1A2 (pressure), M3 (pull-release), and M5 (pressure-release) percussion detonators. Essentially, these are camouflaged tubes (except the M5 which is a box) that are screwed into the explosive charge. When these devices are activated, a powerful spring drives a striker or firing pin into the percussion primer. The resulting mini-explosion is funnelled through the narrow mouth of the firing device and into the main charge.

The M1 can be used as a simple delayed-action device. When the glass ampoule is crushed, it releases acid which burns through a copper wire, restraining the spring and striker. The M2A1 is set at eight seconds, and the M1A2 is equipped with a 15-second delay. These are armed and left behind for an enemy in hot pursuit. The M3 pull-release is rigged to a trip wire. The wire, in turn, is connected to a release pin which restrains the firing pin. The striker in the M5 is held in place by a plate, which is itself held under pressure. When trodden upon, the catch holding the pressure plate is released, allowing it to spring upwards and release the firing pin. The explosive charge is placed under the M5 and both are concealed in a carefully camouflaged hole.

■ Raids and Ambushes

Defined as ". . . a surprise attack against an enemy force or installation." the raid remains the primary offensive technique for forces operating behind the enemy's lines. Raids are designed to cripple the opposition or distract attention from other friendly operations by keeping the enemy off-balance, forcing him to deploy additional units to protect rear areas. Likely targets might include headquarter units, communication centers, radar sites, service units, fuel depots, attack helicopter bases, or heavily defended nodes along the enemy's lines of communication, such as railway and road bridges, and junctions or other choke points such as mountain passes or waterways. The targets must be accessible, vulnerable to attack, and difficult to replace.

The success of the raid depends upon surprise. The raiders must catch the enemy unawares and use the panic and confusion to aid their escape. Small SAS teams, operating behind German lines in North Africa during World War II, crept into German airfields and used delayed-action incendiary bombs to destroy aircraft and fuel stocks. By the time the bombs exploded, the SAS parties planned to be deep in the desert. Lightly defended targets are easy prey for small teams, but heavily defended key installations require a company or battalion-sized attack. In American doctrine this could be provided by partisans led by Special Forces instructors or the 75th Ranger Regiment, whose specialties include deep raids, ambushes, and sabotage.

A large guerrilla or commando force must split into small parties for the move toward the target, but rallying points along the way allow the raid commander to exercise control of the operation. The main assault element is responsible for accomplishing the object of the raid. This includes the "special task" squads, which move ahead of the "main action group" to eliminate guards and breach obstacle belts before conducting diversionary or fire-support tasks. Security elements, moving on the flanks of the main action group, have the job of ensuring that the raiding force has access to the target for the time necessary to complete the raid. This involves blocking communicating roads, to prevent the enemy escaping or reinforcements getting through to the target, and covering the assault element's withdrawal, by fighting rearguard actions. If the raid fails, the security elements have the unenviable task of slowing pursuit and leading the enemy away from the main force. Avoiding prearranged rallying points, the enemy is drawn into difficult terrain in the hope of breaking contact and evading further detection.

The other major offensive tool of the Special Forces is the ambush, defined by *FM 31-20* as ". . . surprise attack from a concealed position, used against moving or temporarily halted targets such as trains, boats, truck convoys, individual vehicles and dismounted troops. In an ambush the enemy sets the time and the attacker sets the place." Ambushes and raids employ similar techniques and can be mutually supporting. For example, enemy reinforcements might find themselves caught in an ambush set by the security elements of a raiding force.

In 1982, as the British Task Force was poised to place its men ashore on East Falkland to begin the recapture of the islands from Argentina, a textbook raid was planned by the SAS. Involving all three services, its like had not been seen since the days of World War II when Combined Operations launched raids against Hitler's "Fortress Europe." The target was the Argentine airbase at Pebble

Island, which, with the materialization of the British war plans, lay dangerously close to the approach corridor of Falkland Sound and the proposed landing beaches at San Carlos.

To the Argentine high command on East Falkland, who were left guessing at where the British would land, Pebble Island was just another dispersion airfield providing a safe haven from the British bombing raids on Port Stanley. Rear Admiral Woodward and the other Task Group commanders had a different appreciation of the airfield's significance. Its Pucaras represented a threat to British helicopters flying outside the air defense umbrella but, more importantly, there were growing suspicions that a mobile American-built ANTPS-43 radar installation was present on the island and well placed to watch the approaching invasion fleet.

The job of totally eliminating the Argentine presence on the island was allotted to D Squadron 22 SAS. As with all well-planned operations, it began with an intelligence-gathering mission. On May 10 two four-man patrols from the Squadron's Boat Troop, specializing in maritime operations, were dropped with their canoes on Mare Rock Peninsula by Sea King helicopter.

From their insertion point on the most northeasterly point of West Falkland, they planned to canoe around the headland and into the treacherous tidal waters of the Tamar Straits which separate Pebble Island from the mainland.

At this point the mission ran into a problem often experienced during waterborne operations. It was immediately clear that canoes could not be launched into the fearful breakers pounding the coastline. An alternative plan was hatched and the helicopter dropped the men into dead ground below a ridge on top of the peninsula.

From there the SAS men were left to their own devices. They carried their Bergens and equipment over the ridge to establish an OP overlooking the straits and the eastern coastline of Pebble Island, and then, tired and cold, they made a second journey to collect their collapsible Klepper canoes.

On the next day, May 11, the reconnaissance party carefully watched Pebble Island for evidence of Argentine patrols. With only

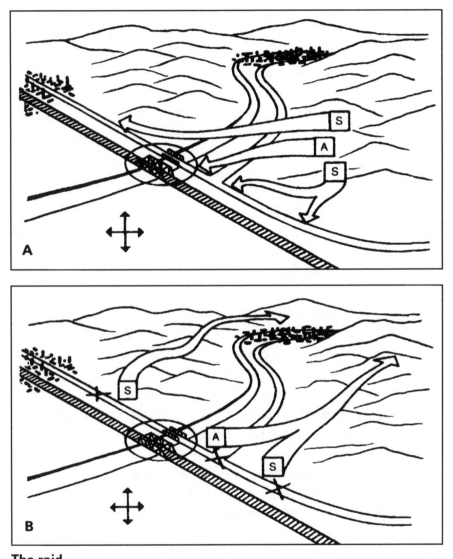

The raid

A raiding force moves out of the hills to destroy a heavily guarded railway bridge. Two security elements (S) move into positions on either side of the bridge to block and ambush roads leading to local towns. Special task details move ahead of the assault group (A) to eliminate the guards and strong points overlooking the bridge (A). When the charges are laid on the bridge, the assault group withdraws with one security element, while the other element withdraws in a different direction to draw away any pursuing enemy forces (B).

wild coastline and seabirds in evidence, the party launched their canoes into the icy currents of the Tamar as darkness fell. Reaching the Island in safety, one patrol remained in a hide with the radio and canoes, while the second set off to cover the ten miles to the airfield in the remaining darkness.

The open moorland offered little cover, except where the elements had etched craters and gullies into the peat. Only the hardy grasses managed to cling on in the face of the frequent gales, and these formed tussocks which made walking with a heavy pack infuriatingly difficult in the darkness.

With dawn the problems multiplied. Lying in a scrape some 2,000 yards from the airfield, the SAS men counted eleven Argentine aircraft: six Pucaras, four Turbo-Mentors (also equipped for the ground-attack role), and a Skyvan transport.

The team's position was precarious; not only was there little cover, but the settlement and grass airstrip lay at a point where the sea encroached on both sides, severely limiting the available escape routes. With their task completed and discovery always imminent, the soldiers abandoned their Bergens and crawled away to lie up in some dead ground. When darkness fell, they walked back to the coast to radio their report to squadron headquarters on the carrier *HMS Hermes*.

On the night of May 14/15, with a gale blowing, the *Hermes* made her way through rough seas to a point 40 miles off the Falkland's coast, moving closer than planned to provide a shorter flight for the Sea Kings of 846 Squadron in the less than ideal conditions. With her went the frigate *Broadsword* to provide air defense. A third vessel, the destroyer *Glamorgan*, sailed to within seven miles of the coast to bring the Pebble Island settlement under the shadow of her guns and to be close at hand in the event of the helicopters being forced to ditch in the sea.

On the island, the Boat Troop reconnaissance party left their hides and moved to within four miles of the airfield. There among the tussocks was an area which they had selected as a helicopter LZ. After putting out identification markers, they moved into all-round defense and waited in the chilling wind and bright moonlight.

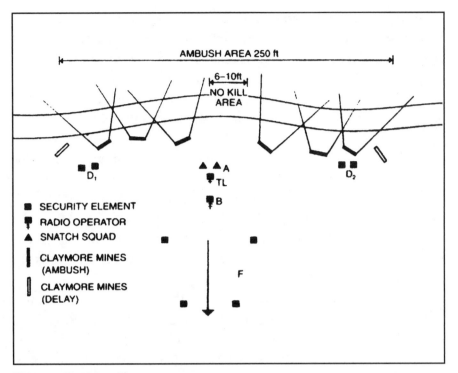

The small ambush

The small ambush is used to harass enemy lines of communication and gain vital intelligence from captured documents and prisoners. The majority of enemy caught in the ambush are killed by area weapons such as command-detonated Claymore mines. If prisoners are a consideration, a "no kill" zone is left in the middle of the ambush. Positioned opposite the "no kill" area are the team leader (TL), the radio operator (B), and a two-man snatch squad (A). The flanks are guarded by flank security with delayed action Claymore mines (D1 & D2). A rear security party (F) or "gatekeepers" are left guarding an escape and evasion corridor. (In Vietnam this usually led to a prearranged helicopter exfiltration LZ.) When the ambush is sprung, the snatch squad move forward to take any prisoners, and the flank security activates their Claymore mines to discourage any flanking attack attempting to surround the small force. The twelve-man Special Forces "A" Team then moved down the E&E corridor, while the "gatekeepers" activated further delayed-action mines to discourage any pursuit.

Forty-five minutes after leaving the carrier, the three helicopters were over the LZ. On board were three sixteen-man troops from D squadron and a Naval Gunfire Support Forward Observer (NGSFO)—a commando and parachute-trained Royal Artillery officer.

The operation was running late and had been reduced to the single objective of destroying the Argentine aircraft. One sixteen-man troop provided security for the LZ and also a protective shield for the NGSFO and the crew of an 81mm mortar which was to provide additional fire support.

A second troop, also acting as security, would seal off the approaches to the settlement. This left one reinforced troop (Mountain Troop) of around twenty men to form the main assault party. The original reconnaissance party from Boat Troop acted as scouts for the move to the airfield.

It was 7 a.m. before the SAS were in position, and time was pressing. Not only would the approaching dawn expose the soldiers, but the Royal Navy ships were left vulnerable to Argentine air strikes.

Without further hesitation, the assault party opened up on the assembled aircraft with small arms and 66mm antitank missiles. The mortar was brought into action, and the NGSFO carefully directed the *Glamorgan*'s shells onto the enemy trench lines. There was some desultory small-arms fire returned from the Argentine defenses. Only later would the SAS learn that the Argentine garrison totalled 114 men, outnumbering the raiders by three to one.

The large ambush

The American Special Forces are trained to use partisans or indigenous forces in larger ambushes with a 200–250-yard killing zone. These employ a thirty-man force with an eleven-man assault team, instead of area weapons. Additional security teams are deployed on the flanks with M-60 heavy machine guns and Claymore mines. Enemy forces are spotted by the flank security elements who radio the information to the team commander and alert the M-60 security team by tugging a communications cord. If the ambush is effective and resistance neutralized, the assault team moves through the killing area and sets up temporary security on the other side of the road.

The flank security then notifies the M-60 gun teams that they are moving onto the road and withdrawing through the center of the ambush area. This ensures that the heavy machine guns have a clear field of fire in the event of a flanking counterattack.

Once flank security has passed through, the assault element moves back across the road, making a hasty search of the dead bodies. The security teams then activate their delayed-fuse Claymores, and the party moves through a checkpoint and on to a preselected LZ.

Ambushes against vehicles are coordinated simultaneously with strikes against the front and rear of the column to prevent reinforcement. Obstacles and explosives are used to bring the convoy to a halt. The assault team opens fire on the vehicles, concentrating on those with mounted automatic weapons and on soldiers leaving the vehicles. Escape routes are covered by machine guns firing on fixed lines, while mortar shells, hand and rifle grenades are fired into the killing zone.

Armored vehicles, such as tanks and armored personnel carriers, are attacked with antitank weapons, mines, and Molotov cocktails, and by hurling grenades into open hatches. Every effort is made to neutralize armored vehicles at points where they are unable to give protection to the rest of the convoy and where they will block the approach of other supporting vehicles.

Trains are ambushed on bridges or steep curves in order to derail as many cars or carriages as possible, maximizing casualties among the passengers and leaving extensive wreckage to block the line. The assault force and heavy weapons groups direct a withering barrage of fire at the overturned carriages, before moving forward to attack the trucks or coaches still standing. If the ambushers are part of a guerrilla army, or are conducting long-term operations in the area, the opportunity is taken to strip the train of its supplies and freight, before setting it on fire. Meanwhile, flank security teams destroy sections of track in both directions to delay the arrival of reinforcements.

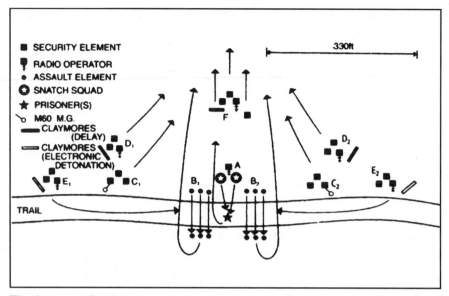

The large ambush

The large ambush is designed to attack an enemy convoy or column. Area weapons are replaced by heavy machine guns such as the American M60 or the British GMPG (C1 & C2). Security groups cover the flanks with electronically detonated mines (E1 & E2), covered in turn by additional groups (D1 & D2) behind a screen of delayed-action Claymores. When the ambush is sprung, the assault element (B1 & B2) moves forward to eliminate opposition and establish fire positions on the other side of the track. The snatch squad (A) then moves into the 15 ft. "no-kill" zone in the middle of the assault element to capture any survivors. This type of ambush places the flank security out on a limb, with Claymore mines and machine guns behind them and dead and wounded enemy troops in front. Approximately ten seconds after the shooting stops, the flank security groups (E1 & E2) tug communications cords connecting them to the machine guns, announcing their intention of moving into the ambush area. They then withdraw with the snatch squad through the center of the ambush. The assault element follows after they have searched the enemy dead for letters and documents of value to Intelligence. Finally, the machine gun (C1 & C2) and security groups (D1 & D2) withdraw behind a screen of delayed-action mines. The last to withdraw down the E&E corridor are the "gatekeepers" or rear security (F).

There is no limit to the size of an ambush, but the site must be chosen well to ensure that a large and dangerous enemy force is funnelled into a killing zone, before they have any opportunity to organize resistance or escape. The area around the ambush site and potential escape routes are sealed with barbed wire, mines, and booby traps. Better still are natural obstacles such as narrow chasms, cliffs, or swamps.

The Communist Vietminh scored a notable victory against the French, on October 1950, by overrunning the Legion fort at Cao Bang and them ambushing the relief force (Bayard Group) at the Coc Xa gorge. When the withdrawing Cao Bang column fought its way through to the gorge, it too was decimated by snipers, ambush and suicide commandos. The fearful battle in this mountainous jungle defile accounted for a number of French units, including three elite Foreign Legion paratroop and infantry battalions.

With the enemy's fuel and ammunition stores exploding under naval gunfire, SAS assault teams then moved onto the airfield to begin systematically destroying the remaining aircraft with demolition charges and 66mm rockets. By 7:15 a.m., the prearranged time for the SAS to withdraw, all the aircraft had been destroyed and more than one ton of ammunition, ablaze in the Argentine stores, was setting off secondary explosions.

The SAS had incurred only one casualty, a soldier hit in the leg by shrapnel. As he was being led off to the helicopter LZ by two comrades, they ran into a party of Argentines, possibly perimeter guards or an outlying patrol. Hearing voices shouting in Spanish, an SAS soldier opened fire in their direction with his M203 grenade launcher. He is believed to have inflicted the only Argentine casualty of the raid. A second SAS casualty was incurred as the soldiers withdrew from the blazing airfield. An SAS corporal was caught in the blast when some Argentines in the trenches command-detonated a land-mine. He suffered a concussion.

The SAS moved down a carefully prearranged exfiltration corridor to a forward RV manned by a captain and the squadron sergeant-major.

By 7:30 a.m., the security elements, mortar team, NGSFO, and the troop which had conducted the assault had withdrawn toward the LZ. When the helicopters appeared precisely at 9:30 a.m., the two casualties and the exhausted reconnaissance team were loaded into the aircraft. Within minutes the rest of the party was airborne and on their way to the *Hermes* and its escorts now streaming out to sea.

This was not the end of the Pebble Island story. After the *Coventry* was sunk on May 25 by Skyhawks operating from airfields inside Argentina, it was generally believed that the elusive radar site on the island had directed the aircraft onto the task force.

Another reconnaissance team, this time from the Royal Marine's Special Boat Service, was inserted by trawler and spent ten fruitless days searching for the installation. Nevertheless, a second raid was planned for June 15. This time two RAF Harriers would attack the airstrip, followed by a force of thirty-four SBS men who were ordered to eliminate any surviving Argentine personnel. When the Argentine forces on the Falklands surrendered on June 14, the waiting SBS moved in to accept the surrender of the Pebble Island garrison.

Nine years later, in the inhospitable wastes of western Iraq, the SAS and American Delta Force teams were to use raids and ambushes to fight a different sort of war.

First, there were the static surveillance teams watching the roads and tracks that ran between Baghdad and the area around the Iraqi airfields at H2 and H3 from which Scud missiles were being launched at Israel. Small and lightly armed, these teams acquired Scud convoys and other Iraqi traffic for American attack aircraft, sometimes directing the A10 Warthogs and F15E fighters onto cunningly camouflaged targets. The problem with using static roadwatch teams was that the Scud convoys were often miles away before the American aircraft could reach their target.

On January 20, the roadwatch patrols were joined by four SAS fighting columns, composed of four-wheel-drive vehicles and scouts on motorcycles. The SAS contingent was drawn from A Squadron (Groups One and Two) and D Squadron (Groups Three and Four). Within four days they had established bases from which the columns would deploy to attack convoys and targets more than 100 miles behind enemy lines.

The SAS operational area ran from Kabala, a mere fifty-odd miles southwest of Baghdad, to Iraq's borders with Syria and Jordan. To the north, the area was bounded by the H1, H2, and H3 airfields which lay close to the main road between Baghdad and Jordan. Further north, the US Army Special Forces Delta Force kept a watch on the roads and harried Scud convoys in an area close to Iraq's border with Syria.

Now the Scud convoys were placed under constant surveillance and attacked again and again by American aircraft. With their impressive firepower the reinforced SAS half-squadrons could also raid targets of opportunity before melting back to temporary hideouts in the desert.

Choice targets included a chain of high observation towers whose guards and electronic equipment kept a careful watch for intruders attempting to penetrate Iraq's borders.

Other targets included the microwave repeater towers and buried fiber-optic cables which provided Saddam Hussein with a secure communications link with Jordan and with his forces in western Iraq. By January 29, two Scud convoys had been identified and destroyed by aircraft, and the SAS had fought a running battle against an Iraqi unit of company strength which had attacked and almost overrun an SAS lying-up position.

The enemy withdrew with ten dead and three vehicles destroyed, but the SAS also suffered casualties and lost two vehicles. Seven SAS survivors of this action, including a severely injured lance-corporal, were cut off from the rest of their column. After walking for two days in the desert, they ambushed an Iraqi vehicle which they drove to the Saudi border.

On February 3, a column of two SAS troops was running parallel to a main highway when it spotted a heavily armed Scud convoy of around fourteen vehicles.

When an air strike by four F15 fighters only resulted in the destruction of one enemy vehicle, the SAS moved closer on a parallel course and raked the convoy with Milan antitank missiles and machinegun fire. Destroying a second vehicle, the SAS were driven off by vehicle mounted anti-aircraft guns; however they continued to shadow the convoy, calling in further air attacks.

Two days later, and in the course of just 24 hours, Group Two targeted a Scud convoy for an air strike, raided and destroyed an Iraqi observation tower, and mauled a second enemy post in a night-time battle.

On the night of February 8, an air strike was directed onto an important strategic radar site, and a patrol from A Squadron raided and destroyed a microwave communications tower. The prisoners from these operations were screened for military information and either released or flown to Saudi Arabia. After January 29, no Iraqi Scuds were fired from the SAS area of operations, and enemy activity was increasingly strangled by air power and guerrilla warfare.

An SAS Land Rover and its three-man crew disappeared during the close recce of a communications center near Nukhayb in the early hours of February 9. Three days later, two of the survivors turned up at an emergency RV.

Ambushed and pursued by the enemy, the crew had abandoned their disabled vehicle and escaped into the desert. The team commander, an SAS sergeant-major who was very badly wounded and unable to walk any farther, had been left to fend for himself. Although listed "missing presumed dead," the NCO was discovered by his pursuers, survived his wounds, and was repatriated at the end of hostilities.

Resupply and support for the fighting columns was provided by a convoy of ten four-ton trucks, escorted by armed Land Rovers and carrying much-needed supplies, armorers, and vehicle workshops ("E Squadron"). Crossing the Iraqi border on February 12, the temporary squadron and the fighting columns met at a rendezvous near the Wadi Tubal, some 70 miles south of "Scud Alley."

Two days later a further two Scud convoys had fallen prey to SAS observers and American aircraft. By February 17, the support column, its job well done, had exfiltrated enemy lines and returned to Saudi Arabia.

With the date for the ground offensive to liberate Kuwait rapidly approaching, and the remaining Scud launchers being withdrawn to bases in other parts of the country, the SAS turned to hitting Saddam's communications equipment. Seven repeater stations along the old highway between Baghdad and Amman were blown up in daylight. On February 21, as the regiment began to withdraw to its base in Saudi Arabia, one of the A Squadron columns ambushed a heavily protected Iraqi convoy in one of the last SAS actions inside Iraq. A running battle developed and, during one intense exchange of fire, the SAS suffered its last casualty of the war. A lance-corporal and motorcycle scout was hit in the chest and killed.

As the British withdrew from the contact, heavily armed Iraqi vehicles gave chase. The battle continued across the desert for 25 miles, with the SAS periodically stopping to ambush their pursuers with heavy Browning machine guns and antitank missiles. Finally, with casualties and vehicle losses mounting, the Iraqis withdrew from the chase and let their quarry disappear into the desert.

By the time the ground offensive to liberate Kuwait began on February 24, the 22nd SAS Regiment's war was almost over. This sustained guerrilla offensive, in an area of Iraq remote from the main theater of operations, had robbed Saddam Hussein of his only chance of bringing Israel into the conflict and possibly splitting the Coalition forces. His missile launchers had fallen prey not only to air attacks by prowling aircraft but to orchestrated ambushes prepared by the unseen eyes in the desert.

At the same time the SAS used two small raids to destroy the secure communications linking with his generals in western Iraq. This forced Iraqi military communications onto the airways, where it was more susceptible to interception by signals intelligence.

Many of the techniques for small-unit ambushes were refined in Borneo and Vietnam. Small reconnaissance patrols would often ambush tracks to obtain intelligence from captured documents and prisoners. The New Zealand and Australian SAS used five- to six-man patrols, while the Americans used seven- to eight-man patrols or twelve-man "A" Teams. All of these units were relatively small and thus relied heavily on "area weapons" such as Claymore mines and grenade launchers to decimate the frequently larger forces caught in the ambush.

The American Special Forces "A" Teams developed the following procedure. Once an ambush site was chosen, the team leader, radio operator, and a two-man snatch element moved into a position where they could observe a long stretch of the track or road.

To the sides, two soldiers, equipped with automatic rifles and M-79 grenade launchers, provided flank security at both ends of the ambush site. Six Claymores covered the killing ground, leaving a 2–3-yard "no-kill area" opposite the snatch element. To the rear of the ambush position, a four-man security or "gatekeeper" force covered the exfiltration route to the helicopter LZ.

When one of the flank security teams warned of an approaching enemy, the team commander lets them move into the killing ground before deciding whether the force was large enough to warrant the effort. On the other hand, if the enemy force was too big, only a fraction of the column was likely to be caught in the ambush. This might have resulted in a running battle, with the possibility of the team being destroyed.

Once the decision was taken to detonate the Claymores, the radio operator made an immediate request for helicopter extraction. Those enemy who survived the mines were dispatched with small-arms fire. Soldiers lucky enough to be caught in the "no fire area" were taken prisoner. The snatch squad also searched the dead for maps, documents, unit identification flashes, or anything that might help build up a picture of the type of enemy forces operating in the area.

When the squad returned, they moved down the escape route with the team commander's group. Simultaneously, the flank elements activated delayed-action Claymores before withdrawing, followed by the "gatekeepers" who left more mines to delay pursuit.

Such detailed and well-oiled professionalism was essential for survival in the jungles of Vietnam. This was particularly true of the "Recce-Ambush" technique employed by the Australian SAS and the attached troop of New Zealand SAS (NZSAS). Once the patrol had lost its "invisibility," the move to the extraction RV could become a race for life itself.

In late 1969, an NZSAS patrol was inserted into an area where the Ho Chi Minh Trail crossed the border into South Vietnam. Its job was to identify those mountain and jungle trails being used by the Communists to infiltrate men and supplies into the South. This information was to be radioed back to the Australian Task Force to assist the targeting of bombing raids.

The first two days were spent carefully surveying a series of narrow tracks that showed little sign of recent use. Throughout their reconnaissance, patrol discipline was strictly enforced: talking was kept to a minimum, LUPs were carefully concealed, and all food was eaten cold. Additionally, the patrol's movement mirrored that of their enemy—moving during the daytime and halting for a two-hour rest at midday. In this way the New Zealanders planned to avoid walking into a VC encampment or ambush.

On the morning of the third day, the patrol discovered another track running northeast. This time the path showed evidence of recent use, and the patrol set up a well-concealed OP. Almost immediately, a five-man party of guerrillas, well armed and carrying packs, passed the hide. They moved quickly and were well spaced to minimize casualties in the event of an ambush. The NZSAS let them pass.

No further traffic was observed on the track until the morning of the sixth day—the day scheduled for the team to be extracted by helicopter. In the early hours of the morning, the soldiers laid an ambush, catching five VC in a devastating hail of projectiles from fifteen Claymore mines. Almost at once, a large Communist force travelling some way behind, possibly a regular NVA unit, made a flanking counterattack. The SAS responded by setting off the rest of the Claymores and laying down a high rate of suppressive fire, to confuse the enemy as to the size of the patrol.

With the counterattack blunted, the SAS slipped away toward their extraction RV. Two hours later, another very large enemy force tried to encircle the New Zealanders. The patrol commander called for an emergency extraction, while he and his men attempted to keep ahead of the enemy.

Fortunately for the patrol, the contact with the enemy was broken again, and the SAS reached the LZ without further incident.

■ Assassination and Abduction

While the museums of many clandestine forces sport weapons such as projectiles dipped in deadly poisons, knives with spring-propelled blades, and suppressed handguns, these can be used only on the very few occasions when an intelligence operative can get close to his or her target. In fact, in the very few instances when a key military or political figure has been liquidated in wartime, he has almost always been caught in a "blood-and-guts" raid or ambush, sprung by commando forces. Because of the security measures taken to protect such individuals, many of these operations either fail or turn into suicide missions.

High-risk targets are rarely caught in an ambush because they vary both their route and times of movement. One of Hitler's key lieutenants, Obergruppenführer Reinhard Heydrich, refused to take these security precautions and so unwittingly set in motion his own assassination.

Every morning Heydrich was driven to work along the same route, in an open-topped car, with only his driver for company. The route took him through the Prague suburb of Zizkov, where the car was forced to slow down as it negotiated a steep bend. It was here that the three-man Anthropoid team ambushed Heydrich on the morning of May 27, 1942. Even a minimum escort would have foiled this operation. Although the three Czechs were intelligence SOF, trained by Britain's Special Operations Executive (SOE), it was no easy matter to carry weapons and grenades around the streets of Prague.

On this morning, Heydrich was late, and when the lookout finally saw the Mercedes approaching, he used a mirror to flash a signal to Sgt. Josef Gabcik, who began to assemble the Sten gun he was carrying in his briefcase. In any event, the submachine gun jammed, and it was left to the third commando, Sgt. Jan Kubis, to throw a bomb which exploded against the rear wheel. The explosion broke one of Heydrich's ribs and drove fragments of horsehair from the upholstery into his body. Even so, Heydrich and his driver, armed only with pistols, routed their attackers.

Heydrich was not mortally wounded but died later of blood poisoning. The commandos committed suicide when the Germans assaulted the Karel Boromejsky Church where they were hiding. As a result of this operation, security measures were tightened, and a later operation, to assassinate the Minister for Education and Propaganda in the Czech protectorate government, failed.

Operation Anthropoid was one of the last successful wartime assassinations against a key military or political figure. In April 1944, two SOE agents kidnapped the German commander on Crete; in retrospect, however, the removal of this unpopular man was seen to provide a significant boost to the island's garrison.

Several attempts were also made, in North Africa and France, to kill General Erwin Rommel, either by the classical commando raid or by targeting his headquarters for air strikes. All of these operations failed. Ironically, providence and an attentive British soldier may have been responsible for Rommel being strafed by British aircraft during the Normandy campaign.

In the months before the Allied invasion of France, the Germans captured some British commandos from a beach reconnaissance party landed to survey the Normandy coastline. Seeking clues to the proposed Allied beaches, the general foolishly interviewed the captives at his headquarters in a château near La Petite Roche Guyon. One of the British soldiers spotted a road sign and managed to smuggle this information back to London from his POW camp in Germany. The Allied fighter-bombers are reputed to have pounced on Rommel's car on the road outside his headquarters.

The former Soviet Union accorded a high priority to assassination and abduction missions in support of wartime operations. Soviet intelligence agents, posing as Polish art dealers selling commercial prints on the doorstep, are believed to have recorded the daily movements of pilots and other key military personnel targeted for assassination in the event of a Soviet invasion of Sweden. Numerous incursions along Sweden's coastline by divers, mini-subs, and mother submarines led to the suggestion that Spetsnaz sabotage and assassination teams might be infiltrated by sea, just before the outbreak of hostilities.

One key operation during the 1979 Soviet invasion of Afghanistan was the liquidation of President Amin and his close advisors. Department Eight of the KGB planned the raid on the heavily defended Darulaman Palace in Kabul. A Soviet airborne battalion eliminated opposition outside the palace, leaving the actual attack on the building to a GRU/MVD Spetsnaz force under the command of Colonel Boyarinov, commander of the KGB sabotage school at Balashikha.

To ensure the total liquidation of its occupants, Boyarinov gave the Soviet Airborne orders to shoot anyone seen leaving the palace during the attack. The order cost him his life. Amin's personal bodyguards fought like tigers, inflicting casualties on the Spetsnaz troopers, who began to run out of ammunition.

When Boyarinov left the palace to get reinforcements from the Soviet paras, he was promptly shot. As Afghan resistance finally faltered, the Spetsnaz overwhelmed the defenders and went on an orgy of killing. Only Lieutenant Colonel Talybov survived. Operating as a Soviet agent, he had infiltrated the household as a cook. During the attack he hid under the stairs until the bloodletting was over. If the Spetsnaz team had operated alone, under wartime conditions, this mission probably would have failed.

The KGB has always maintained departments dedicated to peacetime sabotage and assassination. Many such operations were directed against easy civilian targets, such as Eastern Bloc dissidents living in the West. In early 1961, the KGB dispatched a team to assassinate the Iranian Shah, who had been brought to power by a CIA-instigated coup. The Soviet paramilitaries put a large bomb in a Volkswagen which was left on the route between the Shah's palace and the parliament building. The bomb failed to explode.

Since the fall of the old Soviet Union, military Spetsnaz veterans have been recruited into special units of the KGB Border Guards Directorate. These "Special-Designation Special Purpose Detachments" (OSNAZ) are subdivided into "Alpha Teams," tasked with intervening in hostage rescue situations and civil disturbances. It is thought that during the 1989–91 unrest in the Baltic Republics, Alpha Teams, disguised as paratroops, carried out a series of assassinations against journalists, police officers, and civilian protesters.

The attack on the Lithuanian television station in January 1991 is said to have been spearheaded by Alpha Teams who were responsible for many of the civilians killed during the assault. The murder of eleven Lithuanian policemen and border guards in July 1991 is also credited to Alpha Teams.

An OSNAZ chief instructor, A. I. Dolmatov, wrote a manual for Alpha Team training which was published in 1989. The text, dealing with reconnaissance, abductions, prisoner transportation, and assassinations, shows diagrams of Alpha Team members killing US servicemen such as Special Forces personnel. Evoking earlier Spetsnaz manuals, Dolmatov's text nevertheless has few surprises. It teaches crude but workable commando-type techniques that became the hallmark of the KGB. One illustration shows a four-man vehicle team abducting a person from a street. Two operatives grab the target's arms and legs and carry him to a waiting car, where the driver sits behind the steering wheel with the engine running, while the lookout is ready to prevent passersby intervening in the abduction.

The North Koreans followed the Soviet model for peacetime assassination without much success. After the failure of the 1968 "Blue House" Raid, the North Koreans used bombs for two further attempts on the life of South Korean President Park Chung Hee, one of which killed his wife.

Another commando operation was launched in 1983, to kill President Park's successor, General Chun Doo-Hwan. The attempt took place in Rangoon, Burma, where, during his visit, the South Korean President was to lay a wreath at a shrine known as the Martyr's Mausoleum.

The three-man team arrived disguised as seamen aboard a North Korean freighter. They used a safe house and a cache of weapons and explosives supplies by intelligence support personnel. The security around the shrine was penetrated and a bomb planted, but this exploded prematurely, when the commandos mistook the South Korean Ambassador's car for that carrying the President. The three North Koreans were all killed or captured before they could return to their ship.

The CIA and US SOF are forbidden to carry out peacetime assassinations. The US government also disapproves of abduction missions, the singular exception being those directed at international terrorists. The ruling against assassinations resulted from the CIA's bungling attempts to remove political leaders unfriendly to American interests during the Cold War.

Realizing that only agents could penetrate the security around high-profile targets and make a successful escape, the Agency used Cuban expatriates and mercenaries to make more than twenty-six attempts on the life of Cuban President Fidel Castro. Some attempts failed when the assassin, often a close associate of Castro, experienced a change of heart or when Agency equipment failed. One assassination team managed to land by sea and penetrate Castro's residence armed with an antitank missile launcher, only to discover at the last minute that the bazooka no longer worked.

Both CIA operatives and US Special Forces took part in the Phoenix program to wrest South Vietnamese hamlets from the Vietcong. The cutting edge of the program was provided by the Provincial Reconnaissance or Counter-Terror Teams who would enter the VC sanctuary areas at night, to assassinate or abduct an individual identified by intelligence as being a Communist Party chief, tax collector, or member of a propaganda cadre. Personnel accorded the highest priority within the shadowy, illegal VC infrastructure were the members of the 35,000-strong *Ban-an-ninh* or VC secret police.

This organization conducted assassinations, terror, and kidnappings as well as controlling 25,000 agents in intelligence operations against the South Vietnamese: it was, in fact, the largest spy apparatus in the history of warfare.

The CIA claimed the program was responsible for capturing 28,000 VC, killing another 20,000, and obtaining the defections of a further 17,000 guerrillas. However, operatives have admitted that Phoenix was indiscriminate and became a terror program in its own right. If intelligence could only place a target within a certain area of the village, all the huts within that area would be raided and occupants killed.

Reviewing CIA operations, the US Congress decided that such missions were unacceptable. On February 18, 1976, President Gerald Ford issued Executive Order 11905: "No employee of the United States Government shall engage in, or conspire to engage in, political assassination."

Abduction and assassination are part of the wartime role of the US counterterrorist force, Operational Detachment-Delta. It has trained in this role during NATO exercises in Germany, but the British SAS and units from other Alliance partners have declined to take part.

Combat Rescue

Aircrew are expensive to train and difficult to replace; their loss in combat can leave the air force with more aircraft than pilots. Somebody has to get them back, and this is one mission that the SOF can perform for a parent service. It is a job that requires all the usual SF skills and a high degree of medical expertise, in the event of the aircrew being wounded in combat or injured while leaving the aircraft. SOF units may also be ordered to recover intelligence agents, documents, or special equipment.

In the first instance, aircrew recovery falls to Search and Rescue (SAR) organizations such as the USAF's Aerospace Rescue and Recovery Service, or the USAF's Special Operations Squadrons (SOS). On the basis of lessons learned in Vietnam, it was calculated that a pilot could be extracted successfully if the rescue helicopter reached him within 15 minutes. After 30 minutes, the chances of rescue rapidly diminished. Local forces and small army SOF teams in the immediate area offer pilots a second chance of rescue, rendering first aid and securing their safety until an SAR helicopter arrives.

Specialized ground teams were first used in the Balkans during World War II. Airfields were built in areas held by partisans, and Air Crew Rescue Teams, comprising a doctor, a radio operator, and an OSS officer under the command of an Air Force captain, gathered together evaders and provided prompt medical treatment and evacuation.

Such was the efficiency of this operation that one B-17 Flying Fortress crew was back at its home airfield a mere four days after crash-landing in Yugoslavia. The operation is said to have rescued 3,870 aircrew and approximately 2,000 other nationals on the run from the Nazis.

Pilots shot down over occupied Europe, who were lucky enough to contact a Resistance escape line, were funnelled down a series of safe houses into neutral Spain. Their chances of escape were good if they remained free for the first two hours after bailing out. Some 3,000 aircrew who came down in northwest Europe successfully avoided capture. When the SAS arrived in France in 1944 to support the Normandy invasion, they helped rescue another 366 Allied aircrew, shot down behind the battlefield.

As aerial warfare became more sophisticated, aircrew became an elite whose long and expensive training warranted every effort to recover them if they were shot down behind enemy lines. Britain assigned this role to 23 SAS (V). In Vietnam, American SAR units and highly trained commandos were both used to recover aircrew under a dedicated intelligence program: Bright Light.

British and American forces came together again in the Gulf, but as specialized ground teams and the USAF's Aerospace Rescue and Recovery Service were not deployed to Saudi Arabia, combat rescue fell to Allied forces in the immediate area and to the helicopters of USAF's Special Operations Squadrons. During air strikes inside Iraq and Kuwait, thirty-eight Allied aircraft were shot down, fourteen of them American. Twenty-one US aircrew, who were shot down over cities or concentrations of enemy troops, were captured, while others found themselves in the desert and on the run.

Lieutenant Devon Jones, a Navy F-14 pilot, was rescued by a 20th SOS MH-53J helicopter. Enemy soldiers were already closing in on his

Combat rescue

The structure of the combat-rescue team places heavy emphasis on battlefield first aid as many pilots ejecting from high-speed aircraft suffer injuries during the ejection or subsequent parachute descent. Ideally, first aid is followed by immediate evacuation.

position, using DF equipment to locate his SAR beacon. The helicopter destroyed two Iraqi trucks before lifting to safety. The F-14's other crew member landed elsewhere and was captured. The second successful operation resulted in the rescue of an F-16 pilot shot down in southern Iraq, just 40 miles from the Saudi border. The pilot's rescuers were part of the 3rd Battalion, 160th Special Operations Aviation Regiment, whose helicopters normally support a US Ranger battalion. The other two pilots are reputed to have been rescued from inside Kuwait, one by the Kuwaiti Resistance and the other by an army ground team.

An unsuccessful rescue mission was mounted for the two-man crew of an F-15E who were shot down in western Iraq while hunting Scuds in the H3 area. The 21st SOS, which was assigned the mission, was based in Turkey, which meant that an MC-130 had to overfly Syrian territory in order to refuel the returning rescue helicopters. It took three days to obtain permission from the Syrian Government. Meanwhile, the nearest SAS teams conducted an unsuccessful search for the airmen, who were nearly 10 miles from their last reported position. By the time the Pave Low helicopters arrived, the airmen had been captured.

Army SOF may also be asked to raid security prisons and prisoner of war camps or organize the escape of soldiers and civilians. The Italian dictator Benito Mussolini was rescued from his mountain prison in the Hotel Albergo-Rifugio in 1943 by German Special Forces. As the Italian government moved him from prison to prison after the Italian surrender, German commandos were never far behind. Finally, Otto Skorzeny's crack paratroops landed by glider, stormed the hotel, and flew Il Duce to Germany.

The US 6th Ranger Battalion is credited with the largest ever rescue, releasing 513 POWs from a Japanese camp at Cabanatuan in the Philippines in 1945. Fearing that the guards might massacre the prisoners as Luzon was liberated, a reinforced Ranger company moved ahead of American forces to effect a rescue. Linking up with local guerrillas, the Rangers took the camp in a classical raid, despite a 500-strong guard contingent and the presence of a Japanese division in the immediate vicinity. Two blocking forces of guerrillas effectively isolated the Japanese garrison by laying ambushes on the road on either side of the camp.

At the last moment, they completed the camp's isolation by cutting the telephone wires. Ranger special task squads then moved forward and eliminated the guard towers and machine-gun posts with bazooka antitank rockets. When Japanese reinforcements poured out of their barracks, they too were wiped out by rocket and small-arms fire. Other pockets of guards were pinned down by support fire and, where necessary, mopped up piecemeal by groups of Rangers. Then the assault platoons moved forward to break through the main gate, destroy the camp's radios, and make contact with the POWs. After only 30 minutes, the prisoners were conducted down a cleared lane to freedom. As the Rangers withdrew, the guerillas, who had broken off their battle with an estimated 800–2,000 Japanese, provided flank security for the 25-mile evacuation to the advancing American forces.

During the Vietnam War, Special Forces and civilian irregular troops raided Communist POW camps inside sanctuary areas in South Vietnam or in Cambodia, Laos, and North Vietnam. Conducted with the aim of releasing American servicemen, these 120 or so operations were failures in that they released 368 South Vietnamese troops but only one American, who later died of his wounds. The most spectacular failure was the raid on the POW camp at Son Tay, North Vietnam, in 1970. As US aircraft crippled the North Vietnamese air defense systems, a helicopter-borne force left staging posts in Thailand to mount a daring assault on the camp and nearby installations, only to discover, too late, that the prisoners had been moved.

The most unusual operation took place in 1966, when a U-2 spyplane was lost over Cambodia and the 5th SFG was ordered to do everything to recover the aircraft's black box flight recorder. A mobile guerrilla force, comprised of a Special Forces "A" Team and 250 Cambodian White Khmer guerrillas, slipped through the Communist sanctuary areas and supply routes to a spot in the Cambodian jungle that had been pinpointed by aerial reconnaissance. There, in a long scar in the forest, lay the remains of the high-altitude reconnaissance aircraft, but the Vietcong had got there before them and the black box was gone.

Assuming that the Communists would take the box to a regional headquarters, the mission commander, Captain James Gritz, laid ambushes along the jungle trails to capture prisoners for interrogation. Finally, Gritz obtained his information from a captured VC guerrilla, and Gritz and his men moved close to a heavily guarded encampment, which was aware of the American incursion and on full alert. The only place on the camp's perimeter that was not guarded was the latrine area and Gritz used this weakness to storm the camp and recapture the box. The mobile guerrilla force accomplished this "mission impossible" without the loss of a single man.

As already mentioned, like the operation at Son Tay, the 1980 American operation to free the Tehran hostages ("Eagle Claw") also failed, but American Special Forces are reputed to have rescued an important CIA agent from Gamboa prison during their invasion of Panama (1989). Other notable full-scale parachute assault were used by Belgium (1964) and France (1978) to rescue civilians from rebel troops in the Congo (now Zaire).

CHAPTER 7

Disaster

IT IS NOT ONLY PILOTS AND AGENTS who find themselves on the run behind enemy lines. The aircraft carrying the team to their prearranged DZ may be forced to ditch; or a soldier may become separated during the parachute descent or as a result of an enemy ambush during the move to the operational area. Flank security may become particularly hazardous on raids and ambushes as such offensive actions will provoke a full-blown response against parties conducting long-term guerrilla operations. In particular, American Special Forces may be given frequent opportunities to practice their survival, evasion, resistance to interrogation, and escape (SERE) skills during enemy sweeps through their Guerrilla Warfare Operational Area (GWOA).

The arithmetic of escape

An escaper crawls through the last coils of wire of his POW compound and runs into the trees. An hour later, the escape is discovered. The security forces are now faced with formidable problems in attempting to recapture him. In the absence of well-defined tracks, the soldier may be assumed to have taken any direction, and he has been free for an hour. Assuming that he remained on the move and kept up a pace of around 5 miles per hours, the zone of probability in which he is likely to be found is a circle with a 5-mile radius. This circle has an area of 78 sq. miles. After several hours on the run, it is possible for the evader to cover twice that distance, so that the enemy is faced with searching a circular area with a 10-mile radius: 314 sq. miles. These simple calculations demonstrate the importance of moving away from the focus of enemy activity.

The enemy may give up the chase—hoping that the escaper will betray his own position or surrender when tired and hungry—or attempt to cast a net around him. The static elements in this net include blocking forces, ambushes on roads and tracks, and OPs on high ground. Within the net, mobile elements such as patrols, dog teams, and aircraft attempt to reestablish contact and narrow down the area to be searched. If the escaper keeps away from roads and dwellings and avoids open ground, he should be able to put some distance between himself and the enemy before lying low until things quiet down.

▰ To Run or Not to Run

The evader has three choices in making his escape. The first is to remain in a concealed position and wait for his own forces to arrive. The second is to move closer to the fighting, in the hope of being picked up by the helicopters of a friendly Search and Rescue organization. The last alternative is to make the long and dangerous journey to exfiltration RVs on the nearest border or front line. Border defenses were outlined in chapter 2. The battle area is no less hostile than a border area to the man on the run. One escape and evasion manual offers the following advice:

> If evaders are in the forward edge of the battle area (FEBA) and feel sure that friendly forces are moving in their direction, they should seek concealment and allow the FEBA to overrun their position. Evaders' attempts at penetrating the FEBA should be avoided. Evaders face stiff opposition from both sides.

Some operations leave SOF with only one choice. American and British teams inside Iraq were forced to find their own way home since Operation Desert Storm had the limited objective of liberating Kuwait. The lucky teams, which were still in radio contact with headquarters, arranged an emergency extraction. The others were faced with a long walk. But how do you cover hundreds of miles through a landscape that is more hostile than the enemy?

One essential component in the escape plan is fitness. World War II operations demonstrated that fit, highly motivated commandos could lie up in the heat of the day and still cover 30–40 miles each night even though they had very little food or water. After one of David Stirling's SAS raids on a German airfield in North Africa, Lieutenant Frazer's troop waited six days at an RV for a pickup that never arrived. With their water almost gone, the men began a 200-mile journey home. Forcing the pace on the night marches, they covered the distance in just eight days.

During the Gulf War, more than one road-watch team found themselves in the same position as the earlier SAS raiders. The SAS planners identified three major road supply routes (MSR) running between central Iraq and the three airfields (H1, H2, and H3) close to the Syrian border and within Scud range of Israel. On their initial insertion by helicopter, the surveillance team chosen to watch the southernmost route (Road-Watch South) was dismayed to find themselves on a stark flat stony plain. Once the convoys were attacked, the most rudimentary search would have revealed their hide—and there was nowhere to run. Deciding that a team operating in this area would require their own transport, the insertion was aborted. Road-Watch Central arrived in Land Rovers to find that their proposed OP was also on a flat stretch of stony desert. After calling in an air strike on two mobile radar vehicles, their position became compromised, and they were forced to make their way back to the safety of the Saudi border.

The most isolated team was unlucky. On January 22, Road-Watch North was inserted by helicopter close to the main highway between Iraq and Jordan and close to the heart of what became known as

"Scud alley." With the wind driving sleet and snow into their eyes, the eight-man team moved closer to the road until they could just see the headlights of vehicles on the horizon. They then dug a hide in a small cave and began the monotonous cycle of watching, eating, and sleeping. On the second day, a perverse twist of fate persuaded the commander of an Iraqi convoy that their piece of desert was an ideal site for his anti-aircraft guns. This effectively removed any chance of resupplying or extracting the team by helicopter, short of calling an air strike virtually onto their own position. In the afternoon, even this decision was taken out of their hands. The presence of the Iraqi vehicles attracted the locals, and as happened several times in this conflict, curious civilians virtually stumbled into the hides of the SAS and other special forces. In this case, a child herding goats stumbled on the SAS men in the cave. Like their American counterparts, the SAS men were not prepared to kill children, and the boy was allowed to pass. There was also the possibility that the child would say nothing to the Iraqi soldiers manning the anti-aircraft battery. This illusion was brutally dispelled several minutes later, when the Iraqi camp became a confusion of shouts and vehicle engines. Stopping only briefly to return the enemy's fire, the SAS made their escape. When one of the large anti-aircraft rounds sliced through one of the soldier's packs, the SAS men decided to discard their Bergens, retaining only their weapons and escape belts. Attached to the belts were water bottles and pouches containing ammunition, a little food, survival equipment, and SAR beacons. The men were now on the run in one of the worst Iraqi winters in recent times. The Syrian border was more than 100 miles away, and the specter of capture was ever present. More than a little anxiety must have been generated by the thought that, if taken, they faced interrogation by a secret police apparatus with an appalling record on human rights.

Moving as fast as possible in the dreadful conditions, the inevitable happened, and the team became separated into a group of three and another party of five soldiers. On the second night, the three-man group suddenly discovered that they had lost one of their number. They retraced their route but were unable to find him. Sometime on that night of January 26, Sergeant Vincent Phillips, clad in only light desert fatigues, died of exposure in the snow.

In the early morning light and still only 30-odd miles from the road-watch position, the two SAS survivors decided to split up in order to increase their chances of slipping past the Iraqi search parties. Very soon one of the SAS men found himself surrounded by militia, and after a brief firefight, he surrendered. The last man, Chris Ryan, an SAS corporal, slipped down into the more sheltered valley of the Euphrates River. Moving by night, he followed the line of the river which ran toward the Syrian border. Avoiding roads and habitation, the solider replenished his water bottle by stripping off and crawling across the mud to where the reed beds mingled with the icy green water. On one occasion, he was forced to use the outflow of an industrial waste pipe. There was no food and the capacity to place one foot in front of the other was provided by his superb physical fitness and reserves of mental stamina. On the last two nights, as he moved toward the border, he walked across the desert without water. After covering 117 miles, he finally crossed into Syria. Breaking down his weapon and carrying the parts in a small sack, he made his way to the British Embassy in Damascus.

The other group of five evaders were luckier at first. They reached Al Qaim, near the border with Syria and close to the American area of operations. Then, inside the knot of tracks that ran between the two countries and a mere six miles from the national border, a series of contacts was initiated by Iraqi border guards. During one of these clashes, Trooper Consiglio was hit in the head and killed. A second soldier was wounded in the elbow and ankle. Unable to move, the wounded soldier was taken prisoner. Patrol Commander Andy McNab was captured some hours later.

For the other two soldiers, the only escape route lay across the floodwaters of the Euphrates River. The two SAS men plunged into the fast-flowing river which was swollen by the melting snow from its mountain tributaries and more than 400 yards wide. When they reached the other side, Lance-Corporal Lane collapsed. Weakened by exhaustion and hunger, he fell prey to hypothermia and quickly lapsed into a coma. Remaining with his dying friend, the other soldier, also a lance-corporal, forfeited his last chance of freedom. Trooper Consiglio and Lance-Corporal Lane were both awarded post-humous Military Medals, the SAS sergeant and leader of the five-man group received the Distinguished Conduct Medal.

Evasion is easier than escape and the best form of resistance to in-terrogation is not to be taken in the first place. Evaders are in a better situation than escapers since they are armed and well supplied with survival and navigation equipment, carried in their belt pouches or pockets. The escaper faces a longer journey and, if lucky, he may have been given organized contact RVs before the breakout. If not, he may have to rely on informal meetings with reliable people, such as doc-tors and priests, in the hope of making contact with an escape line.

■ Evasion

Enemy ground and aerial patrols may search for footprints, old camp-fires, survival shelters, discarded equipment, and other telltale signs which indicate the presence of strangers in the area. Civilians, such as farmers, may spot tracks and camp spoils, or notice the theft of stock or crops, and contact the local authorities who initiate an or-ganized search. Other hostile observers may remain unseen. Satellites and aircraft, which take visual or infrared photographs, provide a record that can be studied in minute detail. The main disadvantage of the photograph is that it covers a short period of time, making de-tection of movement difficult. However, successive images of an area may reveal man-made structures such as campsites and shelters. The evader must consider this possibility when selecting rest sites.

For his part, the evader uses the same tools as his pursuers—his ears and eyes, as well as camouflage and fieldcraft—to remain unde-tected. Night is the safest time to move across enemy-held territory, with the evader using the last hour of darkness either to select a con-cealed LUP or build a shelter. This has the additional advantage in temperate climates of allowing the man to move when it is cold and sleep when it may be slightly warmer. However, this may not be

Stealing food

Close to agricultural areas the evader has to take particular care to remain "invisible." One soldier is taking root vegetables from the outermost furrow of the crop, while his companion fills a plastic bag with water from a puddle. No telltale footprints will be left on the field.

possible in difficult terrain such as mountains, jungles, or swamps. Obstacles such as scree slopes, cliffs, tree roots, holes, or branches can cause serious injury and make for very noisy travelling. If forced to travel at night, the evader might find a stout stick to probe the ground ahead or protect his face from branches.

The terrain ahead of the evader will largely determine his route as it must meet his needs for food, water, shelter, and cover. Moorland and open grassland offer little cover and may necessitate night travel. Isolated clusters of alder, birch, or willow and areas of gorse offer concealment; and, during spring and summer, edible plants, berries, and the tops of ferns are available as food. Hills, stony outcrops, and wooded areas usually harbor rabbits, hares, other small mammals, amphibians, and birds.

Living off the land

The evader can gather edible plants as he moves across the country or when he makes his overnight rest stop. Snares, nets, and fishing lines can be left out overnight in the hope of securing a fish or small animal to put in the stew. If the evader moves by night, food and shelter have to be sought in the first hours of dawn. Unobtrusive fishing lines and nets can be left out during the daylight hours while the evader rests.

Mountains and hills are generally bleaker, with a smaller range of wildlife, and sparsely populated, yet they offer good cover. The best evasion route lies between one-half and two-thirds of the way up the slope, following the contours around the mountains. This avoids tracks and roads in the valleys and continual exhausting climbs and descents. Remaining below the summit also ensures the evader is never silhouetted on the skyline. Below the treeline, in needle-leafed forests such as pine, fir, spruce, and hemlock, the trees grow close to-gether, offering cover and concealment. However, these forests harbor few edible food plants. In winter, a snow-covered terrain presents additional difficulties, with deep snow and ice hampering movement and providing a deceptive cover over dangerous obstacles such as crevasses and partially frozen lakes and rivers. Cold, wet conditions, exacerbated by the windchill factor, pose formidable problems in meeting the necessities of food, shelter, and warmth, while a white snowscape strips the evader of camouflage and faithfully records his tracks.

In contrast, deciduous or broad-leafed woods and forests hold a wide range of edible plants and animal life. The forest floor is normally littered with fallen branches and other debris that may be used for firewood and shelter materials. In Europe, scattered woodland often borders agricultural land. Although this provides an opportunity to steal stock, produce, and farmyard garbage, it also represents a danger area for the evader. Fields may be frequented by the farmer and his workers, and provide little cover. The danger of leaving footprints in ploughed or cultivated land restricts movement to hedgerows. The evader is advised to wrap his boots in cloth or other loose material to make his footprints look blurred and old. Root crops are stored in batches after harvesting, and these may be raided. Crops growing in the fields may be taken safely from the outermost furrows. Livestock, such as sheep, may be present, but pursuing, butchering, and cooking them are difficult to hide in such a high-risk area. Free-range fowl provide the opportunity to take eggs and birds, but the farmer usually knows how many eggs his flock lays and counts his animals, although the small, occasional loss may go unnoticed. Dogs will probably prevent the evader from foraging for eggs in barns. Most farmers will also spot the difference between the activities of a fox or mink and a human foray.

The evader's route should dogleg around heavily populated areas such as towns, cities, and their suburbs. Without assistance in the form of clothes, identification papers, and guides, the evader's anonymity will not survive frequent contacts with civilians, soldiers, and police. Where contact is likely, an early British manual gives this advice:

1. Put on a bold front, do not appear "furtive," this arouses suspicion.
2. Obtain unobtrusive clothing and assume a definite identity, if possible, i.e., carry a spade.
3. Keep clean (shave if possible).
4. Make use of bicycles and trains. The destination of [the] train is often marked on the bottom left-hand corner of trucks. Keep away from stations.
5. Beware of *children* and *dogs* (often the first to notice strangers).
6. Never move on roads. If crossing a road, locate sentries and, if necessary, use a diversion. At night, use the noise and light of a passing vehicle to make the crossing.

The enemy's cordon and search techniques are aided in no small part by natural barriers such as rivers, roads, and railway lines. Checkpoints at bridges and ferries can be avoided by fording, swimming, or floating across the water obstacle, using a log or an improvised buoyancy aid. Railway tracks and roads are also crossed at night, after checking carefully for the presence of mobile patrols or sentries. On a railway, the lines can be used as camouflage, if the evader crawls across sideways, keeping his body parallel to the rails.

Survival

Much has been written about survival by the graduates of military survival schools. Most civilian survival situations, however, will differ radically from that facing the military evader or escaper. Both face the common enemies of hunger, thirst, loneliness, boredom, fatigue, cold, and pain from injuries or wounds. In addition, the solider must live with the ever-present danger of capture. "Combat survival" tailors survival training to the realities of life as a fugitive. Food, water, shelter, and cover have to be found along the route to friendly or neutral territory. The evader also needs to know in what direction to travel and how long it is going to take him to reach a feasible destination. Thrown onto his own resources, every day he will become weaker, more lethargic, and less able to combat illness and disease.

Deprived of his map and compass, or the more covert button compass (designed to be hidden on the uniform and, if discovery seems likely, swallowed and later recovered), the evader can fall back on the rudiments of navigational astronomy.

The evader who knows the length of his stride can keep track of the distance covered by counting his paces and knotting a piece of string, or putting a pebble in his pocket, at every hundred paces. Speed and distance will be affected by weather conditions and available light (moonlight, cloud, mist) and the type of terrain to be crossed (open ground, woodland, hills). Even after determining the cardinal points of the compass, a night walk in close ground, with frequent detours to avoid obstacles, can result in the evader becoming disoriented and lost.

On clear nights in the Northern Hemisphere, the Plough (Ursa Major), Cassiopeia, and Orion can be used to locate the North Star (Polaris). A vertical line from Polaris to an imaginary point on the horizon indicates true north, allowing the evader to calculate the other points of the compass and find a reference landmark on the horizon in his direction of travel. As each landmark is reached, the technique is repeated. In the Southern Hemisphere, the long arm of the Southern Cross is extended toward the horizon for 4.5 times its length, bringing the observer to an imaginary point immediately above true south on the horizon.

If the observer cannot find a directional star, any star may be watched over two fixed points (e.g., the sights of a stationary rifle or stakes driven into the ground). The stars travel east to west in great arcs. A star watched for 10–20 minutes and which appears to be:

Falling, is approximately west.

Rising, is approximately east.

Travelling on a flat arc to the observer's right, is in the south.

Travelling on a flat arc to the observer's left, is in the north.

Similar rules can be applied to the phases of the moon with respect to the sun's position:

If the moon rises before sunset, the illuminated side will be in the west.

(A) Temporary rest stop

Resting for 5–10 minutes every hour, the evader carefully chooses an area of natural cover.

(B) The overnight rest stop

In a mild climate, felled trees, a large bush, or the boughs of a fallen pine tree can furnish the evader with an overnight shelter offering some protection from the elements. This saves both time and the valuable energy needed to build a survival shelter.

If the moon rises after sunset, the illuminated side will be in the east.

A full or half moon can be used to find direction, provided the observer knows the local time.

Local Time (hrs)	1800	2100	2400	0300	0600
First Quarter	S	SW	W	–	–
Full Moon	E	SE	S	SW	W
Last Quarter	–	–	E	SE	S

The necessities for life For the short-term evader who retains his equipment, all he needs for survival should be found in his belt pouches. In contrast, the escaper may need to improvise:

- Fire-lighting—magnifying glass, waterproof matches, flint and steel, or cigarette lighter.
- Fishing line and hook and snares—bootlaces, needle, and wire.
- Water container—condom or plastic bag.
- Navigation—button compass, or astro-navigation.
- Cutting and skinning game—knife and wire saw.
- Mugs, mess tin, and cooker—discarded tin cans.
- Windproof coat—sacking.
- Pack, pouches, and belt—old tarpaulin and string.
- Spoon—wood hollowed out by carving or burning a depression.
- Water filter—sand-filled sock.

If the evader moves by day, it may be possible to collect food and water during the journey, spending the last hours of the day finding shelter and eating. This is more difficult on night walks. The first few hours of light may have to be spent looking for food and water. Either way, the construction of elaborate survival shelters consumes too much valuable time, particularly as the area will have to be sterilized before the next move. Moreover, in areas of enemy activity, campsites and shelters will be an unwarranted self-advertisement. Properly insulated with dry leaves or bracken, a range of natural structures can serve to keep the soldier dry and warm. Examples include:

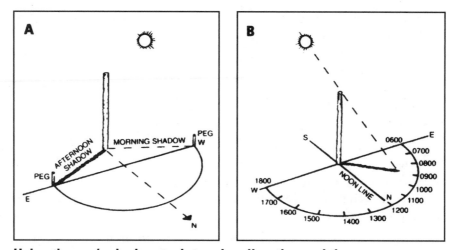

Using the sun's shadow to determine direction and time

A. The sun's shadow can be used to determine direction. A peg is used to mark the tip of the shadow five or ten minutes before noon and when the sun is approaching its zenith. A semicircle is then traced on the ground using the shadow as the radius and the base of the stick as the center. A piece of string or bootlace can be used to do this. The sun's shadow shortens at noon; as the shadow lengthens in the afternoon a second peg is placed where it again crosses the semicircle. A line drawn between the two pegs is the east-west line. The first shadow tip is always in the direction of west. A line drawn at right angles gives the north-south line with north in the direction of the noon-day shadow.

B. A stick set vertically at the intersection of the east-west and north-south lines can be used to find the approximate time. The west part of the east-west line is taken as 0600 hrs, and the east part cast by the last shadow of the day is always taken as 1800 hrs. The north part of the north-south line indicates noon. The shadow of the stick becomes the hour hand of a solar clock.

- The interior of bramble bushes (thorns will deter searchers).
- Hedgerows.
- Small caves or clefts in rocks and hollows between fallen logs.
- The boughs of a fallen evergreen tree with the inner branches removed and placed on the outside.
- Thick dry stone wall.
- Holes in trees.
- Excavated animal burrows.
- Dry steambeds.

Where natural features are lacking, or in cold wet climates, a small sleeping area lined with dry material can be covered with a scaffolding

Obtaining bearings without a compass

Finding himself in an unfamiliar landscape and without the aids of map and compass, the evader can use the sun's movement across the sky as a means of orientation. A stick is placed vertically in the center of a level, cleared area. As the sun rises, the stick casts a shadow, the tip of which is marked by a stone or twig. After 10–20 minutes the shadow tip moves a few inches and is again marked. A straight line, drawn between the two marks, gives an approximate east-west line. As the sun "rises in the east and sets in the west," the shadow moves in the opposite direction, and the first shadow tip is always in the direction of west. A line drawn at right angles to the east-west line provides an approximate north-south line.

A more accurate estimation is obtained by using two shadow tips, one recorded in the morning and the other in the afternoon (equal shadow method). Using the length of the first shadow as the radius of a circle, a half-circle or arc is drawn around the stick. As noon approaches, the shadow shrinks, lengthening again in the afternoon. The second mark is made at the precise point where the shadow again touches the circle.

The shadow tip method is ineffective for use in the polar latitudes (more than 66.5°) due to the position of the sun above the horizon. North of 23.4°N, the sun is always due south at local noon, and the shadow points north. South of 23.4°S, the sun is always due north, and the shadow points south.

Finding local time without a watch

The shadow stick can be used also to find the approximate time of day, important for such purposes as keeping RVs and coordinating the actions of individuals who leave the group to carry out tasks such as searching for food. The stick is moved to the intersection of the east-west and north-south lines and set vertically in the ground. The west part of the east-west line indicates a time of 0600 hrs, and the east part is 1800 hrs (this rule applies anywhere on Earth). The north-south line now becomes the noon line, with the shadow as the hour hand of the shadow clock or sundial. Depending upon the season and location, the shadow may move either clockwise or counterclockwise, but the manner of reading the clock remains the same.

The clock records the "Apparent Solar Time" (AT) ["sundial time"], which varies throughout the year but can be related to the average or "mean solar time" ("Mean Time") by the Equation of Time (ET). This is not an equation but an interval of time, or correction, applied to Apparent Time to obtain Mean Time (ET = AT − MT). Throughout the year, the difference varies between -14 minutes to +16 minutes. A preprepared graph of annual variation can allow the evader to make an instant correction to local time.

of branches roofed with ferns, turf, or moss. Small enclosed shelters, with narrow openings, will trap body heat in the same way as a sleeping bag, particularly if it holds two or more people. Shelters can be constructed in the most desolate areas. One former Parachute Regiment sergeant-major teaches his students to construct an emergency moorland refuge from a framework or woven grass rope covered with grass, bracken, twigs, or moss.

One of the most important mistakes an evader can make is to take shelter in a deserted property or a ruined building. Buildings are obvious features on a landscape, and the first places to be searched by an enemy patrol.

Most experts agree that, despite the increase in environmental pollution, most clear running water and rainwater is safe to drink. In the field, stagnant water is usually filtered by passing it through a

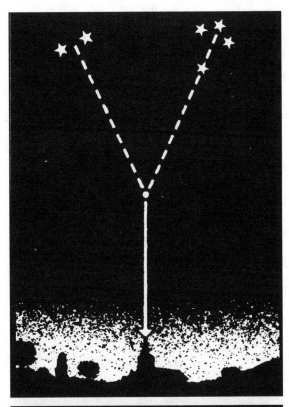

Navigation using the stars

A. In the Southern Hemisphere, lines drawn through the long axis of the Southern Cross and the two Pointer Stars meet at an imaginary point above the southern horizon.

B. In the Northern Hemisphere, the base stars of the Plough can be used to find the North Star which denotes true north with an accuracy of two degrees of the compass.

Using this technique, the evader traces a line down to a landmark on the horizon, which serves as a reference point for the next leg of his walk.

sedimentation bag to remove debris (which apart from being un-palatable consumes purification chemicals) before sterilization with chlorine-based tablets. In the survival situation, standing water can be filtered through a sock containing a fine powder (sand, chalk, charcoal). Alternatively, it can be left to clear overnight. Boiling is the most straightforward way of sterilizing water, but over the last decade filter manufacturers have produced small, convenient water-purification kits. The 2.5 micron filters in these devices remove most disease-causing organisms and some chemicals. In areas without standing water, plastic sheeting can be used to extract moisture from plants (condensation bags) or the ground (survival still).

A fire is dangerous to the evader, greatly increasing the likelihood of discovery and capture. Experts give different advice. The USAF warns its pilots that "fire should only be used when it is absolutely necessary in a life and death situation," while a British manual states that the "importance of fire . . . cannot be over-emphasized." The truth probably lies between the two extremes, as some types of wild food are difficult to eat, and even harmful, when raw, and a fire may be necessary to sterilize water, dry clothes, and provide warmth. Pit fires are the most inconspicuous. The Dakota fire hole is constructed in a pit about one foot deep with a communicating ventilation shaft. The down-draught of air ensures that the fire burns hot with little or no smoke. The pile of tinder is kept small to ensure that the flame remains below ground level. Initial smoke, resulting from moisture in the ground or fuel, can be dispersed by building the fire under a tree.

Most survival courses, military and civilian, demonstrate a range of animal traps, from the simple snare to more complex sprung traps. Time, experience, numerous traps, and luck are needed to snare game. Evaders may remain in an area only a short time, and large numbers of snares increase the probability of discovery. Overnight fishing lines are easier to conceal and are recovered quickly in the morning. Simpler fare is more abundant. Wild plants, snails, slugs, insects, and reptiles soon lose their identity in a stew, helping the evader overcome his reluctance to use unorthodox food sources.

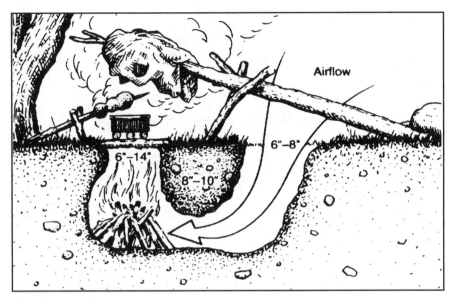

The Dakota fire hole

Most evaders have undertaken a plant recognition course as part of their survival, evasion, resistance to interrogation, and escape (SERE) training and can recognize at least ten edible plants, as well as wild fungi and various common roots, tubers, nuts, and fruits. They are also taught to spot the extremely poisonous plants such as cowbane, monkshood, death camas, the Amanita mushrooms, and four or so other fungi whose toxins attack the liver or nervous system. Familiarity with the edible and inedible species in nature's larder broadens with experience.

■ Pursuit

Quite apart from being seen, the evader's presence can be betrayed by a number of mistakes. While bad weather can cover the sounds of movement, both sound and smell travel for considerable distances on a light breeze or on still and misty nights. An untidy campsite or LUP, with its range of smells and sign, provides an obvious point to start an organized search.

In areas containing hostile patrols, the evader may eat his food raw and take care to bury rubbish and human waste. Even these precautions may not be sufficient to throw off the dog teams travelling in the vanguard of cordon and search parties.

General advice for evading dog teams can be divided into three phases, depending upon the proximity of danger:

Before contact with the enemy While in an LUP, the evader is advised to stay close to the ground. Covering the body with a waterproof article, such as a poncho or groundsheet, contains the scent, allowing it to be absorbed into the grounds. Breathing down onto the ground and remaining still are also said to minimize scent drifting into the air. Before leaving the LUP, the area should be sterilized. Waste should be buried, taking care to use a knife to dig the hole, handling the containers and wrappers as little as possible. This avoids contaminating the earth with body odor. Better still, waste should be weighted down with stones and dropped into deep water.

On the move, the evader should attempt to control his flow of body scent by remaining cool, calm, and confident. Travelling over ground already used by other people and animals forces the tracker dog to work harder, particularly if the evader travels to the side of a path to avoid leaving footprints. A party of evaders can separate for short periods, laying multiple trails to confuse dogs and trackers. Streams and running water also provide the opportunity to disguise the scent trail by crossing the water diagonally and then doubling back and travelling in short loops on both banks before moving along the stream for several minutes. This confronts the dog with an obvious entry point but a large number of dummy exits, any one of which could be the new trail.

Distant contact The first indication that a dog team has picked up the evader's trail is likely to be a distant sighting of search parties or helicopters assisting the ground teams. Less obvious may be blocking forces laying cordons to the evader's front and flanks. The evader's main hope now lies in putting distance between himself and the search teams, moving fast so that the cordons fall behind him, and using various devices to disguise his scent trail. Although the dog, weighing anything between 45 and 100 lbs. and capable of moving silently at speeds in excess of 36 feet per second, represents a formidable hazard, the less athletic abilities of him human partner can be exploited.

Army manuals advise parties to split up. The men should move fast, in different directions, tiring the dog and destroying the handler's confidence that his canine friend is really following a human trail.

Trees, bushes, and hedgerows provide the opportunity to make frequent changes in direction, in an attempt to tangle the running lead, slowing and tiring the dog team. In selecting his route, the evader should be aware of the factors affecting the persistence of his scent trail and consequently the difficulty in breaking contact. Factors favorable to the dog team include:

1. Dense, tall grass and ferns.
2. Wet ground and high humidity.
3. Light wind, rain, and mist or fog.
4. Still water, marsh, and bog.
5. Slow-moving or large parties of evaders.
6. Excess perspiration.

In contrast, factors favoring the evader can be summarized as:

1. Bad weather (high winds, snow, ice, heavy rain).
2. Dry, dusty areas.
3. Sparse vegetation.
4. Hard surfaces such as metalled roads, sand, and rock.
5. Constant evasion, moving through human or animal tracks.
6. Areas contaminated with strong-smelling chemicals (e.g., oil and gas on roads, agricultural chemicals and fertilizers on fields).

Close contact The evaders and their pursuers are now separated by a short distance. The main threat is posed by the combat forces accompanying the dog team. The tracker dog's task has been accomplished, and if released, it will probably shadow the evaders from a safe distance. The soldiers are left little choice but to move fast to separate themselves and their canine shadow from the combat teams.

The war dog and the evader

Dogs see the world in monochrome. They have difficulty in focusing over long distances but are drawn by sources of movement, which are investigated further for sound and scent. Poor eyesight is compensated for by the other senses. A dog's hearing is acute, covering a range of frequencies twice that of humans, while their sense of smell is several thousand times greater than ours.

Military dogs can be divided into two groups. Heavier, more aggressive breeds are used as guard and search dogs, possibly operating with a handler but usually allowed to roam free over a confined area. These animals rely mainly upon air scent to detect their quarry, which is attacked and detained. In contrast, tracker dogs are conditioned to follow ground scent for long distances. By the nature of their task, these dogs are connected to their handlers by long running leashes. Human "body odor" is produced by the sweat glands, particularly in the armpits and groin. Any activity which increases body heat, such as running with a heavy rucksack or wearing too many layers of clothing, increases sweating, as do fear and nervousness. Other factors, such as the use of deodorants and toiletries, or contact with strong-smelling substances such as polish, gas, or oil and the consumption of aromatic spices and herbs, together with infrequent washing, all add to the scent trace.

Airborne scent lingers on still, moist air but disperses more quickly than ground scent. The latter can provide a trail for a tracker dog to follow for up to two days after the evader has passed through the area. Body scent from the soles of the feet, airborne scent remaining on vegetation, vegetation and small animals crushed underfoot, and the gases and moisture released from freshly turned soil, produce the main scent load for the tracker dog. The trained animal can even find the direction of the track, as the toe of the evader's boot makes a deeper impression and remains in contact with the ground longer, leaving a stronger scent at the front of the print.

Attack dogs behave differently, closing with the evaders to immobilize and detain. Consequently, they must be killed. The soldier's

(A) The tracker dog

The vulnerability of the tracker dog team is that the dog and handler are connected by a long leash and the stamina of the animal must be matched by that of the man. The evader's main defenses against the tracker dog are to minimize his scent trail, make evasive movements to destroy the handler's confidence that the dog is really following a human scent, and move faster than the dog team.

(B) The attack dog

The war dog is released to attack and detain the evader. Its main weakness is that it must work apart from its human companions and it tends to be overconfident; in training it is always allowed to win.

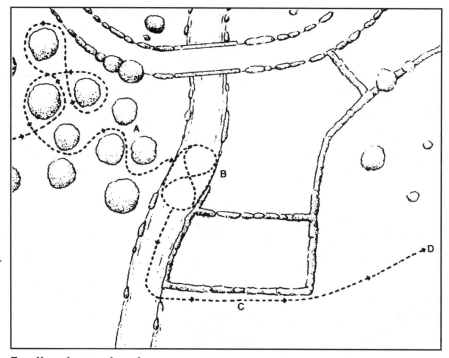

Evading the tracker dog

In this diagram, the evader takes the time to lay a convoluted scent trail in the wood. Obstacles such as walls, fences, and fallen trees may be crisscrossed a number of times to tire and confuse the pursuing dog team (A). Avoiding the road bridge, which may be guarded, the evader enters the stream and lays a series of false exit points, all of which will have to be investigated by the dog (B). The evader leaves the water some distance along the stream. The evader keeps to the hedgerows. Apart from providing cover, this avoids leaving tracks and a scent trail in the crop (C). On reaching open country, the solider moves quickly to widen the gap between himself and his pursuers (D).

slight edge comes from the knowledge that the dog may be over-confident—in training the animal is always allowed to win. While approaching his quarry, the dog dictates the situation, but if the dog attacks an offered target, such as a well-padded arm, he loses this advantage. A primitive spear, fashioned from a pointed stick, can be aimed at the abdomen or a rude club used to crush the skull. An evader caught without a weapon, but still standing, might stun the animal by falling on it, before seizing the opportunity to break one of the dog's legs, by smashing a leg joint. Alternatively, he may beat it to death with a large stick or club. Generalizations aside, this situation is fraught with difficulties. A manual reputedly written for Britain's SAS warns:

> Whichever method is decided upon, supreme physical effort must be exerted. The dog's skeletal system is such that it is virtually armor plated. Go for the soft spots, the abdomen, or the point beneath the chin, and above the breast bone.

CHAPTER 8

Counterterrorism

TERROR HAS LONG BEEN RECOGNIZED as a means of persuasion. Intimidation, clandestine propaganda, street disorder, bombings, kidnapping, and assassination allow a small group of activists to exert an influence well beyond their conventional military threat. Today the techniques of terror are also used by criminals, particularly those organized syndicates heavily involved in drug trafficking.

Most military SOF deploy cadres highly trained in the art of counterterrorism. British SAS squadrons rotate through the Regiment's Counter-Revolutionary Warfare Wing upon their return from operational tours abroad. On 24-hour standby for counterterrorist operations, the squadron is divided into four operational troops or "Special Project Teams" consisting of one officer and fifteen soldiers. Each troop is further broken down into four-man modules, which work as two-man teams during hostage rescue unit (HRU) missions. Operational-Detachment Delta serves as America's national HRU, but the FBI and various law enforcement agencies also deploy their own units. European countries such as France, Germany, Belgium, and Spain have formed their counterterrorist units from police or paramilitary police formations. The SOF of many countries have a fivefold brief in the war against the international terrorist:

1. Some countries, notably Israel, use their intelligence and military SOF in raids against terrorist bases or to hunt down terrorist chieftains.

2. More commonly, military teams are used to "harden" and challenge the security around high-risk installations.

3. To provide close personal protection for VIPs.

4. To intervene in situations where terrorists or criminals seize hostages or some other important or dangerous site or material (e.g., an oil rig, nuclear weapon, or weapons-grade nuclear fuel). Both military SOF and police organizations deploy intervention or hostage rescue units.

5. To train domestic and overseas forces in close personal protection, security, and counterinsurgency techniques. The use of small, and expensive, counterterrorist units on routine security and protection duties is seen as a misuse of these highly specialized troops.

While spectacular, intervention and HRU missions are rare, and much of the day-to-day work of a counterterrorist team centers around unit training and security duties. A Special Projects Team might be asked to harden the security of an embassy or provide close personal protection for a top defector, member of the government, or the Royal Family during periods of heightened threat. The team might also provide training for a range of domestic units. The SAS has provided training courses for Royal Ulster Constabulary surveillance and intelligence units, counterterrorist units of the mainland police, and the Royal Military Police who, in turn, provide teams to protect Britain's embassies and their diplomats. However, a more important role, and one which secured the Regiment's future in the 1960s, is to provide training teams to protect friendly overseas heads of state. First the team will identify the weaknesses in the protection surrounding the head of state, before instituting appropriate security measures and training local units to take over from the team. Occasionally, continuing protection will be allotted to a British firm staffed by ex-SAS personnel and other security experts.

Threat Analysis and Resolution

A central element in protecting an overseas client is assessing the degree of threat to which he or she is exposed. Heads of state, senior politicians, and diplomats are all considered high-risk targets, potential threats materializing not only from criminals and terrorists but from the solitary psychotic with an imagined grudge. Part of the threat analysis is to identify groups within the country which have the organization and will to mount an attack. Their techniques and operations are closely studied, often revealing a particular pattern.

The CIA kept track of more than forty active terrorist groups that might have been tempted to launch attacks in the United States during the Reagan presidency. Analysts at the Dayan Center and the Jaffee Center for Strategic Studies, on Tel Aviv's university campus, have studied the earliest written copy of the Koran to understand the Hezbollah's own perception of its messianic role in Lebanon. They speculated as to whether key passages might provide the moral logic for suicide attacks and hostage taking, or whether such acts of terrorism might create a growing sense of unease among the Hezbollah's leadership.

Criminal organizations kidnap their targets for the ransom. Terrorist groups use abduction or hostage seizure to draw attention to their cause. Some Middle Eastern, Italian, and South American criminal and terrorist groups have specialized in these techniques with great success. Other organizations, such as the Provisional IRA, have been less successful in their kidnapping attempts and favor assassination. While using the gun against "soft" targets, they have preferred to kill with the bomb in Britain and Northern Ireland. The Sicilian Mafia and South American drug cartels also favor the bomb to remove opponents. The Italian Red Brigades used well-planned ambushes to abduct hostages but employed gunmen on motorcycles to kill their targets in the street. Highly disciplined South American terrorists, organized into networks and cells, have carried out complex operations, while smaller cadres of European terrorists have been forced to rely on the simple, brutal approach.

Knowing the enemy and his techniques

It requires a great deal of information, planning, and organization to carry out a successful abduction or assassination, and months, or even years, of careful preparation. Terrorists or criminals need to be able to locate their victim at a specific location and time, and they must have the necessary force or guile to break through the security cordon surrounding the target. The entire mission must be completed in sufficient time to allow the perpetrators to make their escape. If these conditions are not met, the kidnappers or assassins will usually seek an easier target.

Some terrorist groups have used ten, or more, three- to eight-man cells to kidnap a well-guarded VIP, each group being dedicated to one or more tasks. Surveillance and reconnaissance cells gather information on the target's movements and his degree of protection. Diversionary cells cover the actual kidnapping, which is carried out by a snatch squad who bundle the victim into a van hired by a transport team. A logistics cell provides the hideout, and other groups provide guards and interrogators. The whole operation is planned and controlled by a headquarters cell, and if ransom money is paid, this may be laundered by a separate cell with criminal or financial contacts.

Sir Geoffrey Jackson, the British ambassador to Uruguay, became aware of a terrorist reconnaissance and surveillance operation just prior to his kidnapping in 1971. He spotted a young couple and their baby picnicking in the park across from his home, a "courting couple" stationed opposite the embassy gates, and a couple on a motor scooter who regularly followed his car to the embassy, sometimes cutting in front to test his chauffeur's reactions. Despite the terrorists tipping their hand, the size of the abduction operation overwhelmed the security precautions taken to protect the ambassador. The ambush was sprung by a large multiteam terrorist force which trapped Jackson's car in a narrow street and blocked off all the roads providing access to the getaway route. The British ambassador spent eight months in captivity before his release was negotiated.

The former Italian Prime Minister Aldo Moro was targeted by the Red Brigades because he was the only Christian Democrat politician on their hit list whose movements were predictable. In 1978, he and his bodyguards were caught in a classic ambush on the way to the Italian parliament. Fifty-four days later, after the Red Brigades had focused international attention on his mock trial, Moro's bullet-ridden body was left in an abandoned car.

The PIRA (Provisional IRA) has relied heavily on roadside bombs to ambush and murder members of the security forces. Occasionally, terrorist intelligence has been able to obtain the travel plans of senior judges returning from vacation between Dublin and Northern Ireland, killing a judge and his wife in 1987, and a man, his wife, and child a year later, when the car was mistaken for that of another member of the judiciary.

During the Sicilian Mafia War (1981–83), all of the Mafia chieftains invested heavily in automatic weapons, grenades, bulletproof vests, and the very latest in counterterrorist technology. Living in virtual fortresses and surrounded by hundreds of "soldiers" and bodyguards, each capo was better defended than most heads of state. Although bombs are used against judges and policemen who get in their way, Sicily's "Men of Honor" prefer the garrotte, knife, and bullet, when fighting their own kind. Salvatore Inzerillo, boss of two large Mafia "families" in Palermo, travelled in an armor-plated Alfa Romeo. He died when a gunman brought the muzzle of a Kalashnikov close to one of the armored windows and opened fire. Prior to the attack, the assassins had experimented with a jeweller's bulletproof show-case—a short burst of concentrated Kalashnikov fire was all that was needed to punch a hole through the glass.

Don Stefano Bontate lived in a villa surrounded by a range of electronic surveillance devices and closed circuit television. While driving to his similarly fortified country house, the gap between his car and that carrying his bodyguards widened until finally Bontate was left stranded at a traffic light. Seizing their opportunity, trailing assassins drew up alongside and blew half of his head away with an automatic carbine. Top Mafia bass, Carmine Galante, was betrayed from within. He was surrounded by a parcel of heavily armed bodyguards in a New York restaurant when three masked men came out of the kitchens and opened fire. As he fell dying, the chief bodyguard sprang to his feet and fired two more shots into his head.

Most VIPs are killed when they venture out of their heavily protected residence or workplace. Raiding heavily defended residences and embassies can be costly and difficult. Even a small number of elite bodyguards can hold off the assault long enough to evacuate the VIPs or call for reinforcements. When the Multinational Peacekeeping Force was invited to Lebanon by President Gemayal, Hezbollah terrorists looked for ways of attacking American and French installations. Bombs were left near the French and US Embassies on April 18, 1983, killing fifty people. Suicide drivers drove truck bombs into the US and French bases of the Peacekeeping Force, killing 241 US Marines and fifty-eight French paratroopers on October 23, 1983. Two months later, eleven bombs exploded in Kuwait, again hitting the French and US Embassies and killing more than 350 people in fifteen separate strikes. In the following year, the Hezbollah converted microlight aircraft into flying bombs which were used in the sectarian fighting in Lebanon.

As its starting point, threat resolution accepts that most of us, particularly VIPs, live in a triangle. We live at home, go to work, and visit other locations as part of our employment or for leisure activities. The connecting strand between the three environments is travel, and this is the most dangerous part, particularly if daily movements form a predictable pattern or become public knowledge. High office carries a general risk; only three attacks on American presidents have been politically motivated. Periods of specific risks have to be recognized and security precautions tightened. President Lincoln went to Ford's Theater on the fateful night of April 14, 1865, despite the fact that the bloody American Civil War had just come to an end. There were widespread rumors of an assassination plot, and a notice announcing that the Lincolns would attend the play that night had been carried by the local newspaper. President J. F. Kennedy was assassinated in an open motorcade in Dallas (November 22, 1963) in a politically right-wing state and against the background of the Vietnam War. In addition, the CIA was involved with the Mafia in attempts to assassinate Fidel Castro, at a time when the Kennedy administration was mounting a drive against organized crime. Only recently, the Israeli Prime Minister, Yitzhak Rabin, was murdered in the midst of his bodyguards at a highly publicized event. Once again, his murder took place amid troubled political events and his assassin was apparently acting on his own.

Lastly, the VIP is often the last person to recognize that his safety is threatened, and he must be prepared to follow the advice of his security professionals. One of the greatest disasters to befall the CIA was the 1984 kidnapping, torture, and murder of the Beirut CIA station chief, William Buckley. By the time he arrived in Beirut in 1975, age may well have blunted the survival instinct Buckley had developed as a veteran field officer. Security staff in the embassy had noted a number of minor eccentricities, and Buckley chose to live outside the embassy compound in an ordinary apartment block. More importantly, despite having just supervised the training of President Anwar Sadat's bodyguards and in the wake of the car-bombing of the American Embassy in Beirut, Buckley seemed to ignore the threat to his own safety. On the morning of his abduction, Buckley paid attention to detail (he carried a CIA "burn bag" and deadlocked his apartment door, the only other key being held by the American ambassador), but was travelling without a bodyguard team or his embassy driver—a flagrant breach of CIA security. Neither did he seem worried by the stranger who entered the elevator a floor below and travelled with him to the underground garage. The CIA chief was last seen being driven away by three men in a white Renault. That prevention is better than cure is underscored by the fact that the resources of the FBI, the CIA, Israel's Mossad, and covert teams from the US military were unable to recover Buckley. Under interrogation and torture, and pumped full of drugs, he is believed to have told his Hezbollah captors many of the agency's most closely guarded secrets.

◼ The Security Team

The security surrounding a VIP has to be unobtrusive and yet provide a cost-effective screen that is appropriate to the perceived level of threat. Concurrently, local forces are trained and gradually assume these duties. Specialists in close personal protection and security are grouped roughly into three groups:

Headquarters and security section These personnel are responsible for vetting household staff and work associates, and for ensuring that the VIP residence and work area are adequately protected by physical and electronic security measures. The headquarters element is responsible for command, control, and communications between different elements of the security team. The security group travels in advance of the VIP to check for potential threats, and some elements then remain behind to conduct countersurveillance for terrorist reconnaissance and surveillance cells. This section also blocks attempts to gather intelligence by way of electronic eavesdropping (electronic countersurveillance) and conducts improvised explosive device searches for bombs and booby traps.

Escort section These are the escorts of bodyguards who accompany the VIP. Selected for their marksmanship and combat shooting skills, most bodyguards are also paramedics who can provide emergency first aid in the event of an incident or if the VIP is taken ill. The relationship between the VIP and his bodyguards can be difficult. Police agencies, like the German counterterrorist unit GSG-9, select their officers as much for their social graces and ability to blend into the background during formal occasions as for their combat skills. Bodyguards usually adopt a particular formation around their client so that they have clear arcs of fire and all-round visibility. One to three bodyguards might adopt an open "V" formation around the client (open formation), whereas four or more bodyguards are used to surround the client with a human shield (closed formation). The overall risk is a function of the risk assigned to the VIP and the risk allotted to a specific location. Thus a "low-risk" client in a "high-risk" environment (crowded street or political rally) might be assigned a "medium risk" and his escort increased correspondingly.

Vehicle section The vehicle section provides drivers trained in defensive and evasive driving techniques. One driver is assigned to the client's car and each escort vehicle carrying bodyguards. The drivers are also responsible for checking that bombs and booby traps have not been concealed in their vehicles.

▰ VIP Residence

A small number of buildings, and even fewer residences, are designed with security in mind. Most houses are bought for functional and aesthetic reasons, with security aspects considered as an afterthought. Only recently have architects been asked to give a high priority to security in their designs of government buildings, balancing aesthetics with physical and electronic security. Firms like Everett I. Brown & Co. of Indianapolis, Indiana, use computer-aided design techniques to turn architectural plans into electronic 3-D models. The structure is examined for its ability to withstand a wide range of simulated terrorist attacks, then reinforced or redesigned accordingly. Existing buildings can also be tested by means of computer graphics. For example, by rotating the model in the direction corresponding to other buildings in the immediate area, the operator is provided with a potential sniper's eye view of his target.

More frequently, the security man is presented with dense shrubbery, secondary roofs, old locks, and French windows. In his mind, he will superimpose upon the building a series of concentric defenses, designed not to stop suicide commandos but to make a more covert incursion slow, difficult, and dangerous. These defenses also remove any opportunity for a terrorist or criminal to mount long-term surveillance close to his target. The overall plan, here, is to persuade a would-be intruder to choose an easier target.

Outer wall Some military establishments defend their perimeter on the "moat" principle, employing a formidable outer obstacle to deter any potential intruders at the outset (e.g., a guard-dog run contained by two high-perimeter fences). The domestic outer perimeter also should keep the world at bay, restricting passage to access points such as drives and gates. The perimeter defense may take the form of a high fence or wall, well illuminated by strategically placed lights. However, it will act as a real deterrent only if it is under continual surveillance or patrolled regularly.

Gardens Behind the primary obstacle the general idea is to create a cleared zone that offers the intruder little opportunity either to set up a surveillance OP or move closer to the house unobserved. While contrary to the English tradition of creating "secret" gardens, replacing dense shrubbery, wooded groves, and old outhouses with lawn and concrete forces the professional to tip his hand as soon as the outer defenses are breached. Consequently, on a large property, the outer perimeter may be moved close to the house, with more traditional gardens beyond. The outer perimeter and the *cordon sanitaire* are well illuminated at night by powerful lights. On the basis of Murphy's Law (e.g., anything that can go wrong, will go wrong), continuous lighting is preferred over the common passive infrared-triggered lights. With continuous lighting it is immediately obvious that the system is working and adjusted correctly.

For much the same reasons, some security teams discourage expensive hi-tech surveillance devices of the sort discussed in chapters 2 and 6. The overall security of an area resides in the sum of its concentric layers of obstacles, and undue faith in any one barrier risks falling victim to Murphy. The untrained intruder who entered the Queen's bedroom at Buckingham Palace was seen climbing the outer wall by a policeman (whose report was ignored). He jumped over a hi-tech beam and triggered two other alarms that were also dismissed as false. He was then spotted in the corridors of the palace but was assumed to be one of the maintenance staff. It was left to the Queen to keep him talking, while he sat on the end of her bed, until help arrived. A second intruder was able to breach security and enter the royal apartments in 1992.

Securing the client's residence

A. Undesirable security features include outhouses, dense shrubbery, uncontrolled access at the perimeter of the property, an unsecured garage which provides direct access to the house, a garage roof directly below upper-floor windows, climbing plants on the wall providing hand- and footholds for an intruder, old windows, and a pane of glass in the door.

B. In the secure residence, a outer perimeter wall controls access to the house. The wall and gate are well lit, watched by security cameras, and regularly patrolled. Dense shrubbery and outhouses have been replaced by lawns, flower beds, and concrete areas illuminated by continuous lighting. A stout door is equipped with a modern lock, and the windows are fitted with locks and security shutters.

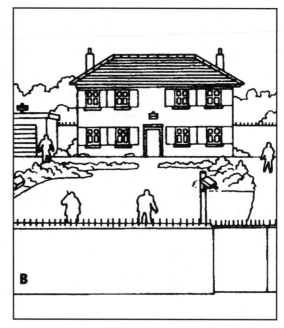

Gaps in the domestic defenses

Holes in the front door are an English obsession and an unwanted feature in the secure house. Mailboxes are a prime point of attack for arsonists. Crime statistics show that 20,000 (18.7 percent) of all fires reported in 1988 were suspected of being deliberately set and, of these, 8,000 occurred in private dwellings. Mailsafe, a fire-retardant mailbox designed by the British Post Office Investigation Department, fits behind the letter-slot and is equipped with an automatic integral smoke detector and fire extinguisher. However, a locked mailbox is better placed on the property's outer perimeter.

The mail is also a favored conduit for bombs. Suspicious packages or letters should never be flexed to determine their contents. The Post Office Investigation Department provides its clients with a list of danger signs:

1. Package is lopsided or disproportionately heavy for its size. Does it have an undue value or number of stamps?
2. An envelope flap that is stuck down completely (there is usually a gap of an eighth of an inch).
3. A postal bomb is unlikely to be less than an eighth of an inch thick or to weigh less than one and a half ounces.
4. Package contains a tightly taped or tied inner package.
5. Protruding wires or small pinholes or grease marks on envelope or wrapping.
6. Almond or marzipan smell.
7. Ticking or hissing sounds.

The Post Office markets a protective container to hold suspicious packages. The Interceptor is constructed to withstand the force of 12 ounces of military explosive. The item is held in an internal net to give easy access to ordinance disposal staff and permits the penetration of X-rays.

Access to the house by bogus officials is prevented by placing the inspection ports for gas and electricity services on exterior walls. In VIP residences these are kept locked, with access strictly controlled. Routine service visits are arranged between the relevant authority and the local police.

Hi-tech systems aside, police records show that simple burglar alarm alerts have a false alarm rate (FAR) of 98 percent. As discussed in chapter 2, security personnel conditioned by a high FAR are less likely to respond to a real incursion. Staff servicing invisible barriers need to identify, and where possible eliminate, intrinsic and external causes of false alarms. For example, where small animals such as squirrels are proving to be a frequent nuisance, these need to be eradicated from the area within the outer perimeter.

▬ The Building

Security starts with portals such as windows and doors. Robust, windowless doors are only as good as their frames. Fire Brigade entry manuals demonstrate a range of techniques to rip doors off their hinges and the use of wedges to lever the entire cylinder from standard locks. Deadlocks and double-action locks may deny the amateur the convenience of removing his loot through a door, but skilled professionals are able to use a variety of techniques to pick locks. These include vibrating tools for bounding the pins on Yale locks and moldable blanks with magnetic bars designed to intermesh with the leaves of lever locks. The latter are then tightened into place to reproduce the key. Even Allen keys can be adapted to open the simpler locks installed on back doors.

Peepholes, which allow the householder to view callers before opening the door, are seen as another vulnerability, as they offer the armed terrorist an almost guaranteed lethal head shot. Professionals prefer miniature surveillance cameras linked to a monitor inside the house. More extensive closed-circuit television networks can be used to watch rooms and corridors and the area around the building. However, the monitor operator's alertness begins to dull after 30 minutes or so, helped in no small part by having to watch a bank of television screens.

Locks are placed on all windows, which may be fitted with reinforced bullet-resistant glass. One security organization favors the continental system of equipping windows with shutters that can be secured at night. These may be manufactured from steel or reinforced resin compounds such as Kevlar. While retaining as aesthetic appearance, they present the intruder with yet another barrier, particularly on ground-floor windows.

Rooms Doors leading to central passages and between communicating rooms should be kept locked when the house is unoccupied. This extends the onion-skin principle of concentric defenses, presenting the intruder with additional time-consuming, and consequently dangerous, obstacles. Interior open-plan designs are not a good security feature. Unoccupied rooms can be protected further by individual anti-intruder alarms, which usually take the form of motion detectors. These may utilize an invisible barrier, normally infrared, which is triggered when interrupted, volumetric devices that sense the presence of air currents, or passive infrared devices that detect body heat. Alarms with mechanical triggers may be rigged to pressure plates placed underneath the floor coverings at the entrances to the room and beneath windows. The windows may be fitted with their own alarms. To overcome the high FAR associated with anti-intruder alarms, the British firm, Pilkington, has developed a fiber-optic system. The thin fibers carry a light beam to a sensor which emits an alarm when the beam is interrupted. Such interruption should occur only when the fiber is broken or crushed. A modified version uses buried fibers that react to pressure without breaking, avoiding the necessity of constant renewal.

Equipping individual alarms with their own power supply and radio link also prevents an intruder from deactivating the alarm system by sabotaging the central control point. One security officer is dismissive about domestic alarm systems which come with an empty burglar alarm box on an exterior wall. While it means to advertise the presence of the alarm as a deterrent, it tells the professional the true nature of the alarm system. Finally, the intruder can determine whether a bell is present by throwing pebbles at the box, or he may just fill it with shaving cream to muffle the sound of the alarm. Second, if the box is empty, the alarm must ring at the police station or some other control point, so he knows to cut the telephone wires where they enter the house or at the nearest junction box.

Safe room A security team guarding a high-risk VIP may advise that a safe room be constructed within his main residence. This is a retreat, used as a last resort in the event of a commando-style assault upon the house, designed to protect the target and his guards until relief forces arrive. The walls, floors, doors, and ceilings of such a room should be constructed from fire-retardant material and must provide ballistic protection for the occupants. The retreat will have its own independent water, telephone, and electricity supplies, extractor fans to remove smoke, fire extinguishers and blankets, a full medical kit and a battery-powered radio as insurance. In the event of the room becoming uninhabitable, an attempt must be made to take the VIP to safety. A high window or hatch, equipped with a chain-link ladder, should provide access to an exterior area of the building that provides some cover.

Garage and car Vehicle booby traps provide the terrorist with a relatively easy and low-risk method of assassinating his target. A security team is likely to institute a series of procedures to guard against this threat. At the end of its working day, the interior of the car is cleaned and stripped of newspapers, handkerchiefs, and other personal effects. Toolboxes and movable accessories are also removed and stored in a locked cupboard. This makes it easier for the team checking the vehicle the next morning and reduces the places where a device can be concealed. Equally, if the exterior of the car is cleaned and polished, it will be easier to spot telltale scratches and fingerprints. Finally, the garage floor is swept, to make footprints and bomb-making debris (wrapping and the plastic coats stripped from electrical wires) more noticeable. The garage is kept locked and protected by internal alarms. The exterior is well lit by continuous lighting.

Before being used again, the garage and car are checked for signs of entry and a thorough search is conducted for explosive devices. This includes the use of mirrors to examine the underside of the vehicle and probes to test the integrity of metal grilles guarding portals such as the gas tank and exhaust pipe. Car bombs used by terrorist groups such as the Provisional IRA are usually self-contained and unobtrusive, being placed under the wheel arch nearest to where the target is likely to sit, and held in position by powerful magnets. The first generation of PIRA car bombs were approximately the size of a lunch box, but more recent devices have been smaller (size of a videocassette) and more difficult to spot.

Mafia hit man ("Man of Valor"), Salvatore "Totuccio" Contorno, was on his way to kill the man thought to have betrayed his boss, Stefano Bontate, when he was arrested by the Italian police in 1982. He subsequently detailed his precarious existence for an Italian court, describing his two bulletproof cars and the electronic devices used to start them from a safe distance. A professional team prefers to start and test-drive the VIP's car, driving it over ramps and up inclines as many vehicle devices are triggered by a mercury tilt switch. They accept this calculated risk, reasoning that these security procedures will force the terrorist to seek another avenue of attack. It is the VIP, and not the security team, who is the assassin's target, and the death of a bodyguard will only drive the client into deeper cover.

▬ Travel

As a VIP is more constrained by time in arriving at his place of work (his return in the evening may be delayed by meetings, dinners, etc.), morning journeys within one block of the VIP's residence are believed to involve the greatest risk. Close to the residence there may be little choice of alternative routes, and additional bodyguards can be met by a larger ambush force. The Montoneros movement used around fifty terrorists to kidnap Jorge and Juan Born in the suburbs of Buenos Aires in 1974. While heavily guarded, the brothers, who were neighbors, usually left home together and drove their children to school before driving into the city. Three cars were used, one bearing the brothers and bodyguards, a second carrying the children and the third containing the rest of the escort section. Setting up diversion signs on the main road for tree trimming, terrorists dressed as policemen diverted all traffic onto service roads. When the convoy appeared, a truck collided with the lead car, while a second vehicle blocked their escape route. Terrorists then shot and killed the chauffeur and bodyguards in the brothers' car, "arresting" and beating the other escorts and leaving them handcuffed to the undercarriage of their car, before driving the brothers away. Leading industrialist Bunge Born was forced to pay $60 million for his sons' release.

Prestigious makes of car can be modified to include an armored body, bulletproof glass, radio transmitter, alarm beacon which permits radio location of the distressed vehicle, simultaneous locking of doors and windows, smoke dispenser, and reinforced front and rear bumpers. However, an armored limousine would provide approximately 30 seconds' protection if caught in an ambush by terrorists using modern small arms and would be defenseless against antitank weapons or road mines. Many security specialists prefer the unobtrusive mid-range executive's car, using speed rather than armor. A vehicle leaving the site of an ambush at only 10 mph puts 14 ft. between the terrorist and his target every second. This is increased to 44 ft. per second at 30 mph.

The VIP's car is accompanied by one or more escort vehicles carrying the bodyguard team. Using defensive driving techniques, the protection vehicles attempt to identify and block potential threats. By keeping the center of the protection vehicle aligned with the off-side of the target's car, and with the rear wheels in sight, the escorting driver can prevent other vehicles from interposing themselves between the two cars and can move laterally to block motorcycles approaching on the inside. This space between the target vehicle and other road users is maintained throughout the journey. When changing lanes, the protection vehicle moves out first to create a space for the VIP car. Faced with making a turn at an uncontrolled intersection, the protection vehicle overtakes and is positioned on a flank to block overtaking vehicles, before sliding back into the rear position once the turn is completed.

In contrast, evasive driving techniques employ many of the skills of the cross-country rally driver. Speed is used to increase the distance

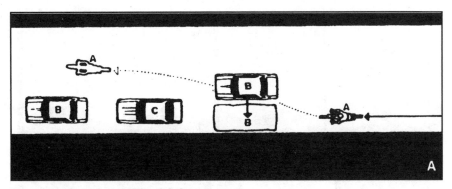

Protective and evasive driving

A. The rear escort vehicle aligns its inside wheels with the outside wheels of the client's car (C). In this position an overtaking vehicle is forced to swing wide of the client's car. If a motorcycle moves to overtake on the inside (motorcycle assassins were a favorite technique of the Italian Red Brigades) the escort car moves across to block it.

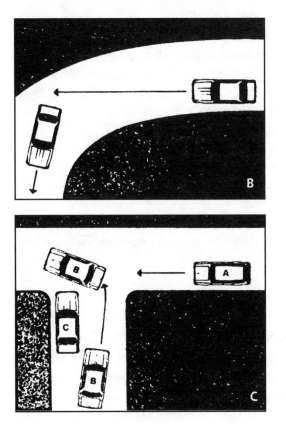

B. Vital seconds translate into hundreds of feet at a bend in the road. The professional uses the finer points of clutch control and the rotational forces acting on the car to spin the back wheels into the line of the road as the vehicle comes out of the turn.

C. At an uncontrolled intersection the rear escort car moves forward to block traffic. When the convoy has passed, it slides back in behind the client's car (C).

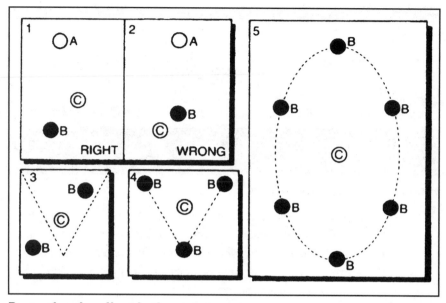

Protecting the client in the street

Diagrams (1) and (2) show the right and wrong ways for a single bodyguard to position himself with respect to his client. In (1) the bodyguard (B) is positioned away from, and slightly behind, the client (C). If an attacker appears from the rear, the bodyguard can position himself between the threat and the client. If a threat materializes in the front, the bodyguard controls the situation, pushing the client out of the line of fire before engaging the attacker (A).

Using the wrong technique (2), the bodyguard finds himself sandwiched between the threat and the client. If the client panics and grabs the bodyguard from behind, vital seconds are lost while the assassin launches a simultaneous attack on both men.

As the threat increases extra bodyguards (B) position themselves in an open V formation (3 & 4) until finally they surround the client in a close double-V formation at periods of maximum threat (5).

between the VIP motorcade and cars in pursuit. The difference in skill between the experienced driver and the professional becomes particularly apparent on bends and corners. The professional aims to lose the minimum of speed and, by using the finer points of clutch control and the rotational forces acting on his car, will spin the back wheels into the line of the road as the car comes out of the bend.

Travelling at 60 mph and gaining a margin of two seconds on a bend increases the distance between the motorcade and the cars in pursuit by approximately 176 ft.

Faced with an ambush or roadblock ahead, the driver has two choices: either make a high-speed 180-degree turn or attempt to break through the blocking vehicles. Allowing for distance, the driver pumps the hand brake while spinning the steering wheel. With the front wheels locked, the car spins on its back wheels (U-Turn). Closer to the threat, the J-Turn provides a slick three-point turn. Alternatively, the K-Turn enables the driver to spin the car while travelling in reverse. If the vehicles cannot be avoided, the driver will reduce speed and, aligning his outside wheel with the axle of the blocking vehicle, push it out of the way. According to the one international organization that has trained presidential security teams in the Baltic Republics, a well-trained driver should be able to perform ramming techniques without scratching his own car and execute evasive driving procedures at speeds of around 40 mph without making his client carsick.

On foot, the client is enveloped by a phalanx of bodyguards. The number of these well-dressed unobtrusive "grey men" is determined by the perceived risk. One to three bodyguards may escort the client in an open V-arrangement, while four or more bodyguards surround the target in a closed formation. One method positions a single bodyguard to the left and slightly behind his client. From this location, the bodyguard can assess the threat, draw his weapon (if armed), and push his client out of the line of fire. Standing slightly behind the client, the bodyguard controls the situation and prevents a panicking individual from interfering with his responses. Presented with two targets, the dictates of personal survival impel a potential assassin to engage the bodyguard first.

A bodyguard team has six main functions in the street:

- Divert, by being an extra target for the attacker to deal with.
- Protect, by shielding the client with his or her body.
- Rescue, by removing the client from the crisis point.

- Neutralize the attacker by combat: but only if this preserves the client's life.
- Render paramedical assistance, if required, until more qualified help arrives.
- Liaise with the agencies of law enforcement and provide a post-action debriefing.

For obvious reasons, open, crowded spaces are considered more dangerous than small, enclosed areas. The most dangerous transit is considered to involve moving the client from a building to his car. If terrorists or a lone assassin have little knowledge of the client's movements or itinerary, his arrival or departure at a private or public function may provide their only window of opportunity. A more detailed picture of their target's movements is built up using surveillance teams. Consequently, the security team will arrive at locations in front of the protection element to check that the area appears safe and to establish counter-sniper OPs. After the client has left, the security element will conduct countersurveillance, photographing and visually scanning crowds and loitering pedestrians to detect the one or more faces which seem to reappear in different locations.

■ Work Environment

Many offices and factories are surrounded by a "moat" of cleared land, some or all of which is used to provide parking facilities and provides the point of primary access to the facility. For reasons of both security and privacy, unauthorized entry in parking areas is usually prevented by manned barriers or automatic systems that respond to a personal card or a coded tag in the vehicle. Since the series of devastating suicide truck-bombings in Lebanon (1983–84), the US security industry has developed a range of counters to the hostile vehicle. Tight bends, speed bumps, and chicanes turn access roads into a "slalom course." A range of sensors, designed to detect a high-speed vehicle, can activate rising barriers and bollards, tire shredders, and even tank traps to block its approach.

The use of identity cards, to prevent unauthorized access to buildings, can be defeated by forgery or theft. Outer doors fitted with electronic locks require the insertion of a key card or personal identification number (PIN). More advanced devices seek "individual-specific" parameters such as fingerprints or the retinal blood vessel net at the back of the eye. Such biometric data, together with a digital photograph and personal details defining access clearance, is encoded and stored on a magnetic strip on the back of the key card ("smart card"). A central computer then compares the data held on the card to an electro-optical image of the fingerprint or laser scan of the retina. Finally, the bio-image and card data can be checked against the information held in the computer's own files.

The security of documents and electronic information is a wide and fascinating subject beyond the scope of this book. Briefly, computers and word processors can be shielded to prevent their output being intercepted by remote electronic eavesdroppers. Direct access to the information held on personal computers and networks is prevented by passwords and encryption (but see chapter 1). Many government organizations are turning to multilevel security systems. These allow a user with security clearance access to the entire computer-based system, while those with lower clearances have immediate access to less sensitive data. This avoids the time-consuming procedure of manually declassifying material and moving it around the network. Britain's Ministry of Defense has invested around £250 million in the Corporate Office Headquarters Technology System (CHOTS), to link 18,000 personnel at more than thirty sites throughout the country. CHOTS is protected by External Guard Devices which interface with non-CHOTS networks and internal Network Guard Gateway Devices which police communications between different CHOTS locations.

The information stored on floppy disks is particularly vulnerable to theft. Floppy and system backup disks containing sensitive information should be given the same protection as confidential documents. Reformatting floppy disks can be a relatively long and irritating chore for the busy executive; however, a range of degaussers are

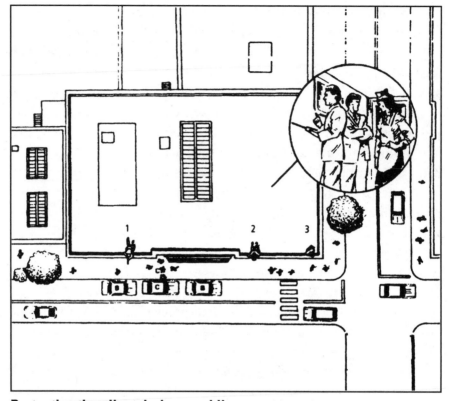

Protecting the client during a public engagement

Long before the client arrives at the building, the headquarters section has vetted the staff and conducted searches for bombs and electronic eavesdropping devices. The team on the roof covering the client's arrival includes an observer with binoculars (2) in radio link to a counter-sniper with a high-powered rifle (1). A third security officer visually scans and photographs the crowds to pick up members of a criminal or terrorist surveillance cell shadowing the client. He is looking for faces which constantly reappear during routine countersurveillance sweeps (3). When the client's car arrives flanked by the escort section, he is very quickly conducted across the pavement and into the building.

now available which remove the information from computer disks and audio and visual tapes. Degaussers act as a sort of electronic shredding machine, destroying the electronic information but leaving the disk or tape intact.

The material from most paper-shredding machines requires further disposal. When the American Embassy in Tehran was seized by Revolutionary Guards, the Iranians used carpet weavers to reassemble painstakingly secret documents from the paper strips produced by the CIA's shredding machines. No doubt, the North Vietnamese were presented with the same opportunities after the fall of Saigon. The theft of documents has been made easier by the photocopier, although it is possible to obtain colored paper that cannot be copied. American intelligence officers transport sensitive documents in briefcases equipped to incinerate their contents in the event of theft or kidnap. Another briefcase, manufactured by an American security firm, has sufficient explosive packed into the handle to amputate a thief's fingers.

■ Electronic Countersurveillance

Electronic countersurveillance is designed to prevent an outside force gathering confidential information, or conducting surveillance of a potential target, by electronic means. The classic "bug" is a concealed microphone equipped with its own means of transmitting conversations to remote eavesdroppers servicing the device. Sweeping for concealed microphones and other aspects of electronic security may be assigned to the security section, also responsible for vetting the household's staff. Comprehensive sweeping for "active microphones," which are designed to transmit continuously, employs the "larsen effect" or electromagnetic feedback. Such feedback is most easily demonstrated by the high-pitched howl when a microphone is placed close to a loudspeaker, or when someone uses a telephone to talk to a radio station while his domestic radio or television is switched on. Western intelligence services employ standard tunable signal generators to sweep rooms, the resulting bugs usually operating at the same frequency as the "howl." Many commercial devices use radio broadband FM transmissions between 5 MHz and 1.5 GHz. One notable sweep led to the discovery of Soviet microphones, embedded in the Great Seal of the United States on the wall behind the ambassador's desk, at the US Embassy in Moscow. The same principle is used by "wands" which are "painted" over walls and objects with measured systematic strokes, while the needle on the meter is watched for evidence of feedback.

Another standard sweeping technique employs audio generators which are tuned to produce a distinctive tone. Generators, each producing a different tone, are placed throughout the building, before scanning the radio frequencies to see if these tones reappear on the airways. If there is a reason to suspect the presence of concealed cameras with a remote link, a similar scan may be performed across television frequencies.

The enemy within: the telephone

The telephone can be used for casual surveillance and to provide detailed intercepts of conversations revealing a subject's future plans and movements. It may also be used as a potent form of harassment.

Casual surveillance includes surreptitious interrogation of the intended victim. A polite but careful approach to answering enquiries seeks to limit the amount of nonessential information passed to a caller. This may be achieved by answering questions with questions. For example:

Answering the telephone: Who is speaking please?
Caller: Is that 0171—?

Reply: Is that the number that you dialed?
Caller: Yes.

Reply: Well that is the number you have obtained. To whom do you wish to speak?

Or, if the caller cannot give the correct number, further enquiries are blocked, e.g.,

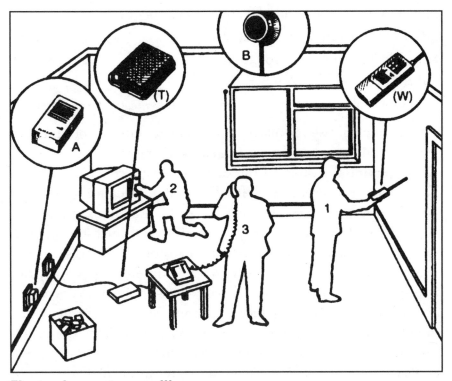

Electronic countersurveillance

Electronic countersurveillance aims at defeating the enemy's attempts to use electronic gadgetry to gather intelligence. A security officer (1) "paints" the walls and fixtures with an electronic "wand" (W) to detect active and semi-active microphones.

One of his colleagues (2) scans television frequencies to detect concealed remote cameras. The third member of the team (3) performs a physical search of the telephone, before installing a device (T) which intercepts calls, surveys the building's telephone network, and rechecks the lines for the presence of "parasite" bugs. The presence of concealed microphones transmitting their information through the building's electrical wiring is checked by using a series of commercial "Baby Alarms" (A) which employ the same principle.

The professional "bug" (B), of the type used by intelligence agencies and which the team will not detect without tearing the room apart, is situated in the wall close to the window. It is command-activated by microwaves and equipped with its own secure landline.

Reply: That is not the number that you have obtained.

Caller: Well, what number is that please?

Reply: What number were you calling?

Caller: (Gives incorrect number).

Reply: I am afraid that you have the wrong number (call is terminated).

The simple answering machine with a prerecorded robotic message performs much the same function, allowing the client to screen his calls or placing the onus on the caller to leave a contact telephone number. Another level of security is offered by telephone interrogators which restrict access to personnel with an authorized pin code which is keyed in after the telephone number. In high-threat situations, the pin code can be changed on a daily or weekly basis, and the systematic release of authorized codes to different personnel can be used to trace internal leaks. Even more sophisticated systems are also available. These include telephones such as the Foil, which provides access to conventional lines and computer networks and can verify identities with reference to a central computer.

Placing a bug inside a telephone is an antiquated method of electronic surveillance. The phone's electrical circuit can be compared with the interior of a similar model, and the presence of additional components quickly identified. Transmissions from such devices can be detected by employing a tone or a service, such as the speaking clock, and scanning the requisite radio frequencies.

The devices employed in modern interception techniques are remote from the target telephone. The civil authorities may use the local exchange for legal wiretaps, while illegal operations may utilize a junction box which services the neighborhood's telephone service. A skilled security technician can trace the relevant cable and perform a physical search for the presence of unexplained components and wires attached to it. The presence of remote microphones, which draw their power from the telephone cable ("parasites"), can also be detected by an increase in electrical resistance (and corresponding drop in voltage); however, most professional devices are equipped with their own batteries.

Searching for the standard telephone "bug" has become automated. The American *Phone Guard* which is connected between the external line and the telephone, automatically searches for intercepts every time the receiver is picked up. A small, inexpensive black box, the device searches for other telephones on the same line that might be off the hook, while scanning radio frequencies for hidden wireless microphones in or near the phone. If a tap is discovered, a warning light comes on. When the receiver is replaced, "white noise" is transmitted along the telephone line, and then the available power on the line is severely restricted, turning off remote "parasitic" taps and tape recorders.

More difficult to detect is the "semi-active" microphone, designed to play dead during sweeping operations and which produces only a momentary flicker of the needle. These devices, together with passive microphones which are command-activated and therefore broadcast intermittently, can be identified by appliances that detect nonlinear electrical junctions such as are found in capacitors. Professional equipment, currently employed by intelligence and security services, may be impossible to detect without an extensive physical examination of the room. Today's hi-tech bugs include passive microphones hidden in window frames and exterior walls. These are command-activated by microwave signals and equipped with their own secure telephone or landline.

Other modern equipment can superimpose a low-frequency FM signal on the current travelling through electrical wiring, this principle being used in the modern type of "baby alarm." It allows someone in the same house or, under certain circumstances, with access to the external power supply, to monitor conversations by means of a concealed microphone attached to the building's electrical supply. Commercial baby alarms of this type utilize slightly different frequencies, and a range of these should give sufficient frequency coverage to sweep for this type of bug.

■ Intervention Teams

The better known and more spectacular aspect of counterterrorism usually results from the failure of security precautions. Often associated with the rescue of hostages held by terrorists or criminals in buildings or vehicles (e.g., trains, boats, buses, etc.), intervention teams may also be tasked with recovering nuclear materials or bombs, recapturing important economic targets, such as oil rigs, or simply blunting a terrorist attack.

For these operations to succeed against an armed and well-prepared enemy, the various elements of the intervention force must work together with well-oiled efficiency.

Perimeter containment team Depending upon the circumstances, this role may be performed by conventional police officers or troops. Their task is to prevent the terrorists from being reinforced or escaping with their hostages. They also cover the advance of the assault team. A second outer cordon is usually employed to keep the public and press from entering the area.

Command element This group is responsible for making the key decisions affecting the command and control of the operations. As in any military or police tactical headquarters, the operation's commander is supported by a range of specialists. Communication specialists maintain a radio net linking the various elements of the intervention team with the command post, satellite radio links to distant decision makers (unit commanding officer and civil authorities), and a secure telephone line to the terrorists. A negotiator may be used to extract concessions from the terrorists, persuading them, perhaps, to exchange hostages for food. Most importantly, he explores avenues that might lead to a peaceful resolution of the situation. A clinical psychologist can use these conversations, together with background information from the dossiers of identified terrorists, to assess the group's likely responses to the intense stress that they are experiencing and the consequent danger to hostages—a major factor in deciding the timing of an assault.

Intelligence specialists may oversee the placement of remote surveillance devices, to build up a picture of the numbers and relative
positions of the terrorists with respect to their hostages. The security
forces may be able to see and hear the terrorists by means of fiber-optic
cables and microphones inserted through the walls of adjoining
buildings. During the siege on a Dutch express train in 1977, combat
swimmers used an adjoining canal to approach the train and place
remote sensors on the carriages. Thermal imagers detected the body
heat from all the people in the train, while magnetometers revealed
which "hot spots" were carrying weapons.

Sniper team The sniper team acts as an additional source of information and may also cover the assault element while positioned to
engage and eliminate the terrorists with precision rifle fire, if so commanded. Faced with a range of light conditions, and the possibility of
a rapidly changing tactical situation, each sniper may be equipped
with up to four personal rifles—"soft kill" and "hard kill" weapons
rigged for day and night shooting.

Some HRU teams favor .22 or .250 "soft kill" rifles for their low
penetration qualities where, say, a number of hostages and terrorists
are in the same room and a heavier 7.62 round may exit the target
and strike a hostage. (When British paratroops opened fire on demon-
strators and gunmen during the "Bloody Sunday"—Sunday January 30,
1972—disturbances, several 7.62 rounds are reputed to have passed
through concrete walls before killing civilians sheltering inside
high-rise apartments.) "Hard kill" sniper rifles, such as the 7.62 mm
Accuracy International L96A1—used by the British SAS—might be
used for long-distance shooting against single terrorist targets, against
other snipers (counter-sniper role), or, on the battlefield, against vehicles, radar and communications installations, and even interconti-
nental ballistic missiles (ICBMs).

The snipers may be the first to locate the terrorists. Each sniper is
assigned a different quadrant of the building, which is scanned by
rifle scope and binoculars, for visible targets and thermal imagers
and starlight scopes to seek concealed gunmen. As each target is

located, it will be assigned to one or more marksmen who keep the sniper commander informed as the target moves in and out of their rifle sights. This may be done verbally, through radio-linked throat microphones, or by depressing a microswitch, located on the stock of the rifle, which changes a light on a console in front of the sniper commander. Only in the rare event of all of the known terrorists being covered at the same time can a siege be terminated safely by precision rifle fire. The French national intervention team, GIGN, ended the 1978 siege at Clairvaux Prison in this manner. During an earlier operation to rescue French schoolchildren from a bus on the frontier between Djibouti and Somalia (1976), snipers also played a major role in the operation (see below).

Support team These personnel are available to secure ladders and abseil ropes and to assist in breaching doors, windows, or walls with sledgehammers, crowbars, shotguns (removing hinges from doors), and explosive charges. The support team may also project CS gas canisters through open breaches before the assault team enters the building.

Assault element The German GSG-9 uses four-man assault teams consisting of a pointman, team leader, and two defensemen. The pointman covers the arc of fire to the front, while one of the defensemen covers the rear. The British SAS further divide their four-man teams into independent two-man modules. The actual assault is often preceded by a diversion, which adds to the element of surprise as assault teams enter simultaneously from multiple access points. During the recovery of a building, abseiling techniques allow a team to envelop the structure and enter all floors simultaneously. This calls for remarkable rope skills and marksmanship as the operator may be faced with shooting one-handed as he swings into the room.

Each assault team is allotted its area of responsibility within the building, sweeping through the rooms and stairwells at maximum speed to locate the hostages. As with a conventional patrol, the individual arcs of fire overlap to provide all-round defense, targets within them being engaged with two- or three-round bursts (American Delta

Force operators are trained to put two bullets in the body and one in the head of the aggressor).

Terrorists close to areas where canisters of antiriot chemicals have landed may already by incapacitated, and these fumes quickly fill the whole building. CS gas vapor burns exposed mucous membranes, resulting in closed, streaming eyes, coughing, difficulty in breathing, and a tightness in the chest. Most victims seek simply to escape their torment, and few are capable of the split-second responses needed to face the assault teams.

Terrorists barricaded inside rooms with their hostages represent an additional problem as there is the real and ever-present threat that they will kill their hostages at the first sign of attack. However, the gunman's advantage has been partly blunted by the advent of stun munitions and frame charges.

The first British stun grenades, manufactured for the SAS, weighed around 250 g and were packed with magnesium powder and mercury fulminate. When the ring was pulled and the device thrown, the mercury fulminate—a percussion explosive—detonated, igniting the magnesium powder which was dispersed by the explosion. Together, these chemicals produce a tremendous bang and an intense flash of white light measured at around 50,000 candlepower. The resulting visual and psychological disorientation may last for around 45 seconds, providing a "window" for the assault team to neutralize the terrorists and secure the safety of the hostages. Although a door can be taken off its hinges with a shotgun blast, and the grenade lobbed inside, modern munitions make this unnecessary. The American M460 ("Thunder-Strip") is a stun grenade in the form of a thin plastic band that can be pushed under a door before being command-detonated. The M465 is a thin rod that can be inserted through a keyhole or a small hole in the wall. The M459 "Starflash" is a modification of the conventional stun grenade. It not only produces intense light and noise but releases a terrifying shower of white-hot sparklets which burn clothing and exposed flesh.

Rescuing the hostages from a dangerous situation, however, while minimizing the risk of assault team casualties, requires more than special munitions. The following scenario illustrates the central principles of a successful rescue: cover; diversion and surprise; speed, accuracy, fire, and movement, and rapid evacuation of the hostages.

Cover While grouped outside the room, the assault team members are concealed from view, but not from high-velocity bullets. Consequently, further protection for the waiting team may be provided by transparent bulletproof ballistic shields.

Diversion and surprise Frame charges may be used to punch two points of entry in the exterior walls. These are directional explosives, in the form of long strips, which are capable of punching precision holes through brickwork, armored glass, and even thin steel. The two simultaneous explosions, which hurl debris and dust into the room, are followed immediately by stun grenades. The terrorists watching the hostages and the obvious portals of entry (windows and doors) are now forced to protect themselves while engaging multiple targets as the assault team enters the room—their opportunity to kill the hostages has passed.

Speed, accuracy, fire, and movement The first members of the assault team close with the terrorists as soon as the stun munitions have detonated. Each team member has an allotted arc of fire and is covered, in turn, by another operator. All have been trained exhaustively on "shoot/no shoot" targets, where, for example, cartoons of civilians pointing or holding various everyday objects ("no shoot") are mixed with almost identical effigies holding firearms. This split-second discrimination is combined with almost phenomenal shooting skills.

One GSG-9 test asks the operator to stand with his back to the target and, on cue, draw his weapon, turn, and fire, hitting the center of a bull's-eye. Some personnel manage this in less than one second. The French GIGN will not even consider accepting a candidate for selection and training unless he is already capable of achieving a 70 percent score with a handgun at 25 yards. The 1–10 percent of candidates who are accepted by the unit and who pass selection will fire around 9,000 rounds with the revolver and 3,000 from the rifle on the range each year. Every "combat-trained" officer is expected to hit a moving target at a range of 25 yards in two seconds with his revolver and similarly place a killing shot on six 25-yard targets in five seconds. Even under the best of conditions, most terrorists, even those trained in the Middle Eastern "commando" camps or by former Eastern Bloc Special Forces, would find themselves outmatched by modern intervention teams.

Evacuation The felons are dead or incapacitated, and the hostages are secure. The major problem now is the asphyxiating fumes from the antiriot chemicals, mixed with the smoke from the many small fires started by the stun munitions. Men left in the stairwell are strategically placed to throw the hostages from man to man to get them out of the building quickly. Wounded and secured gunmen can be evacuated in the same way.

A more formidable challenge is represented by so-called linear situations such as buses, trains, and aircraft, where the hostages are arrayed in rows, presenting a complex of friendly and hostile targets and restricting the areas accessible to explosive entry. Usually, the vehicle is brought to a halt before the assault and rescue can proceed. Some GSG-9 exercises involve the high-speed pursuit of terrorists and their captives along the German autobahns, with pursuit teams following in highly tuned Volkswagens and Mercedes Benz 280E sedans. The pursuit is monitored by HQ staff who adjust operational plans to accommodate new developments, while the Communications Unit controls and coordinates the pursuit teams, helicopters, and supporting elements of the traffic police. Ultimately, the "terrorists" will find their route obstructed by roadblocks, but pursuit teams in Bell UH1D and 212 helicopters are poised to intervene long before this stage. Helicopter-borne snipers have proved themselves capable of stopping a vehicle by firing into the engine block, before surgically eliminating identified terrorists with an accuracy of 85 percent.

One of the most difficult rescues asked of an intervention unit occurred on the afternoon of February 4, 1976 in the small, remote French colony of Djibouti in northeast Africa. A group of terrorists from the *Front de la Côte des Somalis* (FLCS) hijacked a bus carrying

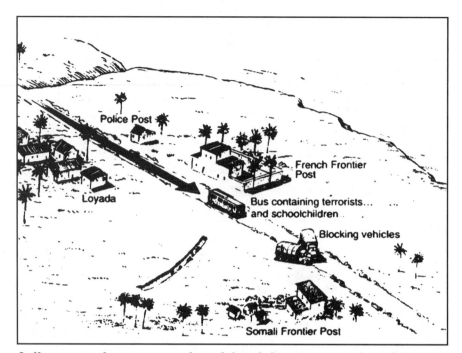

A diagrammatic representation of the nightmare scenario at Djibouti on February 3–4, 1976.

French primary school children and drove it to a desolate frontier post on the Somali border on February 3. The landscape offered no cover, allowing the terrorists all-round vision, and it was difficult to fire on the bus without hitting the Somali frontier post. Other terrorists crossed the border to reinforce the group, which now enjoyed covering fire from Somali troops. The rescue was allotted to the national intervention force, GIGN. *Légionnaire* paratroops of the 2nd REP contained the perimeter. They also provided additional snipers and counter-snipers, who covered the seemingly hostile Somali troops in the border post. As part of the containment, two French army trucks were placed between the bus and the border. Soft sand on either side ensured that the terrorists could not drive around the roadblock and disappear into Somalia with the children.

On the afternoon of the next day, a request from the terrorists for food and water (many of the children were now sick) provided the opportunity to lace the children's sandwiches with a tranquillizer, with a view to removing their silhouettes from the bus windows. Meanwhile, the snipers followed the terrorists through their sights, reporting the movements via their throat microphones. One terrorist was behind the bus, three inside, two in the immediate vicinity, and a sixth on the balcony of the frontier post. At 15:47 hrs, with all of the terrorists covered by snipers, the order was given to open fire. Four of the gunmen were killed instantly, and the fifth was eliminated as the assault team reached the bus. The anticipated small-arms fire from inside Somalia was quickly suppressed by *Légionnaire* riflemen and machine-gun posts; but then the unexpected happened. Using Somali gunfire as cover, the sixth terrorist ran to the bus and turned his automatic weapon on the passengers. He was quickly eliminated, but one child, who was sitting on the conductor's knee, was killed, and five other children, the conductor, and a woman staff member who had remained with the children, were wounded. The remaining twenty-one children were evacuated through the bus windows and into waiting police vehicles.

A similar situation faced the Royal Dutch Marines Close Combat Unit when, on March 23, 1977, South Moluccan terrorists simultaneously seized the Bovensmilde primary school and an express train travelling between Groningen and Assen. The crisis dragged on for three weeks, and most of the schoolchildren were released suffering from the effects of a viral epidemic. The use of combat swimmers to gather pre-operational intelligence on the terrorists holding the train has already been described.

During the night before the rescue, approximately ten five-man assault team using night-vision goggles concealed themselves close to the carriages. Immediately prior to the assault, the pilots of six F-104 Starfighters kicked in their afterburners and flew low over the train to provide a diversion (given the crowded carriages this was considered preferable to stun grenades). Snipers then opened fire on the areas of the train identified as the terrorists' sleeping quarters. As the last shots rang out, the assault force used frame charges to blow open the carriage doors and proceeded to clear the carriages from both ends.

Two hostages panicked and were killed in the crossfire, six terrorists were killed, and another three taken alive. In a simultaneous operation, the Marines drove an armored personnel carrier through the wall of the primary school and into the room containing the hostages and terrorists. Taken by surprise, the four Moluccans surrendered, and the four remaining hostages were released unharmed.

CHAPTER 9

Intelligence SOF and Agent Support Networks

IT MAY SEEM PARADOXICAL THAT, at the end of the Cold War, some Western intelligence agencies are preparing to expand. In many instances, this reflects a realignment toward intelligence collected by human sources or agents (HumInt), but spying is only one agent role. Some intelligence officers are trained in paramilitary operations while some agents may provide support for military SOF missions. This work calls for a different type of tradecraft. While the commando moves silently through a hostile countryside, agents and intelligence SOF must be at home in the enemy's towns and cities—an environment in which their military counterpart can survive, if at all, only for short periods. Here the constant threat is the regime's security apparatus, ever watchful for the small slip in tradecraft which can result in lengthy imprisonment or even torture and death.

Some commando operations are totally dependent upon support inside the target country. Agents can supply equipment, weapons, information, transportation, local currency, identification documents, and civilian clothes or serve as reception/pathfinder teams, guides, or contacts for safe houses and exfiltration routes. In short, the agent provides the only link between the field and the flow of everyday life in towns and cities, The aborted American rescue of the Tehran hostages was launched with only minimal ground support to provide local intelligence and transport for the commandos' journey between Desert Two and the capital. The military attachés and CIA station officers at the embassy, who would normally have provided the basic HumInt, were themselves being held hostage. To compound the problem, the pool of local sympathizers, who might otherwise have been called upon to offer less formal assistance, had either been driven underground or been incarcerated by the new fundamentalist regime. Shortly after the failure of "Eagle Claw," Britain suffered a similar, if far less publicized, failure when plans by the SAS and MI6 to launch an operation into Iran, to retrieve Rapier missile guidance systems sold secretly to the Shah, were discarded due to the lack of available agents inside the country.

The American army's own solution to this problem was the creation of the Intelligence Support Activity (ISA). This highly covert unit, which draws most of its recruits from the US Navy SEALs and the Army's Special Forces, is responsible for providing tactical intelligence support for American special operations anywhere in the world. ISA performs many tasks allotted traditionally to the agent or partisan during wartime: gathering local intelligence, providing equipment, transport, safe houses, and escape lines, and acting as guides or pathfinders for operations in neutral or hostile countries. The 120-man force includes intelligence and communications specialists, deep-penetration agents, and a small team of commandos. In future, the ISA will be complemented by local agents recruited by the CIA as the Americans return to recruiting a global network of agents.

Other countries use intelligence officers to support special operations. The French divers detailed to destroy the *Rainbow Warrior* in Auckland Harbor on July 10, 1985 enjoyed the support of a French secret service team, two of whom were later captured and convicted. During the earlier intelligence-gathering phase of the operation, a woman officer infiltrated Greenpeace to ascertain the organization's plans to disrupt French nuclear tests in the Pacific.

Some groups sharing similar aims have found it easier than the major powers to recruit agents and develop intelligence support

The master players

The blueprint for undercover activities was developed by the master of clandestine work serving the former Soviet Union in its pursuit of world revolution (although the Soviet Union has been dissolved, most of the overseas KGB apparatus is still in place). Between the two World Wars, the organs of Soviet state security were joined by the Third Communist International or "Comintern" which approached foreign Communists and sympathizers with a view to recruiting them as undercover operators. This was often more successful than a direct approach by Soviet intelligence. These willing agents who were organized into effective networks, supported with money and equipment, were controlled ultimately by two types of professional intelligence officers. "Legal" officers were based in the embassy under commercial or diplomatic cover and were recalled to the Soviet Union in time of war. In contrast, the "illegal" officer left the Soviet Bloc by way of several neutral countries before entering his target country, continually breathing life into his carefully crafted cover or "legend." Unless a network or agent became compromised, the "illegal" could go about his work without interference from the police or local counterintelligence agency. Equally, he could and would remain in place during hostilities. This system was eventually adopted by most Western agencies—"official" or "nonofficial" cover, in American parlance.

networks for clandestine operations. Support links among international terrorists are well documented, with groups providing information, passports, arms, training, and safe houses for other terrorist organizations. Similar links exist between criminal groups such as the Sicilian and American Mafias and organized crime syndicates based in Corsica, Turkey, and South America.

▬ "Legals"

Intelligence officers posting as diplomats or other government officers are provided with an official cover, giving them a prima facie reason for being in their target country, and, as such, they are covered by diplomatic immunity. If caught in the act of espionage, they simply lay claim to that immunity and return to the safety of their legation to await the inevitable expulsion order. The Soviet term "legal" came not from their official status but from the privilege of communicating with their intelligence headquarters through safe legal channels.

The intelligence chief within the embassy (American head of station or Russian resident) oversees officers serving military intelligence (American Defense Intelligence Agency or Russian GRU) and the civilian foreign intelligence service (CIA and KGB, respectively). The presence of these officers at the local "station" or "residency" makes it easy for foreign nationals to approach the embassy with sensitive material or information which can then be assessed and dealt with by professional officers.

In a country which restricts its citizens' movements and contacts with the outside world, the embassy can serve as a "post office," providing a vital communications links between agents and the intelligence service.

The military attaché A small but crucial minority of "legals" is comprised of relatively high-profile career servicemen holding appointments within the military attaché's department. They wear uniforms in public and are photographed frequently in the furtherance of public relations. Official visits to military installations are monitored closely by the host country's security service, and, on the face of it, the attachés appear to offer little overt threat. However, all military attachés carry "shopping lists" of military equipment of particular interest to their intelligence departments, and they are often surprisingly adept at taking clandestine closeup photographs in prohibited areas. Vehicles, engine numbers, vehicle suspensions, and even tire pressures may be of great value to technical intelligence analysts in, say, establishing the battlefield mobility of a specific piece of hardware.

The commercial attaché The vast majority of former Soviet "legals" were intelligence agents working under the guise of clerks, drivers, passport officers, or junior diplomatic or commercial attachés. Only a few were known to the security services, enabling this group to mix comparatively freely with the local population without arousing undue suspicion.

The number and grade of "legals" attached to each embassy depended entirely on its political and strategic importance. Viktor Suvorov, a medium-level GRU defector of the 1970s, intimates that, at the height of the Cold War, up to 40 percent of the entire staff of an average Soviet embassy were directly employed by the KGB, while a further 20 percent were answerable to the GRU. Even though this figure will have diminished with the demise of the Soviet Union, it remains a sobering indication of the importance placed by the Russians on agent-infiltration at all levels.

The day-to-day running of foreign nationals recruited as agents falls to the operational officer, supported by a small team of controllers. Once the operational officer has talent-spotted and recruited a local agent, the daily administration will pass to a controller who will get to know the agent intimately. Without the agent realizing it, the controller will study his weaknesses, strengths, and eccentricities to enable the agent to be exploited and controlled. This officer will task the agent, supplying him with the necessary raw materials for his mission, and arrange for the collection of film or information by way of meetings or "dead-letter boxes." The operational officer will keep the names and details of his agents a closely guarded secret. He may call upon the Operational Technical Group—a team within the residency responsible for the provision of dead-letter box facilities, radio transmission stations, photographic and photocopying material—to provide him with logistical support, but will rarely, if ever, ask them to meet an agent.

"Illegals"

A perfect cover and biography has to be found for "illegal" intelligence officers to provide a plausible reason for their presence in the target country. The "illegal" may enter as a refugee or immigrant, or the intelligence service may ask one of their own country's newspapers or business corporations to provide accreditation. However, this latter cover is becoming less common as organizations perceive the risk to their own relations with the host country if the officer is later exposed. Free from interference from the target country's counterintelligence service, the officer can develop agent networks and cover communication channels which take over from the "legals" in the event of a severance of diplomatic relations or a full-scale war. "Illegals" are also well positioned to hide their true affiliations in recruiting agents, who can be led to believe that they are working for a more acceptable humanitarian cause. If identified, the "illegal" may face a long prison or death sentence but is usually exchanged for one of his opposite numbers.

Agents

Nationals recruited to spy or commit acts of sabotage against their own country are also patently "illegals," living a wholly different and far more precarious existence than that of their controllers. To compound their problems, agents will inevitably be disowned if apprehended, and may be discarded, or even compromised, once their limited usefulness is over.

Agents may be given immediate tasks, set upon a long-term career in a target organization, or be left to live normal lives as part of a sleeping network.

Immediate agents By their nature, agents who volunteer their services for money are impatient for rewards. Unless properly monitored, they will soon give themselves away by their sudden change in lifestyle. To increase the opportunities for their clandestine work, and provide a cover for their changed circumstances, they will begin to seek additional overtime and will volunteer for extra routine work during unsocial hours. They will start showing an unusual, often probing, interest in matters that do not concern them and may begin to take an unusual number of foreign holidays to facilitate meetings with their controllers. Inevitably they will be noticed, reported, watched, and eventually caught. As such, they are regarded as expendable.

Profile of an "illegal"

One of the most successful of all postwar espionage cells was run by KGB "illegal" Konon Trofimovich Molody. Molody was born in Moscow but educated in Berkeley, California. After war service with the NKVD, the forerunner of the KGB, he entered Canada illegally and obtained the birth certificate of a dead Finnish-Canadian, Gordon Arnold Lonsdale. As Lonsdale, he travelled to Britain, setting himself up as the director of several jukebox leasing companies, using KGB funds. Technical support for Molody was supplied by Morris and Lona Cohen, alias Peter and Helen Kroger, formerly part of the Rosenberg spy ring in the United States. Only two of the British spies recruited and run by Molody, Harry Houghton and his mistress, Ethel Gee, were ever convicted, although it is certain that other cells existed.

The ideologist He or she is a wholly different kind of agent. Often educated and intelligent, they view their espionage as a duty, rarely seeking payment beyond necessary expenses, and consequently they may be trusted not to attract attention to themselves. Most intelligence services regard such agents as an excellent investment worthy of a carefully constructed cover and professional training. While some ideologists will remain "frozen," others, either because of their vulnerability or their immediate usefulness, will be activated at once. Typical of these was George Blake, aka Behar. Blake was born in Rotterdam of a naturalized British father (of Sephardic Jewish origin) and Dutch mother. During World War II, he served in the Dutch Resistance before joining the British SIS in 1948. A year later he was posted to South Korea, working under legal cover as a vice consul in Seoul. In 1950, shortly after the outbreak of the Korean War, he was interned by the North Koreans and, after a failed escape attempt, interrogated by Soviet advisors. The Soviets were able to "break" and recruit him, so that at the time of his release in 1953 he was a fully fledged agent.

After his release, Blake was offered the post of Deputy Director (Technical Operations) at the MI6 station in Berlin. He used his four-year tour of duty to betray many British and American agents; among them Lieutenant-General Robert Bialek of East Germany's State Security

The most dangerous type of "illegal"

Very occasionally, "illegals" will be planted in the very heart of the opposition's intelligence service in the guise of a defector. Although rare, the perceived threat of a double agent plant led CIA Counterintelligence to send genuine defectors back home to their deaths, discard good intelligence from agents, and prematurely retire tens of experienced foreign operations officers. During the early stages of the Cold War, the major Western nations set up reception centers to screen the thousands of defectors anticipated from the East. Britain's MI5 created a specialist center in Ryder Street in London, in the one-time home of OSS's X-2 section. They also opened a secure compound with a disused RAF airfield at Crail on the Fife coast. In any event, few defectors materialized, and neither establishment was used. Within a few years Ryder Street was closed and sold to the Charity Commission, and Crail passed to the Foreign Office.

Between the creation of the specialist reception center and 1971, only three Soviet experts offered their services to the British. The first, Grigori A. Takaev, defected to the authorities in Berlin in 1948. The third, Oleg A. Lyalin, a KGB "legal" attached to the London trade delegation, told MI6 that his personal task was the destruction of the early warning radar station at Fylingdales. He also claimed to have helped prepare contingency plans for wartime sabotage against Liverpool docks and the London underground. This was considered somewhat fanciful, and his information was dismissed as unreliable. The intermediate, Juri V. Krotkov, is now considered to have been a plant. Since the early 1970s there have been four genuine major KGB defections to Britain: Vladimir Rezun and Ilya Dzirkvelov from Geneva, Vladimir Kuzichkin from Iran, and Oleg Gordievsky direct from Moscow.

Service (SSD). Bialek defected in 1953, living under an assumed name in West Berlin. One evening in February 1956, while walking his dog, he was bundled into a car, taken back to SSD headquarters in East Berlin, and executed. Blake was also responsible for the compromise, show trial, and execution of Lieutenant-Colonel Popov, a GRU agent in the employ of the CIA, and the betrayal of Operation Gold—a 500-yard tunnel constructed under East Berlin to intercept telephone

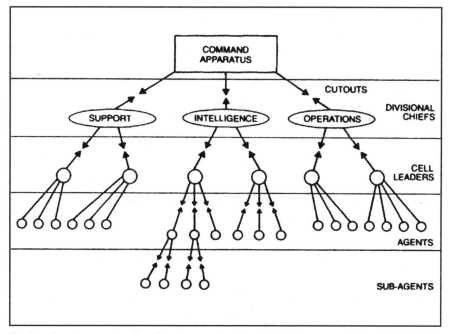

A clandestine organization organized into cells

This apparatus is a model for an "illegal" network inside an enemy country in a time of war, or an urban revolutionary or terrorist organization. At every level the organization is protected by cutouts ($\rightarrow\leftarrow$): couriers or "postmen" who deliver instructions or material between dead-letter boxes or between two members at different levels of the network operating under assumed identities. The Intelligence, Support and Operational Wings are kept separate. The Support Wing controls technical cells (radio operators, document forgers, printers producing propaganda leaflets, and safe house keepers), while the Operations Wing controls paramilitary operations or assists external commando operations by supplying guides, pathfinders, transport, or reception committees. Members of a Support or Operational cell will know each other and may know the identities of personnel in other cells within the same wing as these are brought together to work in concert on operations. In stark contrast, the cells and members of the Intelligence Wing are rigorously isolated to prevent penetration by the local security service. Subagents may even be unaware of the true identity or affiliations of the organization for which they work.

landlines running from the Soviet military and intelligence compound in Karlshorst. Eventually compromised by a Polish double agent, Blake was recalled to London on the pretext of being offered a promotion. He was charged with espionage, tried, and sentenced to a record forty-two years' imprisonment. His next escape, from Wormwood Scrubs, was more successful. Blake made his way to Moscow.

The sleeper As war and the other emergency situations that warrant the activation of frozen networks are rare, many sleepers suffer the frustration of awaiting a call that never comes. Prior to German reunification, the *Hauptverwaltung fur Aufklärung* (HVA), the espionage agency within the East German State Security Service, allegedly infiltrated 20,000 "illegal" agents, many of them sleepers, into Western countries.

The sleeper is the man or woman next door, an agent conditioned to blend totally with their environment. Their behavior and views will be moderate and typical of the community. Their spouse and children may remain ignorant of their double life. Most importantly, they avoid contact with the police or any action that will instigate a detailed investigation into their background. Prior to formal activation, sleepers may be used occasionally to gather low-grade intelligence or to act as messengers, couriers, and guides. These low-risk activities, together with contact through other agents, enable the controller to monitor the readiness of his sleepers.

▬ Cells and Networks

While the agent run by the "legal" residency may operate in isolation, his only contact being his handler or controller, "illegal" networks must contain the necessary skills for independent operations. The "illegal" will recruit his own spies and technical support agents such as couriers, radio operators, forgers, safe house owners, recruiters, and possibly people prepared to carry out tasks such as propaganda, sabotage, and terrorism. Each element is organized into cells, with agents either working alone or in small groups. A cell's link to the rest of the network may be restricted to "dead-letter boxes" or messengers. Couriers carrying messages between different parts of an agent network are called "cutouts." Thus agents never meet agents from other cells, and, at worst, a "cutout" only knows the assumed identity of two contacts. As cells spawn other cells, and agents recruit subagents, the latter may not even be aware for whom they work. In this way, if an agent is taken, he has little information to give his interrogators.

During the 1930s, the Soviets created a cluster of cells in Nazi Germany and elsewhere in Europe staffed by intelligence officers, agents, and anti-Nazi sympathizers. Under the direction of "grand chef" Leopold Trepper, the network grew, stretching from Paris to Bucharest, and produced such a volume of radio traffic that the German Gestapo nicknamed it the *Rote Kapelle* ("Red Orchestra"). A model for clandestine networks, the "Orchestra" later became the subject of a lengthy and detailed study by CIA counterintelligence.

Terrorist groups also operate in small cells. Each Provisional IRA Active Service Unit (ASU) is believed to comprise no more than four or five individuals who arm and finance themselves, selecting their own targets and carrying out their own missions. The cell relies on a central quartermaster for weapons and explosives but, in all other respects, will have no contact with the PIRA command structure. The quarter-master, responsible for the clandestine movement of arms and explosives, will know only the assumed identities of the ASU commanders.

▬ The Operational House

The agent's home must also serve as his operational base. An ideal base should be owned by the agent so that it is not subjected to inspections or alterations by a landlord. Located in a quiet outer suburb, ideally the house should be detached or semidetached and situated where it cannot be overlooked. Clandestine materials should be hidden from visitors, with normal security measures taken against burglars. Radio aerials should be concealed and transmitters suppressed so as not to interfere with local television reception. Ideally, continuous-wave transmitters should be located in areas of heavy radio traffic, such as under airport flight paths or close to shipping lanes, to mask their presence.

The Krogers' property at 45 Cranley Drive, in the London suburb of Ruislip (see "Profile of an Illegal"), was a model operational house. Standing in its own grounds, with playing fields to the rear, it was situated at the end of a cul-de-sac with a narrow pathway leading to Denbigh Close beyond. There was no property directly opposite, making surveillance from any angle difficult. The doors and windows were secured by locks. The house was close to London Airport, and the Krogers' main radio transmitted Morse in high-speed bursts which further defied GCHQ's attempts to intercept their communications.

MI5 and Special Branch officers found two books of "one-time" code pads (see below) hidden in a cigarette lighter, signals plans for three separate types of transmissions from Moscow, and secret-writing and microdot manufacturing materials. A carefully concealed transmitter was hidden in a cavity under the kitchen floor with cameras and other radio equipment. Everything had been carefully concealed in moisture-resistant sealed packages, the whole system being patently designed for long-term use and storage.

After the property had been returned to the Krogers' solicitors, another short-wave transmitter was found under the kitchen floor. Even though the garden had been excavated by the authorities, a third transmitter was dug up by Mr. and Mrs. Sadler, the then owners, nearly twenty years later, in 1980.

■ The Safe House

A network may have a number of safe houses and apartments which can be used to conduct clandestine meetings or store changes of clothes, passports, and money, and provide a sanctuary for the agent on the run. Despite the highest security alert—with police watching operational houses, the homes of friends and family, airports, docks, and ferry terminals—the agent can sit tight in his safe house until security is relaxed and a way is found to get him out of the country. A chain of safe houses can form an escape line, taking the agent toward a port or national frontier. George Blake's escape from Wormwood Scrubs Prison was arranged by sympathizers who hid him in several London safe houses and later transported him to East Germany concealed underneath the bed in a Dormobile camper.

Safe houses are also dangerous, and the agents can be caught like rats in a trap. The following advice on maintaining safe houses is condensed from a section entitled "Advice to Freedom Fighters" from a KGB manual:

1. The agent should set up his own safe house under an assumed identity. The house should not be overlooked, and ideally, the agent can enter and leave unobtrusively using a number of routes—it is easy for surveillance teams to watch a single road or choke-points such as lanes, bridges, or crossroads. Unlike operational houses, safe houses may be less conspicuous in densely populated urban areas, particularly those with transient populations.

   Kilburn, a suburb in northwest London with a large itinerant Irish population has been a favorite base for PIRA ASUs operating in the southern counties of England. Furnished rooms in university towns can provide an agent with both a cover and a constant source of short-lease accommodations.

2. False identity cards should be registered with the police only as a last resort. Identity documents or business cards showing the address of the safe house should never be carried in case the agent is arrested in the street. Rent and bills are settled in cash to avoid leaving traceable tabs such as checks and credit card accounts.

3. The agent's lifestyle should mirror his declared profession. A travelling salesman may be away for long periods, a doctor may be expected to make late-night calls, while students or the self-employed work from home.

4. Maintain friendly but distant relations with neighbors and land-lords. In the event of arrests, these people can provide useful information to policemen or security officers.

5. All clandestine materials must be stored in a remote but secure facility such as a locked garage rented by a third person.

6. Meetings may be held at the safe house, but its security declines with the number of people who come to learn of its existence.

Parties and other innocent social functions can be used to mask the comings and goings of agents and get the neighbors accustomed to the appearance of strangers. Meetings should never appear suspicious by continuing into the night (one group of agents printing propaganda leaflets at night were mistaken by their landlord for currency forgers; and late-night visitors to another Soviet safe house were thought to be patronizing a bordello). Most importantly, other agents should never stay overnight—suspects' homes are often raided in the early hours of the morning, and the police will net several agents for the price of one.

7. Security: If the safe house has been set up to provide temporary accommodations for a number of agents, each must be able to gain access without drawing attention to themselves. (A PIRA safe-apartment in Wandsworth, London, was only discovered when a car thief was shot while trying to steal a car parked outside. It transpired that an armed terrorist was sleeping inside at the time. The police then found the ASU's weapons and explosives in an attached garage.) In this event, the orderly running, maintenance, and security of the safe house are the responsibility of a "safe house keeper." This individual ensures that the premises are regularly cleared of incriminating evidence and that an additional key is held by a third party, who clears and closes the safe house in the event of arrests. The lone agent or a "safe house keeper" also institutes a series of signals, such as chalk marks on a wall or lamp-post, to show that the safe house is "occupied" or "empty," "secure" or "compromised." In this way, other agents are prevented from walking into a trap set by the security forces.

Ironically, the increase in terrorist activity throughout Western Europe has made the task of setting up a safe house far more difficult. Safe houses have been identified by the very security measures taken to protect them. In 1979, the German security service received information that a Red Army Faction (RAF) safe house was operating in Frankfurt. Working on the assumption that terrorists would not risk having their financial transactions recorded by using checks or credit cards, the security service approached the city electricity authority and obtained the names of the 18,000 customers who paid their bills in cash. These were fed into a computer and cross-referenced with the financial records obtained from companies and government departments. After extensive cross-checking, the computer identified only two individuals who settled all of their bills in cash. A background security check revealed that both were using false names. Their properties were raided. One of the houses was being used by a drug dealer, the other was the RAF safe house where Rolf Heissler, a terrorist on the wanted list, was hiding.

■ Countersurveillance in the Street

Are you being followed? Using shop windows as mirrors or turning around quickly in the hope of seeing somebody stop or dart into a shop doorway are a grotesque parody of countersurveillance. You will never spot a professional surveillance team. Part of the reason for this is the use of a technique that the former Soviets called "passing the game." This anticipates the target's route, with "watcher" teams moving ahead along parallel roads, side streets, and around city blocks to place themselves in the agent's path. In ensures that a particular "watcher" follows the target for only a short distance before handing him on to another colleague. The overall emphasis here is on watching rather than following. For example, if the target goes into a tube station, all the exits are covered by surveillance personnel. The target is followed into the station, but if he or she buys a ticket and then moves to an exit, the "watchers" close behind continue to behave like any other commuters. It is not necessary to expose themselves by following the target out of the station—all eventualities are covered.

The surveillance team is divided into ground and mobile elements. The former could by any street vendor, businessman, mother, young couple, or shopkeepers, while the mobile unit might be in a taxi, commercial or public utility van, or just an ordinary family car. A surveillance team will be very cautious. If the target disappears during a regular trip to a suspected clandestine rendezvous, the "watchers" will wait for him at the same place when he makes his next journey. In this way, the route is determined gradually, without alerting the agent. Returning briefly to our shop window, the person who appears to be following close behind and who darts into doorways may be a mugger—or he may be just an innocent passerby who, watching your strange antics, has decided that you are waiting to ambush him! Real countersurveillance seeks to force the "watchers" to reveal themselves or keep spreading their surveillance net to the point where it breaks. The following techniques were taught to KGB recruits:

Countersurveillance sweeps A residency or well-organized agent net will have a team dedicated to countersurveillance which will randomly watch their own people to see if they are being followed. For surveillance to be effective, the various ground and mobile elements must be in radio contact. One technique, which proved effective against Britain's MI5, was to engineer a dummy meeting and scan the airways for the presence of unusual transmissions or an increase in radio traffic. Another ploy was to scan visually or photograph crowds and passersby for the reappearance of the same old faces. Even if the countersurveillance sweep gives an officer or agent a clean bill of health, he will always take precautions against being followed.

Avoid helping the opposition KGB officers and agents were instructed never to make social calls on fellow operatives and to ignore them if they met by chance in the street. They were also advised to avoid using the telephone or postal service for clandestine communications and always to use a nom de guerre when meeting other agents. Large stations and post offices, where a shadowing security officer can question the person behind the counter, and crowded places in general, where surveillance is made easier, were avoided as much as possible.

Buying tickets at airports, stations, and bus terminals is particularly dangerous. If the agent is arrested, the ticket gives his destination. If he is to be followed, the ticket office staff can tell the security officers where to wait to reestablish contact. Tickets can be purchased by third parties and left for the agent to collect. The fare is always paid to a point well beyond the agent's destination. The journey can be further broken at an intermediate point, allowing the agent to change his route and use an alternative means of transport. This is particularly useful when the agent's journey takes him through rural areas where surveillance becomes difficult, if not impossible. On the last day of his interrogation, British MI5 "watchers" did not bother to follow the traitor Guy Burgess beyond the major London station where he usually caught the train home even though they were planning to arrest him when he returned to London on the Monday.

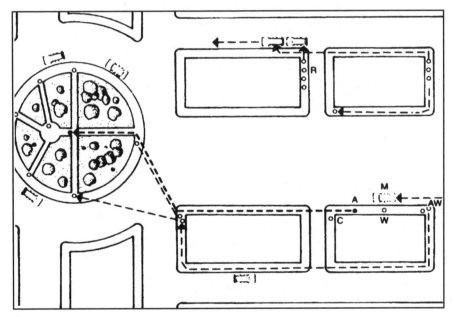

Surveillance

Under surveillance by the local counterintelligence service, the agent (A) is watched rather than followed. As one watcher follows at a discreet distance (W), a colleague waits at the next street corner (C) and other watchers quickly move along side streets to place themselves in the agent's path (AW). The operation is coordinated by mobile element (M) in an inconspicuous vehicle. Other officers and vehicles are held in reserve (R). They move forward only when required, for example when the agent enters the park.

Burgess met fellow conspirator, Donald Maclean, on the Friday night, and the pair drove to a Channel port from which they fled to Russia.

Cleaning The agent or intelligence officer attempts to lose "watchers" by stretching their resources beyond the point at which they can function effectively. An agent might have covered the ground previously to find a convoluted route that can be changed as the situation dictates.

A large department store may have several exits leading to different streets, one of which is a minor road connecting with another road via a deserted courtyard. At this point the surveillance net is starting to become very thin as the "watchers" can no longer predict their target's movements and their resources are starting to become stretched. Continual contact becomes extremely difficult if the agent then hops onto a moving bus or takes a cab for a short distance.

Choke points, such as long, narrow lanes, bridges, or alleys can force the "watchers" to reveal themselves or to end their pursuit. The "illegal" Konon Molody never led the MI5 "watchers" to the Krogers' house. Molody's careful route took him along a narrow pathway connecting Denbigh Close with Cranley Drive, where he finally disappeared.

Following him along the lane or placing the suburban street under surveillance would have been too obvious. His final destination, 45 Cranley Drive, was only revealed when permission was obtained from another resident to use his home to undertake a long period of surveillance.

The agent will probably be unaware that he has been under continual surveillance, but using these standard techniques several times during his journey to a clandestine rendezvous may enable him to lose his "watchers." As his route becomes unpredictable, the surveillance teams increasingly fall behind, and the "game" breaks through their net.

Damage limitation If, from the outset, the sole intention was to arrest the agent, there would be no need to mount a costly surveillance operation. The counterintelligence service uses surveillance to identify the other clandestine operatives in the agent's cell.

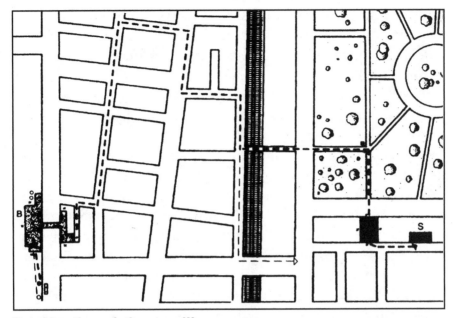

Breaking through the surveillance net

The agent starts his well rehearsed "cleaning" routine by entering a large building with numerous exits, such as a large department store or hospital. The building (B) shown in this example consists of two wings connected by elevated walkways or basement tunnels. Leaving by an exit on the other side of the road, the agent moves into a area well supplied with intersecting roads and alleyways. The surveillance net is stretched to the breaking point as the watchers can no longer predict their target's movements. When the agent uses a narrow footbridge to cross the railway line, he breaks through the surveillance net as the watchers are forced to cross on an adjoining road bridge. With surveillance increasingly falling behind, the agent enters a park only to leave and enter another building with a rear exit. The agent then quickly disappears into an underground station offering connections to two or more different lines. The difficulty with this technique is that if the agent is tempted to use the same routine again, surveillance will begin at the point at which the agent was "lost" on the previous occasion.

By placing these operatives under surveillance they can then identify further cell members and "cutouts," which will lead to other parts of the network. The "watchers" expect the agent to use countersurveillance ploys routinely; therefore his premature arrest is only likely if, by his behavior, he indicates that he is aware of the surveillance and he attempts to escape and alert the rest of the network.

A premature arrest is counterproductive as the cell structure ensures that, even under torture, the agent can only reveal the assumed names of a few people in his cell, and his sudden disappearance will alert fellow agents. The wave of dawn arrests usually only occurs when the network has been penetrated fully by counterintelligence. The spy, Harry Houghton, who was discovered stealing naval secrets, led MI5 to the "illegal" resident Molody, who in turn led the "watchers" to the Krogers. The British Security Service was attempting to piece together the rest of the network when the defection of a Polish intelligence officer forced them into a series of hurried arrests. A KGB manual has the following advice for an agent who had become aware of surveillance:

1. Once an agent became aware that he (or she) was under surveillance their clandestine work was finished. It was a serious offense in Soviet networks not to report surveillance to the agent's immediate controller. An agent's escape and evasion routine was to lose the surveillance, leave a sign to alert the network, destroy all clandestine materials, and then retire to a safe house or contact the network's escape line.

2. If somebody had been followed and then surveillance stopped, their future arrest was assured. If an agent disappeared and then suddenly reappeared, his explanations were initially treated with deep suspicion as he may now have been under the control of the counterintelligence service.

3. Contacts with all such individuals were severed, and their operational house cleared of incriminating materials.

▄ Meetings

Meetings are always dangerous. In high-threat environments a single agent may travel overseas to meet his controller in a low-threat, neutral country (Austria and Scandinavia were used by the Soviets). In Britain, the movement of Soviet diplomats, and hence the "legal" intelligence staff, was restricted to an area within 30 miles of their London embassy.

Meeting points were selected for their blandness and normality— suburban high streets, thoroughfares, open parkland, indeed any- where where individuals might be expected to meet and join in innocent conversation. Usually the meeting point was accessible by two means of public transport, to provide the intelligence officer with the opportunity to throw off surveillance.

Douglas Britten met his Soviet controller, Alexsandr Ivanovitch Borisenko, at the Arnos Grove tube station in north London. There- after they met irregularly, largely to enable Borisenko to keep pressure on his wavering agent. A missed meeting could signal danger. Britten was told that if either should fail to keep a meeting they were to use an alternative rendezvous on the first Saturday afternoon of the next month. Britten was instructed to stand by the notice board outside the parish church in Pinner, Middlesex.

After waiting for five minutes (presumably to allow the controller or a member of his team a chance to sweep the area for surveillance teams), he was to proceed along Church Lane, turn into Grange Gar- dens (both leafy, suburban roads full of respectable semidetached properties) and then return to the High Street. To signify that all was well, he was asked to carry a book and glasses and, when asked the way to the library, apologize for the fact that he did not live in the area. Thereafter, he would be approached by his controller.

Brush contacts In a high-threat situation, materials or instructions may be passed quickly and unobtrusively in a crowded place, such as a street, on public transport during rush hour, or in a crowded build- ing with several exits, such as a large shop or sports stadium. If he thinks the agent is compromised, the intelligence officer will use a countersurveillance team to check the meeting place for any suspicious activity or people shadowing the agent before the contact is made. Oleg Penkovsky, a senior Red Army officer and important Western agent, passed his microfilm to Janet Chisholm, the wife of Rory Chisholm, an MI6 "legal," no fewer than twelve times without attracting KGB suspicion. However, a subsequent brush pass in a Moscow store with Rory Chisholm himself, who, unknown to British Intelligence, had by then been compromised by George Blake, resulted in Penkovsky's arrest and execution.

Dead-letter boxes (DLBs) These provide a means of passing information and equipment without the two agents coming into physical contact. DLBs are always chosen carefully. Sites such as natural fissures in gravestones, walls or everyday objects, such as apparently discarded trash, must offer concealment without attracting the attention of passing strangers or children. The Soviets excelled in the art of selecting or creating DLBs. They used copies of American 7-Up drink cans; narrow plastic wedges that could be pushed into the ground in the agent's local park; underwater DLBs; and natural crevices and gaps in the old brickwork of Brompton Oratory and Coram's Fields in London.

Couriers Individuals who cross international frontiers in the course of their employment, for example merchant seamen, commercial aircrew, and long-distance truck drivers, may be recruited as couriers. This sort of agent is used to service networks in high-risk countries. They carry information, funds, and other material between the agent circuit and a "legal" or "illegal" residency in a low-threat, neutral country.

Signs Inconspicuous signs and everyday objects can be used as covert signals. A small chalk circle on a particular wall may signify that a nearby safe house has been raided or is under surveillance, or it may signify the arrival of a courier. Indeed, the absence of such a mark may mean that a particular agent has been taken. The Soviets used chalk marks when emptying a DLB near the American Embassy in Grosvenor Square. The intelligence officer would make a light blue mark on a

Dead-letter boxes

An agent arrives in an area and signifies his intention to place a package in a pre-arranged dead-letter box (DLB) by using a sign (a "P" placed on a lamppost in blue chalk). The agent emptying the box sees the sign and places another sign to indicate his readiness to empty the box (an "X" in blue chalk on a park bench). The first agent drops the package in the "box" and rubs out the sign on the lamppost. Seeing this, the second agent retrieves the package and rubs out the sign on the park bench. The KGB used a number of different DLBs: containers disguised as discarded soft-drink cans, fissures and cracks in walls and gravestones, and wedge-shaped containers with a flip-top lid carefully concealed behind a shrub in the agent's local park.

lamppost in Audley Square, indicating that he was filling the box that day. Seeing this, the agent would proceed to a predesignated park bench some 250 yards away which he would mark with a small chalk cross. Seeing the cross, the "legal" would then proceed to the DLB, leave his container and return to clean the lamppost. The agent would then collect the package, remove the chalk mark from the bench, and disappear.

Talent spotting

The "legals" are experts in the art of spotting and assessing potential recruits to serve as spies, particularly in the military industries and defense agencies. Potential targets include servicemen and reservists, civilian employees, contractors and outside consultants employed by the armed forces or defense industries, and retired government officials. Civil servants are also prime targets if they have access to classified or sensitive information. Even those on the periphery—family or friends—may be viewed as useful conduits in gaining access to targeted persons, activities, or information. Occasionally, potential agents will be spotted during overseas trips. The former Soviet Union, China, and a few Eastern Bloc republics required visitors to obtain visas. As visa applications, containing full details of the traveller together with the nature of his intended visit, were invariably processed by intelligence officers (the KGB undertook this duty in all Soviet embassies), it was relatively simple to check on the strengths and weaknesses of potential targets by cross-referencing the commercial files routinely maintained inside the embassy.

Within Britain, many talent-spotting sweeps were quite random. In 1962, the Soviets made a detailed survey of British ham radio operators, cross-referencing the names with details of their service in the armed forces. One of the men earmarked for an approach was Douglas Britten, a chief technician in the RAF, apparently living well beyond his means. Britten was recruited by a Soviet "legal" calling himself Yuri, who approached Britten in the Science Museum, addressing him by his radio call sign "Golf Three Kilo Foxtrot Lima." Britten was asked to obtain a model 1154 radio transmitter. Aware that this model was commercially available, he agreed, hoping to deceive the intelligence officer. Alas, it was Britten who was duped, as this seemingly innocent exchange brought him under Soviet control, with the threat of blackmail. Ultimately it earned him a twenty-one-year prison sentence.

Radio Communications

One-way traffic Two-way radio traffic presents the same dangers for the agent as it does for the SAS or any other special forces team. A safe alternative is one-way communications (control to agent) to maintain contact with agents, such as sleepers, who have no direct contact with a controller. The system of sending seemingly meaningless messages over the open radio was first used to communicate with the Resistance during World War II and is still employed by all the major powers. Prior to the unification of the two Germanies, "Magdeburg Annie" (named after the female broadcaster who recited the long, tedious list of five-figure number blocks) regularly beamed coded messages to agents in the West. Although this station is no longer operational, others continue to send messages to and from the former Soviet Union, from China, and between North and South Korea.

Not surprisingly, Western Europe is still the prime target for clandestine messages. Call sign "Papa November," the most vociferous station, transmits on 2.707, 5.015, 7.404, and 11.108 MHz. Transmissions begin at midnight GMT and continue every six hours on the half-hour. Another station, allegedly operating on behalf of the Mossad and using a few bars of the "Lincolnshire Poacher" as a netting-in signal (NIS), transmits on 4.665 and 7.605 MHz at 45 minutes past the hour. A third station, using the tune "Swedish Rhapsody" played on a music box as an NIS, transmits on Saturdays at 8:00 p.m. and 9:00 p.m. GMT.

Controlling Agents

Once recruited, the subsequent control of agents centers on getting them to carry out tasks even at risk to their own lives and liberty. As in the Britten case, blackmail has served as a tried and tested method in many operations. During the late 1970s, Israeli intelligence officers used a French prostitute to lay a "honey trap" for an Iraqi nuclear scientist who was then blackmailed into revealing details of the Osirak nuclear complex in Baghdad. Many agencies use male and female prostitutes to compromise the unwary, and the resulting "honey trap" can have a nasty sting. For example, the single man with little to fear from the casual heterosexual contact may find himself the focus of attention of a strikingly attractive woman. Drunk and with a sedative placed in his last drink, he returns to his hotel room with the woman. After he has lapsed into a deep sleep, the woman is replaced with a young boy, and the two are photographed in compromising positions. The demands arrive later, with the photographs. An equally unpleasant East German ploy was the seduction of lonely secretaries working for the Bonn government.

Occasionally, it is the intelligence service which is left feeling foolish. One Soviet legend recalls how, in the 1970s, a Southeast Asian president was photographed availing himself of the dubious pleasures of a number of young girls while on a diplomatic visit to Moscow. When confronted with the pictures, thoroughly unabashed and far from agreeing to succumb to Soviet influence, the president is alleged to have asked if copies could be provided for the entertainment of his government ministers!

Of the fifty-five Americans associated with the Department of Defense and known to have committed acts of espionage against the United States between 1948 and 1990, more than half were over the age of thirty when they began to spy. Most volunteered their services to the Soviets or other countries and were motivated by actual or perceived professional failure, or general alienation from society. Chief Warrant Officer John Walker, while serving as a communications watch officer on the staff of the Commander Submarine Forces Atlantic, approached the Soviet Embassy in Washington demanding to see "someone from security." As a mark of his future intentions he brought with him a month's key settings for the ultrasecret KL-47 cipher machine. Walker was in many respects a typical spy for money, and his position represented a serious security vetting failure. Walker dropped out of high school and joined the navy after a brief career as a burglar. After the collapse of several business ventures and an attempt to force his wife into prostitution, he approached the Soviets. During Walker's staggering seventeen-year career as an agent, he not only ran his friend Jerry Whitworth as a subagent for nine years

(Whitworth thought he was working for Israeli intelligence) but successfully recruited his son and elder brother. Walker's post-capture analysis intimated that cipher information provided by him had enabled the Soviets to decrypt a staggering one million US messages, including many crucial to the operation of the nuclear submarine fleet.

Two-way traffic There are occasions when it is necessary for an agent to run the risk of transmitting. At least three transmitters were found secreted on the Krogers' property and, sometime in the late eighties, an old Soviet-manufactured transmitter was discovered buried in the Welsh mountains. Transmitting messages in a crowded and technologically sophisticated country such as Britain is danger-ous unless the intelligence service can relay its messages through a communications satellite. Some agents may have the benefit of the new electronic enciphering equipment, but many will still use the "one-time" code pad.

The "one-time" pad has changed little since its adoption by the SOE in September 1943. Used properly, it represents the pinnacle of development in the field of manual cryptology and is mathemati-cally unbreakable. It is extremely quick and easy to use and generates few errors. There are only two copies of each pad, one held by the agent and the other by the intelligence service. There are many vari-ations on the theme of the "one-time" pad. All consist of a cipher pad and a series of numbered code pages. The cipher pad contains a vocabulary of 200 to 300 words, each with a corresponding three-digit number.

The message is first written down and translated into the corre-sponding numerical code. Thus an agent wishing to send the message "Send more film" will find the relevant three words in his cipher and use these to turn his words into numbers. If the relevant numerical codes were to be:

film: 132
more: 186
send: 256

The inscription would read: 256 186 132. The numbers will then be subdivided into groups of five (the signaller's word blocks) with zeros added to make up the missing numbers. Thus the message will now read:

25618   61320

The operator will now turn at random to any one of the unused lines of an outgoing code page. The page consists of vertical and horizontal five-digit numbers drawn at random. Each page and line will be numbered. If the agent were to choose the fifteenth line of the third page, it would appear thus: Page 03

14	13568	27694	45907	46896	69543
15	67935	07538	86574	95725	06936

The agent will transcribe the coded numbers containing his message beneath the random numbers appearing on the line chosen. The lower number will then be taken away from the higher number without carrying across:

67935	07538 (from the code pad)
25618	61320 (the agent's numerical signal)
42327	46218 (the resulting encrypted message)

The resultant number blocks will then be transmitted, preceded by the figures 0315 to show the page and line chosen. Once received, the message will be decoded by reversing the process, using identical figures on the fifteenth line of the third page:

67935   07538

The coded message will be subtracted from these numbers thus:

67935	07538 (code pad)
42327	46218 (signal received)
25618	61320 (signal decoded)

The numbers are now broken into their three-figure constituents (256 186 132) which reveals the original message: "Send more film."

Special operations and the transition to war

Although preparing to assist covert operations may form a small part (if any) of an agent's tasks, some countries, notably the former Soviet Union and North Korea, maintained dedicated covert action support networks. The presence of friendly networks was also assumed in the training of the SAS and other Western special forces during the Cold War era. Such agents will undoubtedly be used in future Western intervention and special operations.

Soviet war plans entailed the use of Special Forces or Spetsnaz teams to paralyze the target countries before the attack by conventional forces. Using a range of minimal-risk overt (commercial flights and ferries) and clandestine insertion techniques, it was understood that the operators would retire to safe houses to await instructions during the transition to war. Teams landing without weapons, explosives, and other military equipment would be equipped by the support networks, who might also have furnished guides, pathfinders, and reception teams. Commandos charged with the assassination of VIPs and attacks on heavily guarded installations (e.g., nuclear weapons) would have required extensive agent help in conducting a detailed reconnaissance of the primary and alternative targets.

The major objectives of the Spetsnaz forces inside Britain may have included power stations, nuclear weapons, command, control, communication, and intelligence (C3I) centers, ordnance depots, and choke points such as the cross-channel "Ro-Ro" ferries. The Royal Family, members of the government, and senior military officers may also have been targeted. The agents required for these tasks would have been totally unknown to the target country's security service, drawn mostly from sleepers and "illegal" GRU officers. Other sleepers, called "agent-saboteurs" by GRU defector Viktor Suvorov, were themselves tasked with gaining employment within economic targets and transportation systems and planning the sabotage of electric power lines, gas and oil pipelines and storage tanks, bridges, tunnels, and railway equipment. These assaults and other attacks immediately behind NATO's lines were intended to cause paralysis and panic, thereby making the Red Army's task that much easier.

If the commandos and saboteurs were successful, the inevitable confusion would have increased their chances of escape. Rather than risk a dangerous extraction, these clandestines would probably have continued to operate from an agent base, retired to a safe house to await the conventional forces, or, in the event of defeat, waited until circumstances enabled them to leave the country by normal transport. North Korean assassins were told to lose themselves among itinerant agricultural workers for six months or more, before making an agent contact to obtain passports and tickets for a commercial flight back to North Korea via Japan. While the use of agents for special operations avoids many of the pitfalls of Western models, it does require a massive and costly espionage effort.

CHAPTER 10

Fighting Techniques of the Special Forces

INTO THE NEW MILLENNIUM

AT 8:45 A.M. ON SEPTEMBER 11, 2001, a bright New York morning, a commercial aircraft, approaching low across the famous skyline, slammed into the North Tower of the World Trade Center. Moments later, a sinister plume of black, acrid smoke began to pour from the gaping wound in the building's superstructure; a funeral pyre for the airline passengers, their terrorist hijackers, and the occupants of some three floors. Horrified commuters watched, helpless, as trapped workers leaped into space rather than face the flames. At 9:03 a.m., a second aircraft flew into ninetieth floor of the South Tower, the explosion raining glass shards and twisted metal onto the streets below. Horror followed horror as a third aircraft hit the Pentagon, while a fourth, briefly recaptured by its brave passengers, disintegrated in a Pennsylvania field.

As the awful images beamed around the world, the first reaction was most commonly denial. Surely it was a movie, a modern take on Orson Welles's radio hoax, *War of the Worlds*. What country would have the intent or means to challenge the world's last superpower? Barely minutes after the attack on the Pentagon, all emotional self-defense evaporated as the South Tower collapsed in a choking cloud of white dust and rubble. Around thirty minutes later, the North Tower crumbled, adding to the terrible death toll. As the world held its breath, commuters fled an ominous cloud of cement dust that threatened to engulf them. As a deadly hush fell on the scene, observers heard for the first time a faint warbling. "What's that noise?" a television commentator asked, but nobody seemed to know. It was the emergency alarm on a New York Fire Department breathing apparatus set. The alarm signals "Man Down," requiring all fire fighters within earshot to cease activities and find the casualty. On this morning, numerous alarms rang from under the rubble, but there were no crews left to locate their comrades.

The perpetrators died in the attack, but there were clear links to al-Qaeda and Osama bin Laden. America's response, Operation Enduring Freedom, toppled the Taliban government protecting al-Qaeda and closed the Afghan terrorist bases. Iraq was then invaded (Operation Iraqi Freedom) but for more complicated reasons. These expeditions used economy of force without a clear strategy for reconstruction and the maintenance of public order, both clearly needed if democracy is to take root, itself a necessary factor in any exit strategy. Growing insurgencies in both countries currently work for the terrorists and against Coalition forces.

■ Mission Preparation: Defining the Enemy, Defining the Mission

A clear understanding of both the enemy and the threat is necessary to define the mission and the consequences of military intervention; however, the huge emotional and psychological shocks of the 9/11 attacks have clouded our judgment. Many believe that we have entered a new era, facing a frightening new enemy, but this is an illusion.

In the 1960s, an American officer went on record declaring that he would rather see America lose in Vietnam than risk destroying the American army. His point was that the main role of professional armies is to fight other armies in conventional actions—in those days the expected scenario was meeting the Soviet threat in Europe—his comments elicited a sympathetic chorus from British generals. In fact, most conflicts since World War II (the last high-intensity war in which America used weapons of mass destruction and Japan attempted to do so) have been either insurgencies or terrorist campaigns. Many incorporated both. These encounters are asymmetric at every level, favoring the guerrilla over the conventional army, which all too frequently blunders around like an enraged elephant.

Faced with a colonial or foreign power, the guerrilla seeks to inflict casualties through either military action or terrorism, often with great success. The body count then influences the political war, weakening the resolve of the aggressor's civilian population to stay the course. France publicly vowed to stay in Algeria, but after losing 39,000 dead and 350,000 wounded, it swallowed its pride and withdrew. The French army had won the military conflict, but with its brutal methods it lost the support of the French people. It lost the political war. Equally, America and its allies never lost a major military engagement in Vietnam; the war was lost at home, where the shift in public opinion reflected both contemporary social changes among the young and a population appalled at the mounting casualty rate in a war made very real for them through the media of newspapers and television.

The insurgent also wages a "people's war." Using "hearts and minds," coercion, and the selective use of terror, the guerrilla gradually seeks to dominate an area. The party, religion, or cause will brook no alternative leaders—landlords, teachers, village headmen, government agents, tax collectors, nongovernmental organizations (NGOs) are either murdered or driven out, and villages are then encouraged to provide food and recruits. The guerrillas establish their own shadow government in the area with guerrilla tax collectors, judges, intelligence officers, and propaganda teams. The village becomes a base, if only for a local guerrilla squad; it becomes part of the struggle.

At the international level, the people's war reaches into mosques and across the Internet. Initial engagement may begin with partisan religious instruction or an informal contact with a recruiter, leading to assessment and vetting and finally to a border crossing in Jordan, Syria, Iran, or Pakistan.

The people's war can also have religious overtones. Some clerics give the current conflicts a religious flavor by teaching that Islam cannot tolerate Christianity or Judaism (or indeed many of the Islamic sects embraced by non-Arabs). The Arab-Israeli confrontation, the eclipse of the Middle East by an emerging West in the 1600s–1700s, even the Crusades, are interwoven into a conspiracy theory so complete it could be termed a worldview. As evidence for this belief, Islamists cite recent events in Afghanistan and Iraq. In contrast, some Arab writers believe that religion is simply a lightning rod for loss of national self-esteem, poverty, and a general lack of opportunity. The Arab intellectual Nazib Ayubi wrote, "The Islamists are not angry because the aeroplane replaced the camel, they are angry because they could not get on the aeroplane." If he is right, the key to defeating the present insurgencies will begin with economic development, nation building, and representative government. Religious differences may then fade into the background.

By their nature, insurgencies also involve an asymmetric economic war. The 9/11 attacks struck at the heart of the West's capitalist system, forcing America and its allies to spend billions of dollars on new security measures. By comparison, the operational security of a guerrilla organization is relatively simple and cheap. Personnel generally remain in the shadows, and money is transferred anonymously around the world using couriers, friendly banks, or the informal banking system in use throughout India and the Middle East.

Nations pour billions of dollars into increasingly sophisticated military technology and the new generation of soldiers required to use it; insurgents make do with basic equipment and minimum training. Second Lieutenant Emily Perez was one of West Point's most promising young officers. A superb all-rounder, she was highly educated to take her place in an increasingly technical and rapidly evolving profession, which recruits its senior managers from the ranks of committed overachievers. The man who took her life, detonating a simple roadside bomb (or Improvised Explosive Device

[IED]) as her medical service convoy passed through his ambush south of Baghdad in September 2006, is probably illiterate and likely to be part of an informal eight- to ten-man bomb-making cell, perhaps centered in a single family or clan.

Expected to learn a simple task in a few hours and perform it well, such a man may have graduated from placing bombs or acting as a lookout, to detonating bombs or collecting intelligence on convoy times and routes; however, he would not have manufactured the IED, as mastering the technical aspects would be beyond him. He may have previously handled and stripped an AK-47 Kalashnikov but would have fired it for the first time in action.

His unit is informal, it has no traditions or doctrines or any need of them. On a nighttime ambush, the group may interface with a reconnaissance cell, responsible for firing flares to mark the progress of an American or British convoy, but these rare actions will involve only raids, skirmishes, and ambushes. The emphasis is on improvised backyard technology rather than on billion-dollar weapons systems.

Most cell members are highly motivated and committed; they will not rotate through Iraq on twelve-month tours. Death is welcomed, jihad a religious duty. Men with military experience control such fighters. At higher levels in the organization, the highly educated are allotted a single infrastructure task such as propaganda, recruitment, fund-raising, transportation, command and control, planning, or operations.

In the wake of 9/11 the most easily recognizable enemy was Osama bin Laden and his al-Qaeda group. Although often portrayed as the greatest threat to Western civilization since Genghis Khan, the intelligence community saw him differently. Many analysts view Bin Laden as a brilliant fund-raiser, a sometime soldier, but an extremely poor strategic thinker. Bin Laden's attacks on US embassies in Africa (1998) and on the USS *Cole* in Aden, Yemen (2000), followed by America's withdrawal from the Somali humanitarian mission (1993), convinced him that America was a "casualty adverse paper tiger." In fact, options after the attacks on the embassies and the USS *Cole* were few as America lacked forward operating bases to launch special operations in an area of extreme political sensitivity, located as it is on the doorstep of both Russia and China. It is a profound irony that this would change after the 9/11 attacks. Equally, the mission to protect the NGOs trying to break the Somali famine succeeded brilliantly. It was only when mission creep changed the goals to killing or capturing General Mohamed Farah Aideed, the most powerful warlord in Mogadishu, that America lost eighteen SOF soldiers, withdrew from its African mission, and armed clans with a street-gang mentality that saw food aid as a way to further clan rivalry.

Prior to 2001, it was difficult to assess the extent of the threat presented by Osama bin Laden. Distant, yet mysterious and menacing, he appeared not unlike the Old Man of the Mountains, the leader of the twelfth-century sect of Assassins—a figure to conjure fear in ordinary people but not a real threat to world peace. The New York attacks appear to have been part of a plan to drive America from the Middle East and end its support of Israel—itself the first step in an impossibly romantic scheme to launch a series of insurgencies to reestablish an Arab caliphate of the sort that existed around AD 670–800. However, bin Laden was in no position to unite Islam in a jihad. Not only was the New York attack condemned by such Moslem scholars as the grand mufti of Saudi Arabia, the head of Al-Azhar (the Sunni premier theological institution), Sheik Yusuf ak-Qaradawi, and Ayatollah Ali Khamenei, but they also questioned bin Laden's authority to declare offensive jihad (the preserve of Moslem rulers). In addition, the notion of a united Islam is belied by the fact that terrorists associated with al-Qaeda attacked Shiite mosques in Iran and Pakistan as a religious duty, while Wahhabism is generally hostile to any sect not sharing its fundamentalist Sunni beliefs.

Although bin Laden's popularity and empowerment increased as a consequence of the invasions of Afghanistan and particularly Iraq, he is becoming as irrelevant to the present security situation as Saddam Hussein soon became to the conflict in Iraq.

■ Mission Preparation: Future SOF Soldiers Will Be Peacekeepers, War Fighters, Experts in Counter-insurgency, and Skilled for a Multitude of Tasks

There are good reasons to avoid entanglement in insurgencies, as a successful outcome requires the involvement of a range of other specialists (those in civil affairs, politicians, NGOs, and law enforcement). However, since the middle of the twentieth century, armies have been asked to perform a range of tasks that risked involvement in armed conflicts with armed groups or insurgents. One of the earliest missions of this type was the rescue by Belgium paratroopers of civilians from the Congo (1964) and when British paratroops were forced to rescue some of their own peacekeepers in Somalia (2000). Even simple, short-term missions risk ensnarement in the underlying conflict for operational or political reasons. Such missions have included fostering stability (Sierra Leone, 1997, 2000), preventing genocide (Kosovo, 1990), providing famine relief (Somalia, 1993), and evacuating endangered civilians (Liberia, 1996). Special Forces have also been involved in disaster relief operations (Zaire, 1997; Kenya, 1998; Mozambique, 2000) because they deploy quickly, operate independently, and are multiskilled and trained to take the initiative. In more conventional conflicts, other high-value missions for the new millennium will include special reconnaissance and surveillance, ambush and counter-ambush, the apprehension of war criminals and terrorists, combat search and rescue, operations to counter weapons of mass destruction, counterterrorism, and helping foreign forces to help themselves.

■ Mission Preparation: Changes in Training and Technology

Armies must both project national power across the globe and refine the art of counterinsurgency and counterterrorism. This is an uneasy marriage. The first requires hi-tech integrated combat and intelligence systems, while the latter must do without them. Conventional operations take place in the physical space of the battlefield, counterinsurgencies in the target population's psyche. Kill five insurgents tomorrow, and next week, or next month, the unit, refitted and rearmed, will be back in action. Remove the "sea" (recruits or support) from the "fish," and the insurgency withers. Conventional forces often make the mistake of only seeing the physical space of the battlefield.

During the Cold War, the center of gravity shifted toward a potential high-intensity conflict in Europe, and much of Special Forces' advanced training at Fort Bragg centered on technological problems and engineering-based solutions. Radios were a case in point. When a Special Forces team acquired a target, high command required a stream of real-time intelligence to allow it to prepare air and artillery strikes and to assess the Big Picture. Radios provided the link, but opening communications on a hi-tech battlefield is akin to firing a weapon—both alert the enemy. In the electronic dimension, the patrol's position is quickly pinpointed using radio direction finding and triangulation. Enemy counterrecon may take an hour to arrive, but air and artillery strikes can be there within minutes.

Immediately after Vietnam, direction finding was slow, and the team radio operator could avoid detection by minimizing transmission time, easily achieved by increasing the speed of Morse transmission from a basic eight to thirty words per minute. As the countermeasures grew more sophisticated, the US Special Forces turned to frequency-hopper radios, which switch very quickly between prearranged frequencies. When the Russians developed "hopper traps," the Special Forces countered with the new technology of "burst transmission," in which messages are sent in an ultrafast burst. Monitoring and direction finding kept pace until the Soviets could detect and triangulate a burst transmission in less than two seconds; then the Americans turned to satellite communication, which can be intercepted only in a small area or "footprint" around the team or by an aircraft flying between the satellite and ground party. Similar developments with regard to Soviet capabilities shaped today's insertion/extraction vehicles, such as the SEAL Delivery Vehicles, the MC-130 Combat Talon, and the MH-53 Pave Low.

In some critical areas, technology will continue to evolve and accelerate. These include unmanned drones, stealth aircraft and missiles, explosive sniffers, aircraft survivability systems, intelligence database sharing, chemical and radiological monitors, Internet surveillance, tracking, and counterstrike capabilities. These are niche areas. On the conventional battlefield, few enemies will possess the technology to challenge America. Unchallenged by a potential adversary, air operations are likely to remain unchanged, particularly as any Western battle plan calls for air superiority and degradation of the enemy's anti-aircraft defenses. Naval Special Forces such as America's SEAL teams have been investing in new submersibles to make them less dependent upon parent submarines, and America's Virginia-class submarines are being built to accommodate special ops as well as conventional submarine operations. However, when confronted with two long-term wars, one in landlocked Afghanistan and the other in almost noncoastal Iraq, it is unlikely that governments will give covert water operations a high priority.

The key to future training is increased specialization (mission and operational area), with Western countries forming more Special Forces schools, enlarging units, and creating new ones. Britain has formed the Special Reconnaissance Regiment for all types of reconnaissance and surveillance including undercover urban operations. It will most likely expand into electronic surveillance, like America's Intelligence Support Activity (ISA), and support the UK Special Forces Group in the same way that Grey Fox supports Operational Detachment Delta's operations. Although Britain's Parachute Regiment could perform the same roles as America's Rangers, the new Special Forces Support Group, or "Ranger Regiment," was created around the First Battalion, the Parachute Regiment with input from the Royal Marine Commandos and the RAF Regiment. The "Americanization" of British Special Forces suggests a commitment to support American operations in the future.

America has restructured and expanded its special operational forces to some 46,000 personnel, with emphasis on small, covert teams and training teams. Under the new structure, Special Operations Command will no longer serve regional commanders in chief but will plan its own operations, its $6 billion budget (2004) reflecting this change. Increasingly, the Federal Army Reserve Special Forces Groups will handle overseas training missions. Under an order signed in early December 2002 by the secretary of defense, Donald Rumsfeld, the ISA is to provide a global intelligence network using local agents and electronic intelligence gathering. When a terrorist cell is discovered, shoot-to-kill teams, drawn from Delta, the Naval Special Warfare Development Group (DEVGRU), and the CIA's Special Activities Division, will be tasked with eliminating the terrorists.

Primary Special Forces training is unlikely to change. During the initial phase of the U.S. Army Special Forces' Qualification Course, the selectors look for reliable candidates with the right physical capabilities, intelligence, and mind-set to adapt to small-group warfare. The instructors look for candidates who can carry heavy loads over long distances while continuing to think and function like soldiers— who will keep going, planning their route to arrive at a distant map reference exactly when ordered; who integrate easily into the family atmosphere of an A Team, yet can operate alone; and who can attempt to complete the mission, even if the rest of the team is killed or wounded.

Phase two of the Army Special Forces Q Course is concerned with occupational skill training. Members of A Teams are assigned the roles of officer, weapons sergeant, engineer sergeant, medical sergeant, and communications sergeant. These are the occupational skills required by a small, unsupported force capable of operating for months behind enemy lines, not only taking the war to the enemy but acting as nation builders to indigenous troops or guerrillas. While other Special Forces units may assign different ranks to the holders of these specialties, or apportion the skills differently between the specialties, these are basic disciplines and are unlikely to change in the future.

One thing that will need to change is the number of personnel fluent in Farsi, Arabic, and the other languages of the Middle East and

Asia. The American State Department refers to these as "Class Five Languages," as they are the most difficult to master, being based on a non-Latin alphabet. Some US units are currently being given immersive (some practice outside the schoolroom) forty-day courses prior to deployment to Iraq, but this will ensure only a basic conversational skill. To master Arabic and its major dialects in its spoken and written forms sufficiently to work undercover takes many years of intensive training.

Green Beret selection culminates in Capstone Exercise Robin Sage where the A Teams lead guerrillas against a technologically sophisticated army invading their country ("Pineland"), conjuring theoretical operations behind Soviet lines during the Cold War and echoes of earlier missions when the Office of Strategic Services and the Jedburgh teams led partisans against the German army in World War II. The paratroop officers playing the role of guerrilla leaders are told to be exacting, suspicious, and hostile to the teams and their missions; however, they are unlikely to emulate Afghan warlords. Recognizing this, the White House made the Afghan warlords more amenable to cooperation prior to the invasion of Afghanistan by sending in CIA covert action teams with suitcases full of dollars. Robin Sage is also unique to the Army Special Forces and is, above all, a test of their ability to recruit, arm, train, and lead indigenous fighters.

In the future, more operators will take the courses designed for urban covert operations in hostile or neutral countries such as the Individual Terrorism Awareness Course and the Anti-Terrorism Instructor Qualification Course, part of the Special Operations Advanced Skills Curricula at the John F. Kennedy Special Warfare Center and School. The Terrorism Awareness Course covers the history and theory of terrorist operations before instilling in students an "awareness" of terrorism through threat analysis and countersurveillance. Thereafter, the course is intensely practical, covering IEDs, terrorist countersurveillance, and surviving as a terrorist hostage. Evasive driving, hostage rescue operations, and narco-terrorism are also included. The students are next introduced to setting up safe houses and operational houses, avoiding security police checks, and surveillance by hostile intelligence services, forging identity papers, lock picking, survival shooting, and the clandestine communications discussed in chapter 9 on intelligence support. These are the skills of the "agent" trying to remain undetected by a hostile populace and security forces, as exemplified by the ground teams that went into Tehran in 1980 to support the planned commando rescue of the American diplomats held in the American embassy. This is also the world of CIA covert ops, Delta Force, the ISA, and the other Joint Special Operations Command (JSOC) mission teams, using exactly the skills that will be required in the savage, dirty wars of the future.

▬ Operating behind Enemy Lines

Special mission terms of the future are unlikely to be concerned with hi-tech national defenses or sophisticated border crossings. Although some countries are surrounding themselves with fences, these constitute only basic perimeter security to deter casual insurgents and refugees. Few countries can afford to build, monitor, and patrol hi-tech borders across, say, the length of Saudi Arabia's frontier with Iraq or America's borders with Mexico or Canada. Even China's borders are marked only by the occasional post with checkpoints on the few major roads, and although the border is monitored by eight to sixteen roving border guards prepared to fire on escaping refugees, the guards can be easily avoided or bribed. China's land borders with Laos, Myanmar, India, Pakistan, Afghanistan, Tajikistan, and Mongolia have become some of the most porous in the world, aided in no small part by China's new market reforms.

Even the North Korean border has become very porous over the last few years, with escapes not only through China but also across the demilitarized zone. There are also new players in the game. Thirty years ago, only a foreign intelligence service or a Special Forces team with intelligence and local support could hope to extract an individual from inside China or North Korea. Today groups as disparate as people smugglers, money traffickers, church groups, and organized crime syndicates have sophisticated networks of safe houses and guides organized into escape systems capable of transporting people into a country (missionaries, gangsters, agents) while funneling political and economic refugees outside the country.

The extraction of a North Korean civilian begins with a validation exercise. The local agent or guide is usually a North Korean Communist Party member with permission to travel freely. The agent arrives at the target's home with travel documents and usually bicycles. The target is told that his or her mother or father or some other relative outside the country wants to talk to the target. Conducted to an area close enough to the Chinese border to access China's cell phone networks, the target is introduced to a money trafficker who allows the target to speak to the relative on a mobile phone. If the target is agreeable, the deal is done, and the man or woman is conducted back home to wait.

The next contact is unexpected; another North Korean will appear at the target's home with an agreed-upon message, such as "Mother is waiting for you." The North Korean will have a forged South Korean passport and travel documents for the target, along with the ubiquitous bicycles. Their journey may lead to a North Korean vessel about to sail or to the demilitarized zone where he or she is handed over to a soldier who conducts the target through the minefields to the Tumen River and the people smugglers waiting on the other side. This can cost around $10,000, but for a mere $3,000 an individual can be conducted across China to the border with Mongolia or Laos—and ultimately to Thailand, which readily grants refugee status. Of the some 8,740 North Koreans who are known to have fled since the end of the Korean War in 1953, 7,000 made their escape in the last four years. With guides and infrastructure commercially available, covert and undercover mission teams that have the physical traits and language skills to pass as locals can, in theory, penetrate any country in the world without the need for sophisticated insertion technology.

The low- and mid-intensity battlefields of the future may be urban nightmares like Iraq, or an inhospitable terrain offering little by way of concealment or natural resources like Afghanistan; others will resemble the Laotian/Cambodian border areas during the Vietnam War. Getting in will be easy; getting out will be the real trick. Foot patrols are vulnerable to the enemy and limited in what they can carry. Food, and particularly water, supplies may limit patrols to three to six days. In the far-flung corners of the world, weather and terrain will always complicate air-insertion operations. The thin, hot air of the desert and the rarefied air of high mountains make it more difficult to evade missiles and rocket-propelled grenades (RPGs), and Iraqi and Afghani insurgents have proved just as proficient as the Vietnamese at bringing down helicopters with concentrated ground fire.

Foot patrols will continue to play a role in mountainous and jungle terrain and possibly in the great northern forests and tundra. Faced with missions in other areas, teams may choose to deploy in vehicles such as Land Rovers and Pinzgauers, which are capable of carrying reserves of food, medicine, ammunition, and water as well as support weapons and an array of additional gear including communications—in effect a mobile team base. Traditionally used in remote areas such as deserts because of their higher profile, armed jeeps were used by the SAS behind the German lines in France in 1944, foraying out from maquis bases in the forests. A year later, they helped spearhead the Allied push into Germany amid a chaotic battlefield and a German army in a state of disintegration. During the Gulf War (Cobra II), Delta (and the Rangers) cut such a swath through western Iraq that Saddam Hussein became convinced that the main assault on Baghdad would come from the west. In all of these cases, the Allies enjoyed air superiority. The situation becomes trickier when the enemy enjoys air superiority or parity.

During the Cold War, Britain experimented with light armored reconnaissance in the stay-behind role. The crews of the light armored vehicles switched between heavily camouflaged surveillance positions and mobile patrols, defying attempts to locate them by electronic triangulation and counterreconnaissance. They also lowered their profile by moving at night and lying up by day. Their success clearly demonstrated that even light armored vehicles could operate covertly in a high-intensity environment without air superiority—at least for a while.

■ The Mission: Reconnaissance or Surveillance?

Toward the end of America's involvement in Vietnam, only 40 percent of MACVSOG patrols placed along the border or inside NVA sanctuary areas, such as the Ashau Valley, lasted longer than twenty-four hours. Some declared an emergency within twenty minutes of insertion, others simply disappeared. This experience gave rise to a belief during the Cold War that LRRPs would have little chance behind Russian lines with their overabundance of internal security and intelligence troops. Therefore, while NATO maintained an LRRP school, most reconnaissance troops were confined to surveillance hides from which they sought to provide continuous real-time intelligence.

Underground hides have two vulnerabilities: the periscope or observation port and the radio aerial or dish. Close to civilian areas, any change in the surroundings is likely to be investigated by children and dogs (two hides in the Persian Gulf War were compromised by children), and if discovered and surrounded, the chances of escape and evasion are low. During NATO exercises few hides positioned to watch roads and other communication links survived longer than four days. In contrast, patrols faced with evading sweeps and moving to a more secure overnight stop risked fragmenting into submodules but tended to survive longer.

Some areas of operations (AOs) have soil types and geography unsuitable for hides (sandy soil, high water table). Other AOs offer a bleak, hostile landscape with little cover and are intrinsically unfriendly to either close target reconnaissance or surveillance. Western forces in Afghanistan have some familiarity with the Russian experience of insertion helicopters coming under fire (Operation Anaconda, March 2002) and patrols and patrol observation scrapes being discovered by the enemy (Operation Mountain Lion, May 2002). High-altitude tracks leading to passes on the Pakistan border may be used infrequently and therefore are a waste of resources for a company or squadron tasked with building up a picture of mujahideen forces in an area. In the valleys, roads and tracks are often heavily used by both civilian traffic and guerrillas, and a small patrol can find itself confronted with a large guerrilla convoy, a counter-ambush force, or plastic mines sown on likely ambush sites. The Russians soon stopped using their Spetsnaz commandos in the recce-ambush role, as the mid- to long-term LRRPs for which they were trained simply did not work in Afghanistan.

The former Soviet Union had little time for value-loaded titles such as "commandos" or "special forces," preferring the more functional terms "forces of special designation" or "special purpose forces"; in this case the reconnaissance companies attached to divisions and regiments. Increasing their reconnaissance strength from 5 percent of their overall force to 20 percent, the Russians switched to surveillance, placing the teams in heavily concealed, aboveground Observation Posts (OPs) at high altitude, predominately ridgelines, crests, and spurs overlooking major routes running through the valleys and the network of trails on ridges and mountain flanks. Each post, which was manned by anything from a four-man team to a platoon, was equipped with powerful binoculars for day and night observation (B-6, B-12, BN-1, and BN-2 scopes) and ground radar (SBR-3, PSNR-1, and PSNR-5). The OPs were echeloned and layered to eliminate dead ground. By day, caravans were stopped and searched while all-night movement was viewed as hostile and pinpointed for artillery or 120 mm and 84 mm mortar fire, also used to support the post in the event of a surprise night attack. Heavy machine guns and AGS-17 automatic grenade launchers were also available to fend off attacks. The arrangement of the OPs, rather like the turrets of a medieval fortress, ensured that each OP could receive protective fire from the others. If the mujahideen responded by bombarding the OPs with rockets, dedicated artillery OPs equipped with laser range finders, and VPZK, SNAR-10, and ARK-1 counterbattery radar, could close down the attack, providing their signals were not overly absorbed or reflected by the mountains. At night, each OP sent listening teams into the valleys to monitor the roads and caravan camps. Central Asian conscripts served as much-needed linguists.

Once established, a post or line of posts maximized the intelligence yield by placing acoustic and seismic sensors (see chapter 6) along the high-altitude trails, interspersed with mechanical ambushes or fields of forty directional mines, each spread over a three-hundred-meter front. Each field was marked with two key sensors, four hundred meters apart, which notified the OP commander when a caravan reached the middle of the minefield. One after-action report details a nighttime detonation that caught twenty men and a line of pack animals. The ambush netted twelve KIA, one WIA, twenty rockets, four rifles, eight antitank mines, and thirty boxes of DShK ammunition. By contrast, human ambushes were slow, ponderous affairs, involving reconnaissance platoons armed with night sights and silenced weapons, often supported by engineers with mine-detecting equipment, flamethrowers, and CBR-3 ground radar. Movement to the ambush site was slow to ensure total concealment and to probe for mines and guerrilla ambushes.

Guerrilla radios were hidden among large caravans, in bases in ruined villages, or in caves. Some OPs were equipped with radio interception gear; however, the mountains made triangulation difficult. The Soviets used Mi-8 helicopters packed with radio intercept equipment, but the guerrillas soon realized their function and their radios went off the air. Consequently, the Soviets resorted to simultaneous air attacks on insurgent bases as such attacks always generated a high volume of excited radio traffic. The frequencies and bearings of the guerrilla radios were quickly fed into the computers of AN-26rr ELINT aircraft, which prowled the skies monitoring and recording enemy radio traffic. The closest analogue to Western Special Forces, the two Spetsnaz brigades under the command of the General Staff's Intelligence Directorate, now served as a reaction force to capitalize on this intelligence harvest—raiding mujahideen bases, using helicopters to surprise large caravans, generally closing down the enemy's supply lines. The former Soviet Union did not lose the reconnaissance war in Afghanistan; it lost the economic war.

Western forces are tied to the recce-ambush role by tradition, one that dates from Roger's Rangers. Despite many assertions that this is a fundamental misuse of such highly specialized units, they have been used in this role in every recent war, and as only a few centers teach

LRRP skills, they are likely to remain the preserve of commando units. One option for restructuring Western forces is to move away from regiments and Special Forces to focus more on function and specialization.

The Mission: Countering Weapons of Mass Destruction

During Exercise Roving Sands, the 5th Special Forces Group plays in the badlands of New Mexico where its desert mobility teams pit themselves against America's finest missile units. The action begins with a long insertion into the exercise area from Fort Bliss, Texas, using high-mobility vehicles, such as the light-strike vehicle and the Pinzgauer. Traveling by night, the Special Forces set up surveillance positions on the remote New Mexico roads, paying special attention to likely concealment sites, such as bridges and dry riverbeds. Within hours the teams were sending back intelligence reports, allowing the planners to assess the enemy's readiness to launch, prepare a response, notify military and civilian authorities in the likely impact areas, and deploy antimissile systems, such as the Patriot.

The scenarios in these exercises reflect the Special Forces' experience in the Persian Gulf War. Within minutes of "launching" a missile, the enemy heads toward its concealment site. Even when there are aircraft over the operational area, the Transporter-Erector-Launchers (TELs) are hard to find and even harder to kill. The enemy's Achilles' heel is the Forward Operating Base (FOB), which may hold up to fifty vehicles. These vehicles are vital to the TEL's operations, and as the Gulf War proved, their destruction is sufficient to stop the missiles, even if the launchers themselves remain intact. Excellent targets include the two crane vehicles that lift the missiles onto the TEL, the fuel trucks, the pressure test trucks, the oxidizer vehicles, the electrical system test vehicles, and the missile transporters. If a Special Forces team catches a TEL at its FOB, it has a seventy-minute window of opportunity while the missile is being loaded, armed, and fueled.

Another target of opportunity is the missile storage site, which may hold up to fifty missiles and is usually located close to the brigade headquarters. Usually such a large headquarters would be clearly visible across the electronic spectrum; however, missile forces use secure landlines for their communications. Locating and destroying the fiber-optic cables will force the headquarters to switch to a more visible means of communication. During the Persian Gulf War, initial attempts to find the cables failed, as the use of helicopters to transport the teams restricted the available time to the hours of darkness. Some later teams, HALO parachuted, enjoyed the luxury of four days in the operational area before being extracted by helicopter.

One little-known aspect of the Persian Gulf War returned to haunt America during Cobra II. Saddam Hussein's plan, immediately prior to the Coalition operations to free Kuwait, was to break the alliance apart by provoking Israel into nuclear retaliation. The provocation would be provided by conventional Al-Hussein ballistic missiles, each tipped with 250 kg of high explosive, under the command of General Hazim Abdal Razzaq Shihab Ayubi. They would target Israeli cities from the desert in western Iraq around the H2 and H3 airfields. In the event of any Israeli response against Iraq, a separate unit commanded by Hussein Kamal, director of the Special Security Organization, was to fire seven missiles tipped with binary nerve agents. The secret missile unit, answerable only to Saddam Hussein, was under the constant gaze of secret police guards at a site in western Iraq known only to senior members of the revolutionary council. Saddam believed that an Israeli attack on Iraq, followed by the mass slaughter of Israeli civilians in Tel Aviv and Haifa, would spark a general Middle Eastern conflict, throwing the Coalition battle plans into disarray.

The UN arms inspectors never found or dismantled these missiles, and lingering concerns were reignited during the run-up to Cobra II by an Iraqi defector who had already provided accurate, high-value intelligence on the Iraqi air force. Once again, the threat involved targeting Israel to provoke a response and draw other Arab states into the conflict. Finding this unit, if it existed, fell to Task Force 22, composed of mobile teams from the 5th Special Forces Group, the Australian SAS (whose job was finding fixed- and rotary-wing landing sites in western Iraq), and the British SAS, initially housed at Ruwaished and Abu-Tarha bases in Jordan but deployed in March to the Saudi-Iraq border. The teams were supported by A-10 Warthogs, F-16 Eagles, and E-3 AWACS operating out of Prince Sultan Air Base in Saudi Arabia.

Breaching the Iraqi border defenses, composed of two large sand berms, Task Force 22 headed north to the areas around Ar-Rutbah and Ar-Ramadi, quartering the ground and paying particular attention to culverts, dried riverbeds, and bridges. Iraqi mobile counter-reconnaissance screens, which were made up of trucks and technical vehicles carrying ten soldiers and armed with mounted Soviet-era DHSK heavy machine guns, attempted to intercept them, resulting in a series of brisk one-sided battles as the Americans called in air support. When it became clear that the Iraqi tactic was to use overwhelming force against the vehicles of individual A Teams and patrols, units combined to meet the threat. The result was the destruction of around eighty Iraqi vehicles and crew, but it was a hollow victory, for behind the screen was just empty desert—no SCUD launchers or forward bases. So, if the Iraqi special missile unit existed, where did it go? The only conceivable explanation is that it evaded across the Syrian border and was concealed by the Syrians.

■ The Mission: Counterinsurgency

When rumors swept Mosul that his men's night-vision equipment allowed them to see through women's clothing, Major General David H. Petraeus avoided the knee-jerk response of simply denying the accusations. Instead, he arranged a dinner for the sheiks and tribal elders where the equipment was passed around and its principles discussed. Then an amazing thing happened; the locals relaxed and began to raise other, more troubling, issues. Discussions followed, then agreements, as the meal became a working dinner. Another dinner followed the next week, and the week after, until it became a regular event with the Iraqis who were as enthusiastic as the Americans.

David Petraeus and his 101st Airborne had been given one of Iraq's most difficult areas. Driving into Mosul, one officer was reminded of scenes from the movie *Apocalypse Now*. With a minority Sunni population imposed on the Kurdish majority, it was a natural flash point for sectarian conflict. Now it was being torn apart by looting and lawlessness. Petraeus had some unusual qualifications for the job. An intellectual with a PhD in international relations focusing on counterinsurgency in Vietnam, he understood the tribal concept of *karaameh*, which embodies dignity and honor. In the Middle East, dignity is held to be more important than life itself, and the loss of personal or family dignity is what makes people join alliances that work against their own interests and ultimately sacrifice themselves. In addition, while Arabs often see Western freedoms as selfish, *karaameh* involves granting others the space, rights, and freedom to participate in tribal affairs without coercion or compulsion. Under Petraeus's command, cordon and search operations became cordon and knock—the suspect was informed that the house was surrounded and invited to give himself up. The Americans worked with local Iraqi leadership jump-starting the economy and local politics, and thereby injecting credibility into the reconstruction process. It has been said of Petraeus that the 101st was engaged in the sorts of strategies in 2003 that other units would be persuaded to follow in 2006.

In Afghanistan, the watchwords of the 19th Special Forces Group are "cultural sensitivity" as they attempt to consolidate NATO gains in the hostile Pesch Valley. When intelligence suggested that a local man working for the Americans had been coerced by the Taliban into hiding weapons in his house, the Green Berets paid an unexpected visit and waited to be invited inside. The man denied concealing weapons, but when threatened with a thorough search, he changed his story and led the soldiers into a bedroom. In a hiding place behind wall shelving, they found a surprisingly large haul of heavy machine-gun ammunition and Chinese-manufactured shells. With the ammunition safely removed, the soldiers gave the man a lift to work, underscoring their philosophy of loyalty and cooperation.

The Special Forces' main points of contact with often distant villages are the team medics, on call twenty-four hours a day and a powerful influence on people who have never seen a doctor. The patients' gratitude often translates into hard intelligence about mujahideen movements. The Special Forces also build schools and wells, but aid and reconstruction remain part of a carrot-and-stick inducement. The Pentagon wants value for its dollars, as reflected by a Special Forces captain who told a CBS television crew, "We take a small amount of tax money and we'll throw them a bone; build a well or something and make sure all the villages around know that, hey, if we're partners with the Americans, we're going to get some assistance too."

However, the odd bone here and there does not rebuild countries or transform tyrannies into democracies. This is one argument NGOs level against military "hearts-and-minds" programs, arguing that only civilian agencies are capable of carrying out a thorough reconstruction of national infrastructure efficiently and at market prices. More disingenuous, NGOs have argued that the Provincial Reconstruction Teams and Special Forces on the ground in Iraq and Afghanistan endanger civilian agencies by driving unmarked four-wheel drives and operating in civilian clothes. While this may be true, insurgents, keen to spoil any government successes, have always targeted NGOs—witness the campaign to eradicate malaria in Vietnam during the 1960s, which withered in a hail of gunfire. Who will control the reconstruction efforts going forward in Afghanistan or Iraq is under hot debate in the hallowed halls of the State Department, Pentagon, and universities—the intensity of the debate underscored by the battalions of new PhDs analyzing the problem.

■ The Mission: Apprehension of War Criminals and Terrorists

Four days after the attack on the World Trade Center, President Bush issued an ultimatum to the Taliban leadership in Afghanistan: surrender Osama bin Laden for trial in the United States or an American-led coalition will invade Afghanistan and take him. Mullah Mohammed Omar's reply was provocative. On September 24, the leader of the

Taliban told President Bush that bin Laden was a guest and that the United States must withdraw its troops from the Gulf and stop supporting Israel if it wished to remove the threat of terrorism. Eight days later, Afghanistan fired the first shot of war when it brought down an unmanned reconnaissance drone searching for al-Qaeda hideouts.

America quickly established Joint Task Force 5 to kill or capture high-value targets. At the top of the list were Osama bin Laden and Mullah Omar. Task force personnel included CIA covert action teams, Delta, DEVGRU, and Air Force combat controllers with attached squadrons of rotary- and fixed-wing aircraft.

The first serious attempt to capture or kill Mullah Omar came on the night of October 20, when Delta and SEALs hit the spiritual home of the Taliban: the village of Baba Sahib, some eight kilometers northwest of the southern city of Kandahar where Mullah Omar had a compound. Simultaneously, Rangers and Army Special Forces, operating as a combined force, parachuted onto the Kandahar military airfield and also a DZ close to the village. There was fierce resistance. and although the Pentagon did not release casualty figures, two Americans died when a helicopter was lost, and heavy casualties were incurred during the assault on the compound. The primary mission failed. Omar and bin Laden were still at large and very much in control of their forces.

The next sighting came in late November as al-Qaeda forces regrouped in the White Mountains (Spin Ghar) just south of Jalalabad, close to the Tora Bora cave complex. Historically, smugglers trafficking in drugs and contraband used these caves, which were ideally situated to store material on its way to Pakistani markets and for contraband destined for the cities of Afghanistan. During the Soviet occupation, the caves allowed many thousands of mujahideen to overwinter in the mountains. Although Coalition intelligence presented the cave complex as miles of tunnels arranged into a medieval fortress, the caves proved to be shallow, often protected by nothing more than a fighting position.

Stories were reaching the task force of a tall man in command of the forces around the caves. In early December, thousands of Northern

Alliance troops massed around the village of Pachir in the valley below the al-Qaeda stronghold. The NSA had informed General Tommy Ray Franks's headquarters that Osama bin Laden was making calls from the area on his cell phone. High above the anti-Taliban forces, B-52s pounded the 11,000-ft.-high mountain ridges with "smart" munitions. The American air force had a new thermobaric bomb, designed to collapse caves and caverns deep within the mountain. Equipped with a laser guidance system, the BLU-118B produces a massive explosion, collapsing caves and tunnels before the white-hot gas sucks the air out of the cave system. On December 11, recon photographs showed some Taliban trying to make the seventeen-hour trek to the Pakistan border. Back at the caves, the remainder played for time by negotiating surrender to the United Nations. By December 12 a combined force of Delta and British SAS had mobile sniper teams infiltrating the area, small forces investigating the caves bombed by the air force, and four-man SAS patrols covering the valleys and high mountain paths to the Pakistan border. However, despite some epic cave assaults and two "confirmed sightings," the operation was poorly coordinated, and Pentagon politics made the commanders hesitant. With the exception of one final sighting, both Mullah Omar and Osama bin Laden disappeared. They have been seen since only in occasional video clips released on the Internet.

The wanted men were probably not heading for the Pakistan border. The last known sighting of bin Laden, by a journalist, was in a cave north of Jalalabad, close to the mouth of the Wakhan Corridor, a fingerlike projection of Afghanistan abutting China and separating Pakistan from Tajikistan. This strange geographical feature is a nineteenth-century creation of the British Empire, intended to serve as a barrier to Russia's ambitions in India. At the end of this corridor lies the Kunlun Shan Mountains and China's predominantly Muslim province of Xinjiang, site of one of the highest border posts in the world.

Osama bin Laden had links to this region prior to 2001. In the late 1990s just a little farther south, where Pakistani Kashmir borders

China, he had met a bemused Eastern European arms dealer, escorted there by the Pakistani Intelligence Service. Bin Laden was in the market for a dirty bomb, and the arms dealer could supply radioactive waste from the former Eastern Bloc. The man's GPS confirmed that he was inside China when he was passed on to al-Qaeda guides who took him to a cave complex serving as bin Laden's headquarters. Reputedly, it was from this base, following America's cruise missile strike on bin Laden's Afghani camps, that two unexploded Tomahawk missiles were sold to the Chinese army. It is said that China paid bin Laden two million dollars for the cruise missiles. China has denied these allegations and accuses bin Laden of trying to destabilize the province by supporting the Muslim separatists. The truth is hard to discern. Many of the Persian or Turkic-speaking non-Han Sunni Muslims of the Xinjiang region, including the five million Uighurs in rebellion against the Chinese, look to Iran for religious and possibly military training; on the other hand, these groups are allotted propaganda Internet sites by groups affiliated with al-Qaeda.

Credible intelligence places bin Laden in this area. For a number of years the Indian government has claimed its satellites have photographed his motorcades in Pakistan-controlled Kashmir. Some of these photographs were leaked to the press in order to embarrass Pakistan. It is possible that China sees bin Laden as an asset or proxy in its rapidly escalating rivalry with America.

Yossef Bodansky, a specialist in Middle Eastern terrorism, believes that bin Laden, his son Saad, and Ayman al-Zawahiri were in Iran in 2003 orchestrating some of the mayhem inside Iraq. He also believes that, with Iranian assistance, they move freely through Asia and the Middle East from Iranian safe houses in Turkey, to al-Qaeda camps in Georgia, to the Fergana Valley in Kyrgyzstan, to northern Afghanistan, and onward through Afghanistan to Pakistan.

Joint Task Force 20 (now combined with Task Force 5 to form Task Force 121) was charged with detaining or killing the major players in the Iraqi regime whose faces were printed on a deck of cards. However, by the summer of 2003 Saddam Hussein and his sons remained at large, and rumors swirled around the Middle East that, helped by the Russians, many high-ranking Iraqis had found sanctuary in Libya. The rumors were bolstered by Saddam's personal secretary, Abid Hamid Humud al-Tikriti, who was captured in Tikrit on June 18, 2003, betrayed by the Baathist agent assigned to conduct him to his next safe house. Humud told his American interrogators that Saddam's family and associates had left the country via Minsk, from which they had flown first to Damascus, then to Chad, before entering Libya overland to avoid American surveillance on commercial flights to Tripoli. However, Kurdish intelligence officer Hoshayr Zabari questioned why Humud was carrying a clutch of Belarussian passports. Surely he had been sent back into Iraq to facilitate the escape of senior Baathists, possibility even Saddam Hussein?

At that time, the Syrian border, which was designated an "Economy of Force" area in the Cobra II plans, remained unsecured, and it was therefore expected that news of the arrest would send the networks racing for the border. Task Force 20 had already stepped up its surveillance of the main highways into Syria—a week earlier, two men had stopped at an American checkpoint near al-Qaim in the early hours of the morning, shooting dead one American soldier, wounding others, and then escaping behind a shower of grenades. It had been a distraction. While American forces searched for the assailants, several convoys had crossed the border.

On the night of Humud's arrest, a predator drone detected a convoy speeding through the village of Dhib in the al-Qaim area. Little Bird helicopters engaged the convoy but only succeeded in demolishing several houses, causing civilian casualties. Part of Task Force 20 took to the air, supported by an AC-130 Spectre gunship and A-10 ground attack aircraft. The convoy was engaged a second time close to the Syrian border where it split into two, three cars crossing the border, the remaining two driving parallel to the border on the Iraqi side. While the A-10s turned south to engage and ultimately destroy the convoy still in Iraq, the Spectre and the Task Force 20 helicopters crossed the border in hot pursuit. Syrian border defenses opened fire and were quickly engaged by the gunship. Meanwhile, as attack helicopters attempted to block the convoy's escape from the border town of Dulaym, Task Force 20 members disembarked inside Syria and moved forward on foot to capture the convoy's occupants. They ran into stiff resistance from Syrian border troops. With the situation deteriorating, attack helicopters destroyed the convoy then joined the Spectre in providing support for the task force operators on the ground. In the resulting firefight, the Syrians lost some thirty killed and five captured (released on June 30). Both countries had made their point. The Syrians decided against lodging a formal protest but beefed up their border defenses.

On the night of July 21, Saddam's sons Uday and Qusay, Qusay's fourteen-year-old son, and a bodyguard turned up at a rendezvous near Tal Afar, expecting bodyguards and guides to conduct them safely across the Syrian border. The RV was deserted. Isolated by betrayal and disillusionment within the Baathist networks, they had no choice but to return to the protection of their father's cousin Marwan Zaydan in Mosul. While knocking on the doors of the sleeping household in the early hours of the morning, they were observed by Zaydan's Kurdish neighbors who alerted the intelligence section of the Kurdish Patriotic Union—one branch of the Kurdish insurgent army. Later that morning when servants reported American activity around the house, Zaydan and his family fled, surrendering to the waiting Americans. Zaydan was persuaded to reveal the identity of his guests. Paratroops from the 101st Airborne secured the house and surrounding streets, and Task Force 20 troops called for the fugitives to surrender. Their demand was answered by a fusillade of AK-47 fire and grenades from inside the house, wounding four Americans and beginning a six-hour siege. Several times, Task Force 20 and the paratroops tried to clear the house, but even with his father, uncle, and the bodyguard dead, Qusay's son, Mustafa, continued fighting. It was only after the complex was partly demolished by TOW missiles, MK-19 grenade launchers, and rockets from two Kiowa Warrior helicopters that resistance ended.

Increasingly isolated and irrelevant to the Iraqi resistance movement, Mustafa's grandfather must have known that his days as a free man were numbered. Some sources claim that by December 2 former

Iraqi army officers, Muhammad Ibrahim al-Omar and Khalil Ibrahim al-Omar, had kidnapped Saddam to strengthen their positions within the Baathist resistance movement, keeping him prisoner in a narrow hole on a farm in the Ad-Dawr area. The capture and interrogation of a key Baathist, Muhammad Ibrahim Omar al-Musslit, on December 12, gave the Americans Saddam's approximate location. Early the next morning, Task Force 20 and elements of the 4th Infantry Division secured and extensively searched the two farmhouses on the estate but found nothing. However, when the former Baathist intelligence officer continued to insist that Saddam Hussein had been hidden on the estate, another search was made, and a soldier's attention was drawn to a straight crack in the ground near a shepherd's hut. He had found the hiding place of the former dictator of Iraq, who was subsequently sentenced to death and executed for crimes against humanity. Saddam loyalists assassinated the al-Omar brothers six days later.

Counterterrorism: Hostage Rescue

The terrorist has two main military strategies—the taking of hostages and the indiscriminate shooting and bombing of soldiers and civilians; however, it is hostage taking that offers the terrorist maximum political advantage and the chance of a prolonged emotionally charged "theater." Traditionally governments have responded with a studied refusal to negotiate with terrorists, combined with the threat of intervention or sending in hostage rescue teams to end the standoff and kill the terrorists. This approach worked for decades until Muslim suicide commandos and the late Shamil Basayev found ways to defeat it, forcing the world's top counterterrorists to rewrite the textbooks. Some analysts in the Pentagon believe that Russia's war against the Islamic Chechen separatists may provide an oracle for our own future. Once again, terrorists seem to hold the winning cards.

Russia faces three major terrorist groups: the Riyadus-Salikhin Reconnaissance and Sabotage Battalion of Chechen Martyrs, the Special Purpose Islamic Regiment, and the Islamic International Brigade, but its most formidable adversary was the late Chechen leader Shamil Basayev. Like many of the Islamic tribes in the former Soviet Middle East, the Chechens are a warrior people with a dislike of foreign oppression. After the revolution of 1917, they fought Stalin's troops and secret police until they were deported to Kazakhstan at the end of World War II. The survivors returned in the late '50s, living relatively peacefully until the Soviet invasion of Afghanistan. This was a poisoned chalice for the Soviets, affecting much more than their economy. Conscripts returned from Afghanistan with glowing reports of the bravery and fighting prowess of the mujahideen, reigniting religious and national aspirations. The metaphorical gun now cocked, pressure on the trigger grew with defeat in Afghanistan and the gradual disintegration of the Soviet Union. The result was an Islamic revival exploding across the Soviet states to the north of Iran and Afghanistan. Like many of these states, Chechnya declared independence under a former Communist Party boss, Soviet Air Force General Dzhokhar Dudayev, in November 1991. Finally, in December 1994, after several clandestine attempts to topple Dudayev, the Russian government sent in regular troops and internal forces to crush Chechen independence.

The late Shamil Basayev was typical of many young Muslims in the former Soviet Middle East, drawn to wherever Islamic guerrillas were fighting to establish a Muslim state. He saw combat in Azerbaijan and Georgia and was trained in guerrilla tactics by the mujahideen in training camps in Pakistan and Afghanistan. He returned to Chechnya in February 1994 to create an elite unit of fighters known as the Abkhaz Battalion, which would force the Russian hostage rescue units to revise their operating procedures. In June 1995, with the Russians winning and the situation desperate for the Chechen fighters, Basayev concealed around 150 of his fighters in two trucks loaded with coffins, supposedly containing the bodies of dead Russian soldiers, escorted by a third disguised as a Russian Militia (police) vehicle. Their target was Moscow, and the plan was to unleash a dramatic terrorist attack that would grab the attention of the Russian government and the world's media. It was a game of bluff. Lacking travel documents or any identity papers that might stand up to scrutiny, they were lucky to get 120 kilometers inside Russia before being stopped at a militia checkpoint and escorted to police headquarters in Budennovsk. Thinking quickly, Basayev had his men storm the police barracks, massacring the occupants. With several men wounded, Basayev's team moved on to Budennovsk Hospital, capturing some 1,500 patients, family members, and medical staff.

The Russian authorities quickly surrounded the hospital with regular forces and paramilitary police from the Department of the Interior. The Chechens released several communiqués, demanding the withdrawal of Russian troops from Chechnya and the opening of negotiations with Chechen leader Dzhokhar Dudayev, but these were ignored.

The siege had come at a very unfortunate time for the Russians, with President Yeltsin on his way to Canada. In accordance with time-honored principles, the Russian authorities refused to negotiate with the Chechens and ordered an Alpha Team to plan a rescue supported by Spetsnaz. Because the hospital was on open ground, the plan called for snipers to provide lethal fire support as multiple assault teams entered the hospital buildings. As if reading his adversaries' mind, Basayev positioned hostages in every window to discourage the snipers from shooting. June 15 and 16 passed in a tense standoff. For Yeltsin, interviewed while meeting Canadian schoolchildren, it was deeply embarrassing. Back in Russia the parliament, or Duma, passed a vote of no confidence in the government. Political pressure now drove matters to a disastrous conclusion. Placating the Duma with news of the "special operation," the minister of defense ordered the attack to proceed immediately. At 2 a.m. on Saturday, June 17, Russian forces attempted to storm the hospital but met fierce resistance and withdrew. Regrouping, they attacked again at dawn. It was a fiasco. Chechen counter-snipers, firing from behind their hostages, lay down withering, accurate fire, forcing the Russians back. Body armor reduced Russian military casualties to a minimum, but the bodies of more than one hundred dead or dying hostages blocked the windows.

Two days later, the world was treated to the humiliating spectacle of the Russian prime minister conducting telephone negotiations with Basayev on live television. The prime minister agreed to allow Basayev and his men to return to Chechnya unhindered in exchange for release of the surviving hostages. With certain key "power ministers" and Russian generals on the verge of revolt, it was also agreed that a number of journalists and Duma deputies ("volunteer hostages") would accompany the convoy. In addition, they negotiated a cease-fire under which Russia agreed to talks with the Chechen leadership. After several tense standoffs, one requiring the direct intervention of the prime minister, the convoy returned to a jubilant Chechnya, where the hostages were released and the fighters were filmed heading for the mountain village of Zandak.

President Yeltsin returned to Russia in a fury. Seizing upon a scapegoat, he informed the Russian people, "The Russians and the whole world saw the low capability of our special services to fulfill the tasks entrusted to them." The Chechen operation caused a furor, not only among the Russian military but also among Special Forces throughout the world. Put simply, governments expect the intervention team to rescue all the hostages unharmed, but this places the Special Forces in a lose-lose situation because the hostage rescue team only retains the confidence of its government and the populace until the next terrorist outrage.

In highlighting the stark choice for governments between negotiating with terrorists or accepting the political fallout resulting from the deaths of large numbers of hostages, Basayev's actions prompted special operators, as political servants, to review their operational procedures. Learned papers, magazine articles, internal reports, and intelligence reports all claimed that the answer to sieges such as the one at Budennovsk hospital lay in the use of "nonlethal weapons systems," particularly war gases, which render terrorists and hostages unconscious while the entry teams take control of the building. The Russians began to look for solutions in the nonlethal gases the former

Soviets had developed for special operations on the battlefield. In particular, they started training with fentanyl, a narcotic some one hundred times more active than morphine.

Meanwhile, in the face of Russia's refusal to grant independence to the tiny republic of Chechnya, the cease-fire broke down, and the Chechens again prepared to test Russian Special Forces' operating procedures. Seven years were to pass before another heavily armed Chechen commando entered Russia. This time the Chechens reached Moscow. At 10:15 on the evening of October 23, 2002, Chechen warlord Movsar Barayev and fifty heavily armed Chechen militants stormed the Palace of Culture Theater during the second act of a popular musical. The cast and audience were taken prisoner, with the exception of those claiming to be Muslim, who were released, the exits were sealed, and guards posted along the corridors. Then some 700 terrified hostages watched as the terrorists assembled a bomb large enough to collapse the theater. Five or six female Chechens, explosives strapped to their bodies, sat down among them. Outside, the Russian police and military sealed off the area.

On October 25, with many of the hostages suffering from dehydration, hunger, and fatigue, the terrorists permitted a doctor and a television camera crew to enter the building. Eight children and seven of the most seriously ill adults were released. The terrorists were engaging in theater of a different kind, watched nightly on newscasts throughout Russia and across the world.

Perhaps sensing they were losing control of the situation, the Russian authorities ordered an Alpha Team to assault the theater. Operators had already taken up positions on the roof and in the sewers under the building. Tiny cameras and microphones were inserted though small holes drilled through the walls. By means of these remote surveillance devices, the security forces learned that the female bombers were under orders not to detonate their personal explosives unless they received a command from one of their male colleagues. It was an edge, a very thin edge, but sufficient to craft a plan. The essential problem lay in the impossible odds against the team being able to break out of the sewers and eliminate the terrorists without detonation of the main bomb or one or more of the suicide bombs. However, if the male and female Chechens could be separated, no command could be given to detonate the explosive belts. Fentanyl would then be used to subdue the terrorists. Even if it worked imperfectly, there was still a good chance the intervention team would eliminate the terrorists before the main bomb could be detonated.

The situation began to deteriorate on the evening of October 25 when, recognizing that the government would never negotiate, the terrorists discussed executing the hostages and destroying the theater. In the early hours of the next morning, the Russian commandos watched as a screaming child attempted to break out of the auditorium, prompting panicky gunmen to fire into the hostages, killing two. The political pressure to resolve the situation increased dramatically. Just as dawn was breaking over Moscow, the terrorists woke hostage Giorgi Vasiliev, the play's author, who had been filming the performance on the night of the attack, demanding to see footage of themselves interrupting the performance as they stormed the theater. Vasiliev and all the male Chechens in the auditorium went to the projection room. Fate had handed the Russians their desperately needed opportunity.

As entry teams hurriedly formed up in the sewers and on the roof, fentanyl vapor was released into the main auditorium. Just minutes later, there was a loud explosion as the first team burst through the roof of the projection room, silently shooting all the gunmen clustered around Giorgi Vasiliev. Simultaneously, teams burst through the floor, eliminating the female suicide bombers. The sound of exploding stun grenades continued to rock the building as Special Forces systematically cleared the corridors and rooms.

Just after 7 a.m., the last shots rang out, and the soldiers turned to evacuating the civilians. It seemed to have been a textbook operation of the highest caliber until it was realized that some twenty hostages, weak and dehydrated, had lapsed into opiate-induced unconsciousness and died. Others, unconscious, died later, raising the death toll to a staggering 117. It is likely to be a very long time before a hostage rescue unit uses an incapacitating agent again.

Premier intervention teams watch each other's operations closely. Those operating under JSOC have come to realize that every complicated operation will be compromised at some point, and the earlier that event, the greater the likelihood of hostage casualties. If the compromise occurs after entry teams have breached the building (or vehicle), then fast, aggressive movement and shooting can save the situation. Although the fantasy may still be current in Hollywood that with the element of surprise elite troops superbly armed and exhaustively trained can, merely because they are "Special Forces," always execute the perfect rescue, it is not to be found in Fort Bragg.

■ Counterterrorism: Countering the Roadside Bomb

Amid the snipers, mortars, and mass RPG-7 ambushes, the greatest threat to the American soldier in Iraq is the simple roadside bomb, or IED. In the first year of the insurgency such devices accounted for one-third of those killed and two-thirds of those severely wounded. The bombers' target was America's supply convoys, and the majority of their victims were therefore drivers, medics, and mechanics. Most IEDs have been planted on the roads leading into Baghdad from the west, north, and northeast—the main supply routes for American convoys entering or leaving the capital, about 250 miles of pavement.

The first bombs, modified 155mm shells or mortar shells, appeared when piles of garbage began accumulating on the capital's streets. Hidden inside chocolate boxes, old tires, or even a dog's rotting corpse, the bombs were hardwired for manual detonation. Coalition forces responded to the threat by stopping the convoy before it reached the bomb, following the wire, and killing the bomber. The bombers responded by using decoys. A small, visible device or perhaps a broken-down bus or truck would be left on the road, prompting the convoy to halt some two hundred yards up the road from where the main device was hidden. The convoys learned not to stop, instead driving up on the sidewalk or into the oncoming lanes.

Meanwhile, foot patrols were trained to recognize signs of potential bomber activity, including lookouts loitering idly and men with handheld video cameras, ready to film the outrage for training and propaganda purposes.

The next generation of devices used the electronic components from a toy car, or other commonly available circuitry, linked to a radio-controlled detonator and wrapped in C4 explosive. US forces countered this threat by fixing toy-car controllers (or garage door remotes or cell phones) to their dashboards with the "on" switch taped down. In addition, these frequencies were routinely jammed or, alternatively, broadcast to cause a premature explosion. Sniper teams were deployed at night to kill the bomber as he or she planted the device.

The insurgents again changed tack, resorting to hardwired bombs linked to buried command wires. Sniper and spotter teams initially watched for people with shovels, but later they were ordered to eliminate anyone breaking the curfew and behaving suspiciously. Bulldozers plowed the sides of the road to expose the wires. The Humvees were given armored protection; tanks and armored vehicles patrolled the roads, so the terrorists brought in Chechens who had cut their teeth blowing up Russian tanks. A shaped charge destroyed an M-1A1 tank on October 28, 2003, forty miles north of Baghdad—providing a sinister example of cooperation between the Baathists and Islamists.

Simultaneously, the next mode of attack, the suicide car bomb, was telegraphed when the Americans picked up an unwitting suicide bomber—the driver, who was carrying a Syrian passport and pockets stuffed with banknotes, had been asked to deliver a car equipped with a bomb. However, the device was timed to explode before the end of his journey. Within days, five martyr-driven car bombs had exploded in Baghdad, outside government buildings, police stations, and the Red Cross headquarters. Doctors and medics would soon come to recognize the terrible injuries resulting from such attacks, the blast virtually liquefying the soft internal organs of those caught in the lethal radius. Brains came away with helmets.

Outside Baghdad, the bombers began placing their devices in the fronds of roadside palm trees. Those injuries too were characteristic:

multiple shrapnel injuries from metal and glass as the bombs shredded vehicles above the armor plating. In response, an extensive network of closed-circuit television cameras was rolled out, patrols and sniper teams were deployed, and some freight was moved by air, so the insurgents switched to softer targets: Iraqi army, police, and civilians. One army general likened it to a cruel, destructive version of the children's game Rock, Paper, Scissors. Security specialists likened it to a spiraling conversation between bomber and counterterrorist. The only question concerning them was, "What is the bomber doing when the countermeasures are still effective?" In other words, what form will the next mode of attack take? There will always be a new move until the bomber has achieved his or her aims or his or her organization has been eliminated.

Intelligence Support: The Internet

Computer skills have become increasingly important to American Special Forces. The communications specialist in an average Army Special Forces A Team is expected to be more than computer literate, the specialist is expected to understand and manipulate computer networks for hardwire communications with the command structure and access to intelligence databases. More specialized units, like Delta, have computer cells composed of soldiers trained in the theory of cracking and hacking, while in the ISA these skills are widespread. Beyond Special Forces, whose skills are offensive in nature, Military Intelligence and Signals maintain *defensive* units to prevent hackers, terrorists, and foreign powers from penetrating America's defense computers, while the FBI's National Infrastructure Protection Center has primary responsibility for identifying and assessing attacks against America's networks. The center has the lead role in providing early warning of computer attacks and pursuing cybercriminals but liaises with Space Command at Peterson Air Force Base, Colorado, in the event of cyberattacks and espionage by terrorists and foreign powers. Other service branches contribute in various ways to this new challenge, primarily the Joint Task Force-Computer Network Defense

(JTF-CND) in Virginia, which serves as the focal point for defense of Department of Defense computers.

Arrayed against them are some powerful operators. Over the past decade, China has directed an intense espionage offensive against North America in both the physical context and cyberspace. Missions have included military and commercial espionage carried out by intelligence officers, supported by highly trained offensive computer units from the People's Liberation Army. Other operations may have included reconnaissance of the computer networks controlling vital utilities such as water and power. An aggressive Internet presence has supported and complemented operations in the real world in which intelligence cells and Chinese gangsters under the control of China's intelligence service targeted Canadian and American businesses in what investigators described as "part of an overall plan to win an unconventional war." This may be economic competition seasoned with espionage, but intelligence analysts are more concerned about an electronic Pearl Harbor prior to conventional hostilities. In this scenario, computers rather than teams of commandos would carry out paralyzing attacks on high-value targets.

The trickle-down model of technology holds that what is the preserve of nations today will become available to terrorists and criminals in the future. The open, universal nature of the Internet, the employment of former servicemen as contractors or mercenaries, and the establishment of terrorist training schools as netherworld universities, hyperaccelerates the transfer of technology and ideas. Consequently, an intruder inside a heavily protected defense computer could just as likely be a terrorist or teenage hacker as a spy.

In the post-9/11 world, with so many real threats facing Western countries, tolerance for hackers has markedly decreased. Both the FBI and intelligence circulate through the American hacker community developing contacts and informants while maintaining active professional links with foreign law enforcement. The technology is in place to track hackers "phreaking" through dial-up connections into ISPs in South America before disappearing into labyrinthine university nets to reemerge inside defense computers. These advances made it possible to track, identify, and apprehend the two foreign hackers who illegally entered the Air Force's Rome Lab in New York in March 1994. If the culprits are terrorists rather than geek teenagers, the orders for their apprehension or elimination are likely to be passed to a small, covert action team.

The Internet has other security aspects. The hidden alleyways of cyberspace offer many more methods of passing secrets and information than a dead drop in Central Park or a brush contact on the Paris Métro. Private chat rooms with direct computer-computer (DCC) links can offer a quick, efficient method of transferring any material converted into a digital format. Tracing is possible but difficult if the chat room is in, say, Estonia, and the two parties are in other countries, and more difficult still if the IP addresses of the individuals are deliberately obscured (for example by using servers that offer this service). Far more efficient than radio messages, one-time Hotmail accounts, created and dissolved in a few minutes in an Internet café or library, leave few traces. Alternatively, operational codes, hidden inside seemingly innocuous texts, can be left on any one of millions of Web sites.

Some messages are open and easily accessible. Claiming to speak on behalf of the Iraqi Baath Party, the Dhe Qar Directorate of Operation "Special Operations" issued orders (September 6, 2006) to "commanders of special units" to assassinate a list of Iraqi politicians and Shiite leaders. Other communiqués have listed the names and addresses of witnesses and lawyers involved in the recent trial of Saddam Hussein. Some of those witnesses were murdered. In other cases, the poorly trained local assassination teams were satisfied with killing extended family members.

Suicide bomber Abu Mufadh (a Saudi whose real name was Sa'd bin Saleh Al-Janubi) left a ten-minute video in which he demonstrated how to assemble a car bomb. Next, the actual attack is shown, followed by a eulogy for the bomber. On October 19, 2006, a number of Islamist Web sites published a list of German Web sites that they claimed had defamed God and Islam. Links provided instructions for denial-of-service attacks in which the target server or computer is overwhelmed by other computers attempting to access it (most easily achieved by a dedicated network of computers or by inserting a "Trojan horse" to hijack innocent computers).

As previously mentioned, the Internet also serves as an important venue for proselytizing, recruitment, fund-raising, and propaganda. Recent videos soliciting funds and volunteers have shown a sniper at work in Baghdad and Uighur guerrillas training in the red-sand desert somewhere inside Xinjiang (couriers carry digital video clips across the border, so avoiding the Bamboo Firewall). Hits on these Web sites show their immense popularity.

The Internet has become the virtual battlefield of the future, but it remains uncontested by Coalition forces. There are no videos showing the human cost of the carnage inside Iraq or scholarly minidocumentaries questioning whether the Koran can be used to justify the indiscriminate killing of innocents. We have not attempted to harness the skills of Arab-Americans to argue a different point of view in the Arab media. Despite all the hard-earned lessons of Vietnam and other brush-fire wars, our civil affairs companies and psychological warfare teams remain a military curiosity, staffed predominately by reserve personnel. We see very little beyond our domestic political arenas and the physical battlefield.

Appendix

The World's Major Special
Operational Forces

Country/Unit	Role and Notable Operations
ARGENTINA	
Buzo Tactico	Naval Special Forces. Saw action against the British Royal Marines during the invasion of the Falkland Islands (April 1982).
Halcon (Falcon) 8	Permanent cadre of Army Special Forces (40–45 men). Counterterrorism and counterinsurgency.
Army Commando Coys	Trained to conduct mountain operations and LRRPs. As a result of their skill at arms, they were also used to deploy anti-aircraft missiles during the Falklands conflict. On the Falklands they were joined by the Air Force's Special Operations Group and the police Gendarmerie Special Forces Squadron. A forward patrol of army commandos were defeated by the British Royal Marines Mountain and Arctic Warfare Cadre at Top Malo House on May 31, 1982.

AUSTRALIA

Army Commando Coys

Party of Citizen's Military Force (Army Reserve). Roles: reconnaissance, raids, special assault tasks, and training indigenous forces. Some NCOs and officers were attached to the American Civilian Irregular Defense Program during the Vietnam War.

Special Air Service

Roles: strategic and operational intelligence gathering (LRRPs and LRS), harassing the enemy in depth with raids and ambushes, combat rescue operations, and counterterrorism. The regiment has seen combat in Borneo and Vietnam.

Regional Surveillance Units

NORFORCE, the Pilbara Regiment, and the 51 Far North Queensland Regiment are army reserve units trained to conduct surveillance and reconnaissance operations and fight in a stay-behind capacity.

BELGIUM

Para-Commando Regiment

Formed in 1952 to amalgamate the army Commando Regiment and the 1st Parachute Regiment SAS. Acts as rapid reinforcement for NATO while maintaining specialist reconnaissance, maritime, and mountain warfare units. The Para-Commandos also provide support for counterterrorist operations. In November 1964, the 1st Parachute Battalion and 12th Coy, 2nd Commando Battalion, rescued European hostages caught up in the Congo civil war.

Special Intervention Squadron

National intervention unit drawn from the paramilitary police or *Gendarmerie Royale*.

CANADA

Special Service Force

Rapid reaction force trained for international operations and internal defense. Also provides support for counterterrorist operations.

Emergency Response Teams	Royal Canadian Mounted Police national intervention teams.

COMMONWEALTH OF INDEPENDENT STATES
(FORMERLY, THE USSR)

Forces of Special Designation (Spetsnaz) Russian Army (2nd Directorate of Military Intelligence)	1) Independent Companies attached to each army. 2) Long Range Reconnaissance Regiments. 3) 16 Special Operations Brigades attached to each Group of Forces or Military District. Each brigade has a headquarters company of elite professional troops for sensitive missions.
Russian Navy	Four Naval Spetsnaz Brigades attached to each of the Northern, Baltic, Black Sea, and Pacific Fleets. Each consists of a headquarters company (special operations), midget submarine group, three combat-swimmer battalions, a parachute battalion, a signals company, and technical support units.
Ministry of Internal Affairs (MVD)	Dzerzhinskiy Special Operations Motor rifle Division—internal security.
Committee of State Security (KGB)	1) Spetsnaz forces, probably drawn from elements of the KGB Border Guards. 2) Alpha Teams. Counterterrorism and special operations. Transport and technical support provided by Border Guards Directorate and controlled by the Urgent Action Crisis Head-quarters in Moscow.

FRANCE

2nd Foreign Legion Parachute Regiment	No. 1 Coy—urban warfare, night and helicopter operations, including commando raids. No. 2 Coy—mountain warfare. No. 3 Coy—maritime operations.

No. 4 Coy—sabotage, demolitions, and stay-behind operations. Commandos de Renseignement et de l'Action en Profondeur—special operations. The 2e Régiment Étranger de Parachutistes was virtually wiped out during the siege of Dien Bien Phu (Indochina) and reformed for the Algerian War. In May 1978, elements of the Regiment parachuted into Zaire to rescue European hostages held in the mining town of Kolwezi.

Groupement d'Intervention de la Gendarmerie Nationale

GIGN, the French national intervention team, is drawn from the Gendarmerie Nationale. Hostage rescue operations have included the release of French schoolchildren at Djibouti (1976), the rescue of hostages at Clairvaux Prison (1978), and the training of Saudi forces prior to the recapture of the Great Mosque at Mecca (1979).

GERMANY

Fernspahetruppen

The Bundeswehr deployed three LRRP companies, which drew many of their recruits from the airborne and alpine divisions. Since the reunification of Germany, these have presumably been joined by East German Special Forces such as the 40th (Willi Sanger) Parachute Battalion.

Grenzschutzgruppe 9

GSG-9 is the German national intervention team and, like many European counterparts, is drawn from a paramilitary police force: the Federal Border Police. It has conducted domestic operations against the Red Army Faction (RAF) terrorists, including the rescue of hostages from a Lufthansa 707, which was hijacked by the RAF and flown to Mogadishu (1977).

HOLLAND

Royal Netherlands Marine Corps

Rapid reaction force which supports NATO under the command of Britain's 3 Commando Brigade. Also provides the national intervention team or Marine Close Combat Unit. Notable operations include the termination of the 1977 sieges on the Depunt train and the Bovensmilde primary school.

INDIA

Para-Commandos

Formed from the Army Commandos and the 9th Parachute Battalion. Conducts independent operations and actions in support of the two parachute brigades. Intervention force operators of the Special Counterterrorist Unit are drawn exclusively from the Para-Commandos.

INDONESIA

Amphibious Recon Para-Commando

Coastal reconnaissance.

Air Force Special Forces

Airfield security, capture of hostile airfields, search and rescue, pathfinding, and forward air control.

Unconventional Warfare Force

"Para-Commando" operations and training indigenous forces. Indonesian Special Forces were in action against the British in Borneo and spearheaded the 1975 invasion of East Timor (Operations Lotus).

ISRAEL

Naval Commandos

Maritime raids and reconnaissance.

Sayeret units

Reconnaissance.

Sayeret Matkal

Foreign special operations. Numerous wartime and counterterrorist operations, including the Entebbe raid (1976).

Yaman	Border police national intervention force.
Shal-dag	Technical and intelligence support.

ITALY

San Marco Marine Battalion	Amphibious and rapid reaction force operations.
Commando Reggrupamento Subacquei ed Incursori	Underwater warfare.
Folgore Brigade	Parachute-trained assault and sabotage force.
Groupe Interventional Speciale	National intervention team drawn from parachute-trained elements of the paramilitary police or Carabinieri. Also specializes in underwater or "Incursori" operations.
Nucleo Operativo Central di Sicurezza	National intervention team which achieved international fame after their rescue of US Army General James Dozier (1982).

NEW ZEALAND

SAS Squadron	Full spectrum of special operations including mounting intervention teams for counterterrorist operations.

NORTH KOREA

Special Purpose Forces	Approximately 70–105,000 personnel organized into diversionary, assault, reconnaissance, and special operations units. Twenty-four light-infantry brigades comprising airborne, amphibious, and reconnaissance units, five combined-arms brigades, and 35 divisional-level light infantry brigades. North Korean Special Forces have conducted numerous operations against the Republic of Korea.

PAKISTAN

Army Special Services Group

Para-Commandos who also provide the national intervention team.

PHILIPPINES

Army Special Warfare Brigade

Modelled on US forces, the Brigade consists of Scout Ranger battalions (reconnaissance/raiding), Special Operations Group (urban warfare), and Home Defense Forces (village and regional militia).

Special Action Force

Philippine Constabulary commandos organized into mobile strike forces.

Special Warfare Group

Naval unit modeled on US Navy's SEAL teams.

Aviation Security Commando

Air Force counterterrorist team.

THE REPUBLIC OF KOREA

Ranger Battalions

Modelled on US Rangers.

Army Special Warfare Command

The training of indigenous forces and special operations. 707th Special Mission Battalion deploys national intervention teams.

SOUTH AFRICA

Reconnaissance Commando

Reconnaissance, tracking, and sabotage operations.

South African Police Special Task Force

Primary national intervention force.

Special Task Force of the South African Rail and Harbor Police

Transport intervention team.

THAILAND

Royal Thai Special Forces

The Special Warfare Command consists of five Special Forces Regiments, organized into two SF Divisions, with an independent LRRP company, Airborne Resupply Battalion, and Psychological Operations Battalion. The Command is organized along American lines with Ranger units deployed for reconnaissance and raiding tasks and Special Forces troopers training indigenous militia for counterinsurgency operations.

Royal Thai Marine Corps Reconnaissance Company

Coastal reconnaissance. The Thai Recons also deploy an intervention team.

Royal Thai Navy Sea-Air-Land Teams

Waterborne wartime and counterterrorist operations.

Police Aerial Resupply Unit

Counterterrorism and remote area counterinsurgency operations.

Border Patrol Police

Counterterrorism and operations against drug traffickers.

UNITED KINGDOM

22nd SAS Regiment

Full spectrum of special operations including providing the national intervention teams. The regular SAS saw extensive action during WWII in North Africa, the Mediterranean, Italy, France, and Germany. In the postwar era, the Regiment has seen action in Malaysia, Borneo, the Oman, Aden, Northern Ireland, and the Falklands.

23 SAS (V)

Combat rescue and intelligence gathering.

21 SAS (V)

Intelligence gathering.

264 SAS	Regular Signals Squadron.
63 SAS	V Signals Squadron.
Special Boat Service (RM)	Royal Marines maritime operations unit of swimmer/canoeists. Specialize in operations lending themselves to seaborne insertion, undersea warfare, and maritime terrorism.

OTHER UK SPECIALIST UNITS

Mountain and Arctic Warfare Cadre	Royal Marine cold weather and mountain specialists. Roles: LRRPs, pathfinding, specialized cliff assaults, and the provision of instructors to the Royal Marine Commandos.
Commacchio Group (RM)	Royal Marine unit tasked with the defense of Britain's oil rigs and nuclear arsenal.
Pathfinder Platoon	Parachute Regiment's airborne pathfinder and reconnaissance specialists.

UNITED STATES

United States Special Operations Command	1) US Army Special Operations Command: Five regular and four reserve Special Forces Groups, 75th Ranger Regiment, Special Operations Aviation Brigade, 160th Aviation Battalion, 4th PSYOP Group (four battalions), 122nd Signal Battalion, and 96th Civil Affairs Group. 1st Special Forces Operational Detachment (Delta Force)—intervention, counterrevolutionary warfare tactics, and aggressive special operations.
	2) Navy Special Warfare Command: Two Naval Special Warfare Groups consisting of Sea-Air-Land (SEAL) Teams (amphibious and underwater commandos), Special Boat Squadrons (specialized

maritime craft), SEAL Delivery Vehicle Teams and the Inshore Undersea Warfare Groups (surveillance and protection of beaches, anchorages, and harbors against enemy special forces). SEAL Teams Five and Six—naval component of Delta Force.

3) Air Force Special Operations Command: 1st Special Operations Wing provides five Special Operations Squadrons of fixed- and rotary-wing aircraft for special and psychological operations, fire support, and long-range low-level night troop movements.

4) Joint Special Operations Command: Doctrine, techniques and requirements of all services and oversees the command and control of all multi-service special operations.

OTHER SPECIALIST US UNITS

Intelligence Support Activity

Intelligence support for counterterrorist and special operations. Part of Intelligence and Security Command.

Technical Analysis Team

Electronic countersurveillance and security of US Army bases and American defense facilities. Rapid reaction support for counterintelligence teams. Part of Department of Defense Technology Management Office.

Seaspray

Clandestine US Army/CIA aviation unit.

Long Range Surveillance Companies

Assigned to armored battalions as part of Military Intelligence Brigades' Combat Electronic Warfare Intelligence Effort.

Long Range Surveillance Detachments

Attached to armored cavalry squadrons.

Eskimo Scouts	Regional surveillance (Alaska's Army National Guard).
10th Mountain Division (Light Infantry)	Stay-behind operations.
US Marine Corps: Reconnaissance Battalions	Conduct LRRPs for Marine battalions. Pathfinding and reconnaissance for amphibious landings and intervention operations.

US NATIONAL INTERVENTION TEAMS

Treasury Department's Secret Service	Executive Protection Division provides bodyguard teams for the president.
Nuclear Emergency Search Team (Energy Department)	The recovery of nuclear weapons or weapons-grade fuel stolen or illegally obtained by terrorist groups.
Federal Bureau of Investigation	The FBI deploys one national Hostage Response Team and smaller counterterrorist teams in each US state.
US Marshal's Service	Intervention team.
US National Park Police	Intervention team.
The Secret Service	Provides close personal protection for the US president.

Bibliography

Adkin, Mark. *Urgent Fury: The Battle for Grenada*. Leo Cooper, London, 1989.

AF Regulation 64–4, Volumes 1 and 2. *Search and Rescue Survival Training*. Department of the Air Force.

Amundsen, "Kirsten." "Spetsnaz and Soviet Far North Strategy." *Armed Forces Journal International*, December 1989.

Andrew, Christopher and Gordievsky, Oleg. *Instructions From the Center*. Hodder & Stoughton, UK, 1991.

Archer, Bob. "After the Storm." *United States Air Force Yearbook* 1992.

Bermudez, Joseph S. Jr. "North Korean Special Forces." Jane's Publishing Company, UK, 1988.

Bermudez, Joseph S. Jr. "North Korea's Intelligence Agencies and Infiltration Operations." *Jane's Intelligence Review*, June 1991.

Bosiljevac, T.L. *SEALS; UDT/SEAL Operations in Vietnam*. Green Hill Books, Lionel Levanthal Ltd, UK, 1990.

Burnett, F.R., Tovar, Hugh B., and Schultz, Richard H. *Special Operations in US Strategy*. National Defense University and National Strategy Information Center, Inc.

Casey, William. *The Secret War*. Simon & Schuster, New York and London, 1988.

Clutterbuck, Richard. *Terrorism and Guerilla Warfare*. Routledge, London, 1990.

Collins, John M. *Green Berets, SEALs & Spetsnaz*. Pergamon-Brassey's, London & New York, 1987.

Combat Survival: SAS Escape & Evasion Course Notes. Paladin Press, Boulder, Colorado, USA.

Cooper, Dale. "Bulldog Balwanz and His Eight-Man Army." *Soldier of Fortune*, May 1992.

Devereux, Tony. *Messenger Gods of Battle*. Brassey's UK, London and New York, 1991.

Dolmatov, A.I. *Special Physical Training*. Central Council of the Dynamo *Physical Culture and Sports Organisation*, 2nd revised edition. Translated into English and published as *KGB Alpha Team Training Manual*. Paladin Press, Boulder, Colorado, USA, 1992.

England, James. *Long-Range Patrol Operations: Reconnaissance Combat and Special Operations*. Paladin Press, USA, 1987.

Ernst, Bernhard F. "Traffic-Control and Radiomonitoring Direction Finders Covering HF to UHF." *News From Rohde & Schwarz*, Vol 29, 124, January 1989.

Hamilton, Nigel. "The Price of Independence" in *Frontiers*. BBC Books, London, 1991.

FM 7-93. *Long Range Surveillance Unit Operations*. Department of the Army.

FM 31-19. *Special Forces Military Free-Fall Parachuting*. Department of the Army.

FM 31-20. *Special Forces Operational Techniques*. Department of the Army.

FM 31-24. *Special Forces Air Operations*. Department of the Army.

FM 31-45. *Special Forces Waterborne Operations*. Department of the Army.

Fielding, Xan. *One Man in His Time*. Macmillan, London, 1990.

Friedman, Colonel Richard S. "Intelligence and the War on Land." In *The Intelligence War*, Kennedy Colonel William V., (Chief Editor). Salamander Books Ltd, London, 1983.

Geraghty, Tony. *Who Dares Wins: The Special Air Service, 1950 to the Gulf War*. Little, Brown and Company, London, 1992.

Grabau, Rudolf. "Radio Direction Finding II." *News From Rohde & Schwarz*, Vol. 29, 124, January 1989.

Hackwork, Colonel David and Sherman, Julie. *About Face*. Sidgwick & Jackson and Guild Publishing, London, 1989.

Hyde, Montgomery. *George Blake, Superspy*. Constable, London, 1987.

KGB. *Essential Handbook for KGB Agents*. USSR Committee for State Security, Moscow, published in English by Industrial Information Index, London, 1991.

King, Patrick. *The Black Box*. Combat & Survival, July 1992.

Kutter, Colonel Wolf D. "Deep Behind Enemy Liens." *Military Review*, June, 1990.

Langmuir, Eric. *Mountaincraft and Leadership*. The Scottish Sports Council and The Mountainwalking Leader Training Board, 1984, UK.

Livingstone, Neil. *The Cult of Counterterrorism*. Lexington Books, USA, 1990.

Long, Helen. *Safe Houses Are Dangerous*. William Kimber, London, 1985.

Lonsdale, Mark. *Advanced Weapons Training for Hostage Rescue Units*. Specialized Tactical Training Unit, California, 1988.

Mangold, Tom. *Cold Warrior*. Simon & Schuster, UK, 1991.

McGee, Eddie. *Complete Book of Survival*. Stanley Paul and Co. Ltd, UK, 1988.

McLoughlin, Chris. "Internal Security: Special Ops '91'." *International Defense Review*, November 1991.

Micheletti, Eric & McColl. Colonel Alex M.S. "Dragoon Scouts." *Soldier of Fortune*, May 1992.

Office of Air Force History. *Search and Rescue in Southeast Asia*. Office of Air Force History, Washington, DC, 1980.

Paschall, Rod. *Low Intensity Conflict 2010: Special Operations and Low Intensity Conflict in the Next Century*. Brassey's US Inc., New York and London, 1992.

Plugge, Matthias. "Soviet Special Forces Used to Maintain Law and Order." *International Defense Review*, March 1991.

Quayle, Anthony. *A Time To Speak*. Barrie & Jenkins, London 1990.

Robinson, Mike. *Fighting Skills of the SAS*. Sidgwick & Jackson, Great
   Britain, 1991.

Shortt, Jim. "Spetsnaz." *Soldier of Fortune*. June 1992.

ST 31-91B. *US Army Special Forces Medical Handbook*. Department of
   the Army.

Stoll, Clifford. *The Cuckoo's Egg*. Bodley Head, London, 1989.

Suvorov, Viktor. *Soviet Military Intelligence*. Grafton Books, Great
   Britain, 1986.

Tusa, Francis. "Soviets Feared Battle for Berlin might have Pushed Allies toward Minsk." *Armed Forces Journal International*, February
   1992.

US Special Forces Reconnaissance Manual. (United States Institute for
   Military Assistance, 1972), Lancer Militia, USA, 1986.

Welham, Michael. *Combat Frogmen*. Patrick Stephens Ltd, London, 1989.

West, Nigel. *GCHQ*. Weidenfeld & Nicolson, London, 1986.

Wright, Peter. *Spycatcher*. William Heinemann, Australia, 1987.

Index

Note: Italicized page references indicate illustrations.